Onondaga County Post Offices and the Postal System

by Robert W. Bitz

I0170695

Copyright ©2017 Robert W. Bitz
Published by Ward Bitz Publishing

All rights reserved. Printed in the United States of America. This book may
not be duplicated in any way without the expressed written consent of the
publisher, except in the form of brief excerpts or quotations for the purposes of
review. The information contained herein may not be duplicated in other books,
databases or any other medium without the written consent of the publisher or
author. Making copies of this book or any portion for any purpose other than
your own, is a violation of United States copyright laws.

LCCN: 2017910547
ISBN-13: 978-0-9859504-6-0
First edition, published 2017.

Ward Bitz Publishing
Baldwinsville, NY

The author may be contacted at:
2470 Virkler Trace
Baldwinsville, NY 13027

FRONT COVER: *Omnibus in front of the post office in the third Baldwinsville
Seneca House circa 1890. Courtesy of McHarrie's Legacy.*

BACK COVER: *LaFayette Post Office and rural mail carrier Clayton S. Baker
circa 1910. Courtesy of J. Roy Dodge.*

Preface

It is a daunting task to write about an institution that has been part of the life of almost every person that has lived in Onondaga County since the county was established in 1794. That institution is the United States Postal Service. But, it is far more than an institution. It is, and has been, an integral part of each of our lives. It brings us messages telling of the loss of a loved one and the birth of a new life. It brings messages of love, anger and remorse. It brings those inevitable bills that have to be paid, but sometimes puts money back in our pockets.

For over 100 years, when the US was mostly rural, the post office was often the community meeting place where friends gathered and local news was shared. It even served as the local resource center and food bank, before they existed. When neighbors heard of a neighbor in difficulty, help was offered to them, and food, if needed. It was non-denominational. Everyone was included without exception.

In the early 1900s, when Rural Free Delivery was established, many people were opposed because it meant losing their beloved local post office. Delivery to the home benefitted the greater number who had a long trip to the post office and RFD won out. Today there are still thousands of these rural post offices providing a community service that amounts to much more than just postal service. The need is less now, though, due to radio, telephone, television and the internet.

It is difficult to comprehend the extent of the changes in the postal system that have occurred during the past 200 years. Mail was first carried by a man on foot, by a horse or in a small boat powered by oars. Soon stagecoaches pulled by four horses, carrying both mail and passengers, were bouncing along rough roads at the rapid speed of four miles an hour. Next, steamboats were plying our larger lakes and rivers, followed by trains that carried the bulk of the mail for over 100 years. They were followed by airplanes and the trucks we see on our highways each day. It has been an amazing evolution!

We cannot overlook the millions, yes millions, of postal workers, who have diligently served the public over these years. They have fought their way through rain, snow, floods, hurricanes, heat and cold to deliver the mail. Postal workers are performing their tasks 24 hours a day to get the mail delivered in a timely manner.

In writing about Onondaga County post offices it is interesting to see how our county has changed over the years. Many small communities were established and then disappeared as industries came and went, gradually gravitating to larger centers of population where water power was available and shipping opportunities were superior.

We have seen a dramatic change in communications during the past 30 years. The internet is replacing much of what the Postal Service had done in the past. It provides instant communication for ordering goods along with electronic payment. Newspapers and magazines, long delivered by the Postal Service, are gradually disappearing. The Postal Service is attempting to remain as an important institution for Americans, and must continually adjust to the changes occurring. No one knows what lies ahead, but change is inevitable.

The information in this book, regarding the post offices in Onondaga County, comes from numerous sources that are believed to be accurate, but undoubtedly there are errors. The main source of post office names, date established, date discontinued and name of the first postmaster is: *New York Postal History, The Post Offices and First Postmasters from 1775 to 1980*, by John L. Kay and Chester M. Smith, Jr. (© 1982 American Philatelic Society).

A supplementary source is a compilation assembled by Fred L. Scholl, in 1954, directly from photostats of official US Post Office Department records in the National Archives on which were penciled notations made by Richard Wright, director of the Onondaga Historical Society. This source provides the date of many of the postmaster appointments. The lists of postmaster appointments is in the appendix. Some of the lists are incomplete because of lost records or not finding a source that could provide the information.

The dates for the establishment of post offices are often not accurate to the precise date because their establishment was sometimes not recognized until the Post Office System received a deposit of money from the post office. In the early 1800s little money was collected by small post offices so it is possible that dates could differ by several months depending upon the source. In addition, records, over that length of time, may have been misplaced or lost due to fire. Even though the information has been carefully compiled, clerical errors may also have occurred.

The author hopes that the readers will receive some enjoyment as they read these pages and look at the pictures, many of which leave much to be desired, but they were all that was available. It is unfortunate there was no such thing as photography for most of the first 100 years. The pictures from that period will have to be envisioned in the minds of the readers.

About the Author

The author enjoys history, maybe because he has seen so much! But, because he has always enjoyed history, it must be in his blood. He has always looked toward the future while enjoying the past, and receives pleasure in writing about what has happened and why. His livelihood was farming and if a farmer doesn't continually learn from experience, he will soon have another occupation.

He has lived his lifetime in Onondaga County except for a few years at Cornell University and some pleasurable winters in a warmer climate. He has written ten books about the Baldwinsville area, agriculture and family. Most of them are available online at Amazon or Barnes & Noble.

The fact that there is so much forgotten history associated with post offices, attracted him to writing about the post offices of Onondaga County. He was not disappointed and he hopes that the readers will find enjoyment as well as a little bit of learning.

Acknowledgements

When I first started to research material about the post offices of Onondaga County, I had little idea of their complexity and how much I would have to rely upon help from others in order to put a book together. My first break was a call from Maureen Marion of the US Postal Service in response to my request for information from the Syracuse Postmaster. Maureen told me that there was a compilation of Onondaga County's post offices assembled by Fred L. Scholl in 1954, with penciled notations by Richard Wright, former director of the Onondaga Historical Association (OHA). After a successful call to the OHA, I soon had a copy which was full of helpful information.

My next piece of good luck was purchasing, online, a used copy of *New York Postal History* by John L. Kay and Chester M. Smith, printed in 1982. This book has a chapter listing all the post offices in Onondaga County up to 1982.

A call to Bonnie Kisselstein, Town of Lysander historian, resulted in her kindly providing me a list of the town historians in Onondaga County as well as some information regarding post offices in the Town of Lysander. I cannot speak highly enough of the help I received from many of these historians whom I have acknowledged after each chapter regarding that town's post offices. The town and village historians go to great efforts, with minimal renumeration, to preserve knowledge of the past that otherwise would be lost forever. My hat is off to them for all their fine work.

In Onondaga County we have a tremendous historical resource in the OHA. I obtained information about many post offices from their file of old newspapers. This was information often not available from any other source. I also used photos from some of these articles to help the reader obtain a visual image of a few of the old post offices. When researching for material regarding local events, one begins to realize how important newspapers are in recording the everyday happenings of our lives. I have gained greater respect for the service they provide.

During the year spent assembling and writing this book, I sometimes posed questions to Maureen Marion of the Postal Service, probably to the point of annoyance. She graciously responded with what information she was able to share. My thanks also go to the Postal Service for information from their various postal bulletins which helped provide a comprehensive history of their more than 200 years of service. My thanks go also to Jacquie Olmsted for typing the lists of postmasters, both past and present, from each of the post offices which are listed in the appendix.

Finally, a book of facts that reaches back over 200 years is the result of the work of generations of historians and involves hundreds of people who have taken the time to record some of their daily experiences. My thanks go to these people. Although most of them are long gone, their work lives on!

Table of Contents

CHAPTER 1

Early Methods of Communication Prior to Colonial America

Not unlike animals and birds that we are commonly associated with, man's first communication with each other was by sound. With time, what we now call words evolved, and eventually two or more words were spoken in sequence to provide a clearer message.

To communicate by sound to someone a distance away, the best a communicator could do was shout. The effective distance that one could normally expect another person to hear and understand what was being said would be about the length of a football field. Of course, with the wind at the communicator's back or from a hillside looking over a large valley, with nothing to interrupt the sound waves, a shout might travel much farther.

If a person wanted to communicate with someone more than a few hundred feet away, there was no recourse other than to walk or run to within vocal distance. At some point in history, bonfires were lighted at night to pass on an important message, such as danger. In daytime such a warning might be communicated by the waving a branch or flailing one's arms at an observer some distance away. Later, after fire came into common use, smoke signals were sent by periodically interrupting the smoke emanating from a fire.

During times of warfare, generals sent messages by runners to communicate between their various forces. The runners exhibited not only speed in running, but also the ability to remember and relay the message accurately to the recipient. The sender, usually the military commander or ruler, also chose men as runners who were unfailingly loyal and refused to share information with an enemy even under excruciating torture.

Writing, as a form of communication, came into existence a few thousand years ago. The first written messages were carved on stone pillars or were inscribed on clay tablets. These were too heavy to be conveniently transported long distances, and if there was any time urgency, writing messages on these objects was a slow process.

No one knows exactly when couriers first delivered written messages, but archeologists indicate they delivered the decrees for Egyptian Pharaohs before 2,000 BC. The oldest surviving Egyptian piece of mail, however, dates only to 255 BC. Most certainly couriers were delivering messages for rulers in China, India and Persia in a similar period of time.

The first credible claim for the development of a real postal system was in Ancient Persia. The invention of such a system, in about 550 BC, is attributed to Persian King Cyrus the Great who mandated that every province in his kingdom organize the reception and delivery of post to each of its citizens. One can only guess what proportion of the population used this system. Quite likely it served very few of its citizens.

Cyrus's son Darius improved this postal system by building a network of roads across the Persian Empire to enable troops and messages to move with remarkable speed for this time period. The central road of the system was 2,000 miles long. Post stations were set up along the roads at intervals where the messages were passed to another courier with a fresh horse. It is stated that a distance of 200 miles could be covered each day using this system.[1]

These messages were written on papyrus which was made from a reed that grew along the Nile. The papyrus, somewhat similar to heavy rough paper, was relatively light making it a convenient way to carry messages long distances. There was little more that could be done for many years to speed the sending of messages other than improving roads and breeding faster and more durable horses.

---

[1] Gascoigne, Bamber. *History World. from 2001, ongoing.* www.historyworld.net

In the 11th century it was discovered that certain domesticated pigeons, when moved to a distant location and then set free, flew back to their original location. This made it possible to send condensed messages by pigeon back to the pigeon's home base. Genghis Khan used them to send news of each new conquest back to his homeland in Mongolia.[2]

The invention of the Gutenberg printing press with its movable type, in the 15th century, was a giant step forward in communication. By the year 1500 it is estimated there were about 1,700 presses in 300 cities scattered throughout Europe. Books were first printed, but pamphlets and single sheets soon followed, numbering in the millions. The Reformation, resulting from Martin Luther's challenge to the Catholic Church, was a major factor in the rapid proliferation of single sheet and pamphlet printing.[3]

Pamphlets printed on the printing press were the forerunner of news sheets which slowly evolved into newspapers. Newspapers gradually came into general use in the 1600s and in later years, postal systems became an important means for their distribution.

In 1516, King Henry VII of England established 'A Master of the Posts' to oversee his need for communicating to multiple points. This position gradually evolved into the English office of Postmaster General. It was in 1635 that King Charles I of England opened the use of his mail service to the public. Quite likely, as mail service evolved in the American Colonies some of the ideas, including the name 'Postal Service,' came from the English postal system.

---

2 Ibid.
3 Ibid.

CHAPTER 2

The Colonial and Early United States Postal System

Note: The information presented in this chapter is condensed from the Bulletin 100 'The United States Postal Service, An American History 1775-2006' by the United States Postal Service.

Until the American colonies became more numerous and geographically distant, no mail service was needed. A message could be sent to a neighboring settlement whenever a friend happened to be going in that direction. A letter might be left with a merchant to give to a specific person when he came to the store, even though he might not be there for several weeks. If a settler wanted to send a message to family back in England, he would send it with someone traveling on a ship that would soon be sailing.

In 1639, the General Court of Massachusetts designated the Fairbanks Tavern as the official repository of mail brought from, or sent, overseas. This followed the European practice of coffee houses and taverns serving as mail stations.

As more settlements developed in the colonies, the earlier practice of sending a message by a friend was no longer sufficient. As a result, local authorities operated post routes within the colonies. In 1673, the English-appointed Governor of New York set up a monthly post between New York City and Boston. This old post rider's trail became known as the Old Boston Post Road and is now a portion of U.S. Route 1. Governor William Penn established Pennsylvania's first post office in 1683. Other systems were developed in the colonies as the need became apparent.

It was after 1692 when a central postal organization came to the colonies. Thomas Neale received a 21-year grant from England for a North American postal system. The franchise was passed to different parties over the years but never became much of a success.

A former lieutenant governor of Virginia, Alexander Spotswood, became the deputy postmaster general of America in 1730. Likely his most notable achievement was to appoint Benjamin Franklin postmaster of Philadelphia in 1737. Franklin was only 31 at the time and served until he was dismissed by England in 1774 because some of his actions showed sympathy to the colonies. During his 37 year tenure, Franklin did much to improve the postal system. He made new surveys that shortened and improved routes, set milestones on principal roads, and in 1760, even made the first profit for the system. When he left office, post roads operated from Maine to Florida and from New York to Canada.

After Franklin was dismissed, William Goddard set up the Constitutional Post for intercolonial mail service. He employed only reputable postmasters and required each post rider to keep his mail under lock and key. When the Continental Congress met in 1775, Goddard had 30 post offices operating between Williamsburg and Portsmouth, New Hampshire. England still provided postal service in the colonies, but Goddard warned that their system was not to be trusted. The Constitutional Post operated by Goddard, that bypassed the English-controlled postal system, played a vital role in bringing about American independence.

On July 26, 1775 the Continental Congress created the position of Postmaster General and appointed Benjamin Franklin to that position. This appointment was made about three months after the battles of Lexington and Concord, and almost a year prior to the colonies' Declaration of Independence from England. For the next several years, the main duty of the postal system was to carry messages between Congress and the armies. Franklin still held the position when the Declaration of Independence was ratified making him the first Postmaster General of the United States. He left that position in November 1776 when Congress sent him to France to negotiate its support for the war against England.

In 1782 Ebenezer Hazard, Postmaster of New York, was appointed by the Continental Congress to be the third Postmaster General. Hazard expanded post routes, reestablished monthly service to Europe and contracted with stagecoach companies to carry mail on heavily traveled routes. When Hazard left the office in 1789, the population of the United States had reached almost four million, was served by 75 Post Offices and had about 2,000 miles of post roads.

When one considers the fact that there were 13 states extending more than 1,000 miles north and south, as well as several hundred miles east to west, the Post Office was critically important in holding these widely separated states together. As this time, the electronic advances of telegraph, telephone, radio and internet were inventions waiting to be discovered long into the future.

In 1792, when newspapers became more widely read, Congress formally admitted newspapers to the mail. At that time, Congress also passed laws prohibiting postal officials from opening mail and provided rules for the future development of the Postal Service. When Washington, D.C. became the seat of government in 1800, two horse-drawn wagons were all that were needed to move all of the postal records, furniture and supplies from Philadelphia to Washington.

The United States was growing rapidly, fueled to a great extent by the growth of its Post Office System. By the end of 1819, post offices served the citizens of the 22 existing states with 60,000 miles of roads on which the mail traveled. By 1828, the number of post offices had increased to 7,530, more than 100 times the number that existed in 1789. There were 29,956 postal employees at that time making the Postal Department the largest employer in the executive branch of government. Only three years later, United States Postmasters outnumbered soldiers 8,764 to 6,332.

CHAPTER 3

The Growing United States Postal System

NOTE: *The information presented in this chapter is condensed from the Bulletin 100 'The United States Postal Service, An American History 1775-2006' by the United States Postal Service. Facts stated after 2006 come directly from Postal Service releases.*

The United States was growing rapidly, stretching further and further to the west. New settlements were being formed, some of which later became villages or cities. Each of these settlements wanted a post office, although the cost to the Postal System might be greater than the revenue received. Sometimes these settlements grew and provided a profit to the System. More often than not, though, their growth was not substantial and they became an additional expense. However, Postal Department decisions made during the 19th century reflected its desire to provide excellent public service and as a result the Postal System mushroomed in size.

In 1829, President Jackson recognized the potential value of patronage and invited William T. Barry, the existing Postmaster General, to sit as a member of the President's Cabinet. This appointment became a precedent that continued until the reorganization of the Postal System in 1971. Postal System patronage permitted the political party in power to make thousands of postmaster and rural carrier appointments. This system provided many political workers and thousands of votes for the appointing political party.

Until 1829, during Andrew Jackson's presidency, postmasters were appointed by the President. At that time, Jackson elevated the Postmaster General to a cabinet position in the executive branch of the government. From then until 1971, when Congress created the post office as an independent agency, postmasters were appointed throughout the United States based on their patronage.[1]

In the Post Office Act of March 3, 1847 the Postmaster General was authorized to produce stamps which, when attached to any letter or packet, proved payment of postage. Until then, the only stamps used were privately produced by mail companies or independent carriers. Before 1847, mail was sent either by the sender prepaying the postage at the post office or by the recipient paying the postage without the use of stamps. It was not until nine years later, in 1856, that stamps were required by the Post Office Department.[2]

As post offices increased in number and the country expanded, the transportation of mail underwent numerous changes. Originally, the mail was carried by a runner or person on horseback. Although stagecoaches were more costly and sometimes less suitable for transporting mail than by a rider on horseback, sending mail by stagecoach was a means of subsidizing stagecoach routes in order to improve the country's transportation system. Congress continued this practice until 1845 when it cut costs by awarding contracts to the lowest reliable bidder. Throughout the Postal System's history, as new improved methods of transportation came into use, such as steamships, railroads and airplanes, they were used to expedite mail service, and indirectly subsidize these methods of transportation. This practice permitted new forms of transportation to be more cost effective and resulted in lower costs for passengers and freight.

It was in 1811 that mail was first carried on steamboats, which gradually replaced packet boats, rowboats and rafts. By the 1820s there were more than 200 steamboats serving communities on the water, so in 1823

---

1 Crowell (Kathy), Moore (Ann) & Schiffhauer (Nancy), *A History of the Fayetteville Post Office*, p. 4
2 Ibid., p. 13

Congress declared waterways as Post Roads. Their use began to decline after 1853 as railroads came into greater use.

Railroads moved the majority of mail volume over the next hundred years. The first mail carried on railroads occurred in 1832, about 20 years later than the first steamboats. It was only six years later that Congress designated all United States railroads as post routes. Soon there were postal system employees riding in mail cars sorting the mail while traveling from city to city. After the mail was sorted, some was left at the cities along the way while other mail, designated for cities on different routes, was transferred to the appropriate trains serving those cities. By 1930, more than 10,000 trains moved mail. In 1958, Congress decreed that railroad trains losing money could discontinue mail service. This substantially decreased the number of trains moving mail. The last railway post office made its final trip in 1977. The movement of some classes of mail on railroads still continues, but is relatively small compared to a century ago.

As the country expanded west in the 1800s, the standard method for mail traveling from the east to California had been for it to be transported by boat to Panama, then across Panama by packhorse and finally by boat up the western coast of North America to California. It was a long distance for the mail to travel and took a month or more. Later, when it was transported across the southern United States by stagecoach, the time required dropped to 20 days.

Although it moved only a very small fraction of the mail, the Pony Express became an important segment of the Postal Service for thousands of Americans living in the west. The romanticizing of the Pony Express in novels and motion pictures has made it larger than life. In 1860, when the Pony Express was founded, St. Joseph, Missouri was the furthest point reached by railroads carrying mail from the east to destinations further west.

The Pony Express traveled through portions of Missouri, Kansas, Nebraska, Colorado, Wyoming, Utah, Nevada and California. The first Pony Express trip from St. Joseph, Missouri to California took 10 days, one half the time it had taken when carried on stagecoaches. The owners of the Pony Express had searched the West for sturdy and fast horses. Before being employed, the riders had to swear on a bible not to cuss, fight or abuse their horses. Relay stations were established every 10 to 15 miles where riders changed horses. A rider averaged 75 to 100 miles on his shift each day.

The Pony Express parent company began operating under a contract with the United States Postal System on July 1, 1861. Although they charged as much as $5 for a half ounce of mail, when ordinary postage was no more 10 cents, the private company operating the Pony Express was soon deep in debt. Four months later the Pony Express came to an end, only two days after the transcontinental telegraph line was completed. There was no way it could compete with the telegraph and the railroad in either cost or speed of delivery. Transporting mail almost 2,000 miles through desolate, unsettled country was a super human feat which should always be a valued part of the history of both the United States and the Postal System.

Often, because it has been an important part of our lives for over two centuries, we look upon the Postal Service as huge business and ignore the fact that it is composed of people like you and me. An interesting example of its human element is exemplified in Owney, a dog that served as the mascot of the Railway Mail Service from 1888 to 1897.

Owney was a stray pup that walked into the Albany, NY Post Office in 1888. The postal workers allowed Owney to stay and soon he became a fixture in the post office. He shortly began to ride the mail train, gradually traveling to more and more distant points served by the Postal Service. The clerks purchased a collar for him so that if he wandered too far postal employees who hadn't seen him before would know where his home was located. Clerks in other cities fastened metal baggage tags to his collar to identify the numerous rail lines he traveled on. Owney's collar became so weighted down with metal tags that one of the clerks made a small jacket for him in order to distribute his load of tags more evenly.

Owney's travels took him not only to many points in the United States, but also to Canada, Mexico, Japan, China, Singapore, Suez, Algiers and the Azores. After his demise, railway clerks donated money to have a taxidermist preserve him for posterity. For many years he was on exhibit at the postal service headquarters in Washington. In 1998, he moved to a new home at the National Postal Museum in Washington. You can only imagine the smiles Owney brought to hundreds of postal workers throughout the world, the dozens of newspaper articles about him and the fame this wandering little pup achieved.

Post office names have a fascinating history. Originally the hamlet or village that desired a post office suggested the name it wanted in its application. If the Postal System determined that the proposed location was worthy of a post office, the name requested became the name of that post office. By 1825, there were often two or three post offices with the same name in the same state. By the 1840's, duplicate names were recognized as a serious problem and the application to establish a post office was changed to read as follows:

> *The name of the candidate for postmaster should not be applied as the name of a post office. It is preferred to have some LOCAL or PERMANENT name, which must not be the name of any other office in the State; and you should aim to select a name not appropriated to any office in the United States.*

This statement illustrates that quite often the person applying for a post office name wanted not only to be the first postmaster but to also have the village named for him.

The last post office formed in a state where there were duplicate names was usually the one required to choose a new name. Even after these changes were made, the mix-ups in mail going to the wrong post office often continued due to many post offices with similar names. Often, one of these post offices was required to choose a new name.

Inconsistent geographic names were recognized as a serious problem. In 1890, President Benjamin Harrison created the United States Board of Geographic Names to bring uniformity to the names of places. The Post Office Department was recognized as a major source of this geographic name confusion. The Post Office System changed the names and the spelling of many post offices after the Board's report was issued.

Did you ever send a letter to someone with a Star Route address and wonder what it meant? In 1845, Congress, in an attempt to lower the Postal System's costs, authorized putting mail routes out for bids. The contract went to the lowest bidder that could provide 'celerity, certainty and security'. Post clerks shortened these three words to asterisks, or stars, and these routes became known as Star Routes. The successful bidders were required to furnish their own equipment, whether horse, dog sled, boat, truck or whatever transportation method was necessary, for the delivery of the mail. In 2006, the Postal Service had 16,707 highway contract routes. Almost half of these routes provided service to customers who lived along them. The term 'Star Route'

is occasionally used as part of a recipient's address today, but is not common.

Free postal home deliveries did not come into general practice until 1863. An act of Congress that year stated that free home delivery could be provided in cities whose income from local postage was more than needed to cover those expenses. Initially, the mail was only delivered if the customer was present for the letter carrier to put it in his hand. If the customer was not home, the carrier returned later to try again. This policy became too expensive, so in 1923 it was required that all customers have a mail slot or receptacle for the carrier to leave the mail.

Rural Free Delivery (RFD) was authorized by Congress and became a permanent part of the Postal System on July 1, 1902. City residents had received free delivery for a number of years. However, in 1890 about 65% of the population lived in rural areas. John Wanamaker, Postmaster General at the time, stated that it made more sense to have one person deliver the mail than to have 50 customers each have to travel to a post office. Studies were made and experiments conducted over a period of 12 years before RFD finally became a permanent service.

Initially a variety of mail receptacles were used: everything from tin pails to potato crates. Very soon the postal authorities asked manufacturers to design standardized boxes according to prescribed specifications. These boxes were required to be installed by those living in rural areas in order to receive mail.

RFD became a very important service for rural Americans in many ways. The rural carriers sold stamps, money orders, and registered letters. In effect they became mobile post offices that came almost to the door of rural residents. Their travel on thousands of miles of unimproved roads accelerated the movement for better roads in rural areas.

As the number of rural delivery routes increased, the number of post offices in the United States decreased. One post office usually served several of these new rural routes, which eliminated many existing post offices. In thousands of counties throughout the United States, little country hamlets that once had a post office began to be served by rural letter carriers. Without a post office in existence, the name of these little settlements was no longer used and many have disappeared into the past.

At the time RFD was authorized, by law the Postal System could not carry parcels weighing more than four pounds. In the mid 1800s, private express companies began to flourish to fill this need. In 1910, 54% of the country's population was rural without any package system readily available. The mail order companies of Montgomery Ward and Sears Roebuck were becoming popular, but delivery of goods to rural route residents was lacking. Finally, effective January 1, 1913, Congress authorized Parcel Post to provide this much needed package service. It became an instant success with 300 million parcels delivered during its first six months.

By 1901, the miles of roads in the US traveled by RFD carriers had increased to over 100,000, but nine years later 40,997 RFD carriers were covering nearly a million miles of road a day. In 1913, with the introduction of parcel post and the national distribution of newspapers and magazines, millions of dollars of mail-order merchandise was delivered to the homes of rural residents.

There have been many changes in rural delivery since its beginning around 1900. One change is that RFD became RD, Rural Delivery, without the "F" for Free, in 1906 as the free was understood by then. The RFD service was never free as customers always paid for their stamps, as they do now. Most likely the word "Free" was originally used to make the new service more palatable to postal customers.

In 1899, when RFD was still in its infancy, the Post Office Department experimented in county-wide application of RFD. In Carroll County, Maryland 63 small post offices were discontinued along with 35 contract routes. These were replaced with county-wide delivery which proved viable. The writing was on the wall. In Onondaga County there were numerous small post office closures as they gradually were discontinued. This practice that is still occurring today, but now with fewer post offices remaining there are fewer small ones to discontinue.

In 1901, the number of post offices in the United States reached a peak of 76,945. The following year the number had dropped by 1,000 and the numbers continued to decline. In 2012, there were over 40 million homes and businesses served by rural carriers.

As had occurred in the past with stagecoaches, steamboats and railroads, the Postal System played a key role in the development of transportation by air. In 1911, it experimented using a plane to transport mail on Long Island with daily flights between Garden City Estates and Mineola, New York. The bags of mail were dropped from the air and then picked up by the Mineola postmaster. Experiments in using airplanes to carry mail continued, but it wasn't until May 15, 1918 that the Post Office Department initiated the first scheduled airmail service. On that date, there were simultaneous takeoffs of mail planes from Washington's Polo Grounds and Belmont Park, Long Island, with both flights stopping in Philadelphia to leave mail.

The early planes carrying mail had no instrumentation. Pilots only had a compass, eyesight and the time since takeoff to determine where they were. Forced landings were common in bad weather, but there were few accidents because of the small size of the planes, their maneuverability and slow speed.

The Postal Department had long range plans for a transcontinental route from New York City to San Francisco. The first leg between New York and Chicago was established in 1919, with a transcontinental route completed in 1920. At this time mail was carried on planes during the daytime and on trains at night.

In 1920, the Post Office Department began installing radio stations at each airfield to provide pilots with the latest weather information. When the radios were not busy passing information to pilots, they were used by the Department of Agriculture to transmit weather forecasts. The utilization of radios made both day and night airmail possible.

The first time mail was flown over the transcontinental New York to San Francisco route during both day and night was in 1921. Congress was impressed by this feat and authorized the expenditure of money for additional landing fields, towers, beacons, searchlights and boundary markers on air fields across the United States. The airplanes were also equipped with luminescent instruments and navigational lights. Without question, the many improvements made to improve airmail service also speeded up the use of planes for passenger service and increased flight safety for passengers.

In 1925, Congress passed legislation to encourage commercial aviation and authorized the Postmaster General to contract with commercial aviation companies for the transportation of mail. The commercial companies eagerly signed contracts and soon all mail traveling by air was carried on commercial flights. The Post Office transferred its lights, airways and radio service to the Department of Commerce and its air fields to the municipality where they were located or to other government departments. The Post Office planes were all sold and by September 1, 1927 all airmail was carried under contract.

With the advancements in airplanes, the time it takes today to move mail from New York City to San Francisco is only six to seven hours compared to the month or more it took in 1849 by the way of the Isthmus of Panama. One only needs to look into the improvements in mail service over the last 200 years to marvel at how rapidly change has occurred. Not only is the mail moving more rapidly, but the cost of moving it is far less.

ZIP codes came into use in 1963. Mail volume had been increasing rapidly after the 'Great Depression' of the 1930s and as the economy of the United States boomed in the 1950s following World War II. Centralized billing also increased the volume of business mail as companies consolidated and computers came into general use.

The Post Office System was still using their old-time methods of sorting and handling mail, which were totally inadequate. Because many postal service employees had gone to serve in the military, the Postal System, in 1943, began using a simple numbering system to help inexperienced employees sort the mail. This had proven helpful, and in 1962 a study was made to devise improved methods of mail handling utilizing a numbering system. As a result of this study the ZIP code system went into effect on July 1, 1963. The first digit designated a broad geographical area of the United States ranging from 0 in the northeast to 9 for the far west. The next two digits pinpointed population concentrations accessible to common transportation networks and the last two digits represented small post offices or postal zones in larger zoned cities.

Crisis had been approaching the Postal System for many years, but was generally ignored by Congress and the postal leadership. In 1966, the Chicago Post Office almost came to a halt because of an unwieldily amount of mail. The situation was bad enough to bring recognition that changes were needed throughout the Postal System. Congressional hearings were held and President Johnson appointed a Commission on Postal Reorganization. The Commission recommended:

A self-supporting government organization; Elimination of patronage; Rates be set by a board of directors; That labor-management impasses over contracts and pay be referred to the President.

On August 12, 1970 after two years of discussions, meetings, work stoppages and compromises, President Richard Nixon signed comprehensive postal legislation into law. It transformed the Post Office Department into the United States Postal Service, an independent establishment of the executive branch of the United States Government. The Postal Service officially began operations July 1, 1971. The Postmaster General was no longer a member of the President's Cabinet.

Throughout the history of the United States Post Office Department thousands of changes had been made to improve service and lower costs. As mail volume increased mechanization became necessary. A parcel sorting system was introduced in 1956 and a letter sorter in the late 1950s. New and faster methods were gradually introduced as technology increased. A ZIP+4 code was added in the 1980s with the first two added digits denoting a delivery sector and the last two a segment of that sector. With these added digits, new sorting machinery was then able to eliminate a great deal of sorting by postal delivery employees. Automated equipment permitted the Postal Service to deliver 32% more mail with nine percent fewer employees in 2006 than in 1988.

In the 1990s, the Postal System lengthened the ZIP+4 by two more digits to permit sorting machines to sort letters directly to specific addresses, and reduce the amount of time needed by the mail carrier to sort mail. The recipient or the sender of a letter doesn't use these digits, but will often see a bar code at the bottom of a letter. This bar code, printed by a sorting machine, uses those numbers to help mechanize the delivery process.

In 1997, robotics were introduced for use in handling the mail. They helped eliminate much of the lifting and repetitive motions that were previously performed by human hands. Optical character recognition now reads over 98% of the 155 billion pieces of mail sent in the United States each year. As of 2014, there were 244,365 delivery routes to deliver to over 150 million specific delivery points. Almost half a million employees make the Postal Service the largest retail network in the United States.

Making the use of the Postal Service easier and more convenient for its customers is a continuing and ongoing goal. As technology evolves, whatever will be of benefit to the customer by providing better service and improving efficiency is sure to be adopted. No one knows what inventions await development in the future, but it is certain that the United States Postal System will continue to innovate and remain on the cutting edge with its adoption of new technology.

A few other interesting facts concerning the United States Postal System are:

- Two United States Presidents were postmasters: Abraham Lincoln and Harry Truman.

- In the United States Postal System's early years postage was not paid by the sender, but rather by the recipient of the mail.

- The first postage stamps were issued in 1847. Self-adhesive stamps didn't arrive nationally until 1992.

- Letter carriers originally worked 9 to 11 hours a day, 6 days a week, 52 weeks a year. Beginning in 1888, they received 15 days of leave each year. In 1935, a 40-hour work-week was implemented.

- The first commemorative stamp, printed in 1893, honored the Columbian Exposition.

- There were usually two deliveries a day to city residences until 1950.

- In 2006 there were 224,400 letter carriers in our nation's cities.

- The number of post offices reached its peak of 76,945 in 1901 and has gradually declined to less than 30,000 today.

CHAPTER 4

The Early Development of Postal Service in Onondaga County

Onondaga County was formed by the New York State Legislature on March 5, 1794 from a portion of Herkimer County. It included portions of Cayuga, Cortland and Oswego Counties, which were formed at later dates.

The first post office formed in Onondaga County was on January 1, 1795 at Scipio, which became part of Cayuga County on March 8, 1799. Three months later, on April 1, 1795, the first post office in what is now Onondaga County was established at Onondaga (today usually referred to as Onondaga Hill) with Comfort Tyler as its postmaster. As late as 1812, letters were being distributed from this post office to people living in the towns of Camillus, Pompey, Marcellus, Otisco, Spafford, Lysander and Manlius.[1] A post office was next established at Marcellus on April 17, 1797. Two other post offices established in the late 1700s were Cayuga on December 28, 1797 and Aurelius on August 11, 1798, both becoming part of Cayuga County on March 8, 1799.[2]

Each of these post offices served a large geographical area since Central New York was just beginning to be settled. As small settlements developed, the residents applied to the United States Post Office to request a post office in their area. Some requests were approved. Others were turned down if the Post Office Department felt the number of residents was too small or that the community could receive reasonable service from a nearby post office. Needless to say, the number of post offices in Onondaga County steadily increased as the county was settled.

The number of post offices increased rapidly in all parts of New York State during the 19th century, but at somewhat different times as the population gradually moved west, to the north and to the southwestern part of the state. The first New York post office was established in New York City in 1775 followed by Albany in 1776. By 1800 there were 105 post offices scattered throughout New York State. In 1820 the number had increased to 670, and in 1850 there were 2,032. The number of post offices in New York peaked at 3,498 in 1895 prior to the establishment of Rural Free Delivery and the gradual consolidation of the many smaller post offices. By 1980, the number of post offices had decreased to 1,889.[3]

Mail arrived at the early post offices in a variety of ways. Before there were roads, it often was delivered by a runner or a man on horseback. If the post office was near a lake or a river, it came on a small boat powered by a man using oars or, if the water was shallow, by poling.

During the first decade of its existence, before highways were cut through the forests to permit stage-coaches to travel, mail coming to the Onondaga Post Office from the east, where most of the population lived, usually came by boat, except when the water was frozen. At numerous points along the routes there were portages, where both the mail and the boat were carried past rapids or waterfalls. At other points the mail was transported several miles over land to a navigable spot where it could again be carried on a boat. Three Rivers, a point where the Oneida and Seneca Rivers meet to form the Oswego River, provided a waterway to Onondaga Lake with Onondaga Hill, only a few miles to the south. Mail could then be sent to the post office by runner or horseback. During the winter, mail traveled from the east carried by a man on a horse.

Before there was a regular mail route an itinerant traveler stopping at the Onondaga Post Office might pick up whatever mail's destination was in the direction he was traveling and leave it along the way. In the Town of Lysander there were at least two such locations. In Columbia, later named Baldwinsville, there was a hollow tree east of the settlement where messages were

---

1 *History of Onondaga County* by Professor W.W. Clayton, p. 275
2 *New York Postal History* by John L. Kay and Chester M. Smith, Jr. pp.215-221

---

3 *New York Postal History* by John L. Kay and Chester M. Smith, Jr. p.11

Village Post Office by Thomas Waterman Wood (1823-1903) painted in 1873. The country general store and post office depicted in this painting is typical of many similar ones that existed in Onondaga County during the 1800s. One lady is picking up her mail while another is busy bartering her eggs for cloth. Others are sharing news while the men in the background are enjoying a game of checkers. Everyone feels at home including the two dogs. Courtesy of the Fenimore Museum in Cooperstown, NY.

left for the recipient or one of his neighbors to retrieve when passing by. There was also a hollow tree, used as a depository for mail a mile and one-half south of Wilson's Corners, later named Plainville. Letters and messages might remain in these locations for a number of days before they were retrieved and relayed to the proper recipient. David Bruce, who came to Salina in 1794, carried mail on horseback from Onondaga Hollow to Oswego. He found his way through the wilderness by trees that had been marked to show the way.[4]

In 1807, when the Onondaga Hill to Oswego highway was laid out, the first runner carrying the mail was an Onondaga Indian Chief named Oundiaga. Prior to this time, mail was simply left at Three Rivers or taken to Onondaga Hill, where it remained until someone came to pick it up. Oundiaga made the 40 mile run to Oswego and back twice a week. The night before his run was spent in front of Judge Foreman's fireplace with Oundiaga's head resting against the mail bag. At four o'clock in the morning he started out, stopping at various locations along the way to drop off mail before reaching Oswego 10 hours later. A tradition states that one of his regular stopping points was the Halfway Tavern located about three miles north of Baldwinsville on what is now State Route 48.[5]

Oundiaga spent the night in Oswego and the next day made the 40 mile trip back to Onondaga Hill carrying mail in that direction. He made this trip two times a week regardless of the weather. Tradition indicates he was never delayed or failed in his trust as a mail courier.[6]

Roads worked like magic in bringing people to Upstate New York. Where two roads crossed, settlements often came into existence bringing tradesmen, churches, schools and post offices. Roads came slowly because of both lack of funds and people to use them, but when a road was opened through the forests people

---

4 *History of Onondaga County* by Professor W.W. Clayton, p. 262

5 *Historical Review of the Town of Lysander* by Miss L. Pearl Palmer, Part 45
6 *Historical Review of the Town of Lysander* by Miss L. Pearl Palmer, Part 45

came and communities developed. The earliest roads had no bridges to cross rivers and streams. Originally these roads headed toward a spot on the rivers where access in and out was relatively easy.

The first road to cross Onondaga County was what later became known as the Great Genesee Road. Around 1790 a party of emigrants led by General Wadsworth cut a road through land that was little explored and virtually wilderness from Whitestown (slightly west of Utica) to Canandaigua, a distance of over 100 miles. On the east it crossed the Onondaga County line north of Deep Spring (approximately where Route 173 crosses from Madison County into Onondaga County), passing through today's Manlius village, crossing Butternut Creek a mile south of Jamesville, through Onondaga Hollow to near General Hutchinson's home, about a mile west of Onondaga Hill, on what is now Route 175. After this road was cut through the forests, traffic of settlers heading west greatly increased. As early as 1800, the settlements along this road from Utica to Canandaigua attained some consequence.[7] The route from Deep Spring to Onondaga Hollow was almost the same as the Indian trail of 1756.[8]

In 1793, John L. Hardenburgh, Moses De Witt and John Patterson were appointed to the newly created Board of Commissioners for laying out and opening public roads in the Military Tract, of which the current Onondaga County is a part. The principal road passed from Deep Spring to Cayuga Ferry with others located in different parts of the Military Tract. The roads were to be laid out four rods wide (66 feet) and the sum of $2,700 was appropriated for that purpose.[9]

Joshua Clark provides detailed descriptions of the early roads in Central New York in his book *Onondaga*, published in 1849, as follows:

"In 1794 an act was passed by the legislature of the State of New York appointing Israel Chapin, Michael Myers and Orthniel Taylor, commissioners for the purpose of laying out, and improving a public highway, from Old Fort Schuyler, on the Mohawk River to the Cayuga Ferry, as nearly straight as the situation of the country would allow. Thence from Cayuga Ferry to Canandaigua, and thence to the settlement of Canawagas (Avon), on the Genesee River. Road

to be six rods wide (99 feet) and the sum of 600 pounds (approximately $3000) was appropriated for the expense of opening and improving so much of the road as passed through the Military Tract. In 1796, the Surveyor General was authorized to sell certain lands on the Indian Reservation, and from the proceeds of the sales, appropriate 500 pounds for improving the Great Genesee Road through the County of Onondaga."

Another act passed by the legislature in 1796 was the appointment of Seth Williams, William Stevens and Comfort Tyler (the first postmaster in Onondaga County) as commissioners to make and repair the highways of Onondaga County. The legislature appropriated $4,000 and directed that half of the money be used to improve the portion of the Great Genesee Road that passed through Onondaga County. This money was to come from surplus from the sale of State lots in the various towns. The following year the New York Legislature authorized three lotteries to raise $45,000 for the further improvement of roads and specified that $13,900 of it was to be used to improve the Great Genesee Road from Old Fort Schuyler to Geneva.[10]

A letter written by Captain Charles Williamson, an agent for English owners of lands in 'Genesee Country', written in the later part of 1797, shows the need and effectiveness of the appropriations by the State for road improvements.

"By this generous and uncommon exertion, and by some other contributions, the State Commissioner was able to complete this road of near 100 miles, opening it 64 feet wide, and paving with logs and gravel, the moist parts of the low country. Hence the road from Fort Schuyler on the Mohawk River, to Genesee, from being in the month of June 1797, little better than an Indian path, was so far improved, that a stage started from Fort Schuyler on the 30th day of September, and arrived at the hotel in Geneva, in the afternoon of the third day, with four passengers. This line of road having been established by law, not less than 50 families settled on it in the space of four months after it was opened."[11]

In 1800, the Seneca Road Company was granted a charter by the Legislature authorizing it to improve the old State Road, which in Onondaga County passed

7 Clark, Joshua V.H. *Onondaga* p.383
8 Beauchamp, Rev. William M. *Past and Present of Syracuse and Onondaga County New York* p. 241
9 Clark, Joshua V.H. *Onondaga* p. 384

10 Clark, Joshua V.H. *Onondaga* p.385
11 Bruce, Dwight H. *Onondaga's Centennial* p. 198-199

Changing Horses by E. L. Henry painted in 1880. In the early 1800s most of the mail in Onondaga County was transported by stagecoaches similar to the one shown here. Until trains were available, stagecoaches were the fastest method of moving both people and mail. About every ten miles, at a country inn which was also a post office, a fresh team of horses would replace the tired stagecoach horses. At each post office, mail was dropped off and picked up. Courtesy of the Haggin Museum in Stockton, CA and Richard Palmer.

through Manlius, Jamesville, Onondaga Valley and Marcellus, now a combination of Routes 173 and 175. The capital stock of the Company was originally $110,000 but was increased by another $50,000 later. In 1801, an amendment to the charter gave the company some discretionary right to deviate from the old road. When a number of residents living along the old road heard this they, through devious means, prevailed upon the company to maintain the same route as the old road. In 1806, when the Seneca Road Company discovered they had been misled, they secured a further amendment to their charter authorizing them to build a new road from Sullivan to the Onondaga Reservation, near the Salt Springs to Cayuga Bridge. This new road was finished in 1812 and was known as the North Branch of the Seneca Road, but was later called the Genesee Turnpike. The road passed through Fayetteville, Syracuse, Camillus and on to the West.[12] (Later this road became Route 5.)

In 1797-8 the mail was carried on horseback. Later it was carried by horse and wagon. The first four-horse mail coach was established in 1804 and made one trip weekly from Utica to Canandaigua. In 1805, the State

Legislature granted Jason Parker and Levi Stevens the right to run stages between Utica and Canandaigua for seven years with the requirements of two trips a week with a maximum of 48 hours, accidents excepted, and with a maximum passenger fare of five cents a mile. By 1808, stages were running daily.[13]

Because stagecoaches only averaged three or four miles an hour, and individuals traveling with oxen pulling their possessions averaged less than three miles an hour, travelers on these new roads needed taverns to provide food and lodging. As a result many taverns were established along these major roads.

From the book *Old Line Mail* by Richard F. Palmer a list of Inns from Utica to Canandaigua is shown as taken from *William Williams' Almanac* of Utica. There are 18 Inns listed over 18 miles of the highway beginning with Warner at mile 38 in Manlius and continuing with Dyer at mile 39, Dwight at mile 40, Barrit at 40, Gumver at 43, Olmsted at 45, Cadwell in East Hill at 47, Brown at 48, Longstreet in Onondaga Hollow at 50, Johnsons in West Hill at 52, Brownsons also at 52, Hutshinson in Marcellus at 55, Leonard also at 55, Lawrence at 58, Beach in Nine

---

12 Bruce, Dwight H. *Onondaga's Centennial* p. 199

13 Bruce, Dwight H. *Onondaga's Centennial* p. 199-200

Mile Creek at 60, Gumver at 63, Hall in Skaneateles at 66 and also Sherwood at 66 in Skaneateles.

Most of the Taverns or Inns provided food and lodging for not only the travelers but also for the horses and drivers. Sometimes the stop at an Inn would only be long enough to change the horses and for the travelers to stretch their legs, but late in the evening the stagecoach driver and passengers would all spend the night. In the early days of stagecoach travel the mail was sorted at each post office stop with the thru mail going on to the next post office. There was a relatively small amount of mail in the late 1700s and early 1800s due to the size of the population, many people didn't know how to write, there were few newspapers and junk mail had not come into existence. As the years passed, the volume of mail gradually increased as all of the above factors changed.

As the number of stagecoaches and travelers on stagecoaches decreased, many of the Inns and Taverns along the major highways were forced to close. The ones remaining were those in small villages, often where the post office was located or the ones in the larger communities where the railroads passed through.

The opening of new roads was important in the movement of mail, bringing the stagecoach era into existence. The peak for the use of stagecoaches to move mail over long distances ended with the arrival of railroads. Stagecoaches, however, remained active for about 75 years after railroad use began, carrying mail over short distances from rural post offices to post offices that were located on a railroad. A number of small post offices in Onondaga County received and sent their mail by stagecoach until the early 1900s. Some of them will be mentioned in the chapters relating to the post offices in each of the towns in Onondaga County.

CHAPTER 5

The Postal Service in Onondaga County

Notes to the readers

The author has done his best to provide accurate and reasonably complete information about the post offices, past and present, of the various towns in Onondaga County. There will be errors and omissions because much of the information comes from old newspaper articles and verbal information from individuals.

The dates for the establishment of post offices are often not accurate to the precise date because sometimes their establishment was not recognized until the Post Office System received a deposit of money from the post office. In the early 1800s little money was collected by small post offices so it is possible that dates could differ by as much as several months depending upon the source. In addition records, over that length of time may have been misplaced or lost due to fire. Even though the information has been carefully compiled clerical errors may also have occurred.

It is well to stop looking into post office history and take a brief look at where Onondaga County fits into the US Postal Service of today. There are approximately 33,000 post offices in the US that handle 200 billion pieces of mail a year and have a gross revenue of $67 billion. Making this all happen are about 617,000 post office employees.

To manage this gigantic operation efficiently, the US is broken down into eight areas with 74 district offices divided among these areas. The post offices in Onondaga County and much of Eastern NY are administered from the Albany district office. Our Albany district has 726 postal locations of all kinds and 678 post offices with approximately 6,600 employees. The district extends roughly from Plattsburgh to Binghamton and from Albany to Waterloo.

These 726 postal locations have a variety of designations. The most common designation in Onondaga County is post office. In the county there are 29 post office locations; 28 outside the city and the main Syracuse Post

Office which is on Taft Road. It has window service in front but most of the 24 acre building is designated for the service of its many carriers. In Syracuse seven locations are stations: Downtown Syracuse, Colvin Elmwood, Eastwood, Teall, Franklin Square, Syracuse Carrier (part of the Taft Road facility), and Syracuse University. In the county there are a number of branches which include Bayberry, Solvay, Mattydale, DeWitt, Onondaga and the Federal building on Clinton Street. At Mattydale, the Federal building, Downtown Syracuse, Eastwood and Syracuse University there is window service only. There are also two Inspection Service/Office of Inspector General locations on Taft Road and the Syracuse Vehicle Maintenance Facility, which provides service to hundreds of postal vehicles on a regular basis. Mottville is classed as a community location with postal boxes and retail sales inside a non-postal facility. (There is a table with this information in the Appendix.)

— • —

Now we move back in time again to the early 1800s. Additional post offices gradually came to Onondaga County. A post office came to Fabius in 1800 (in Cortland County at that time), Manlius 1800, Pompey 1803, Tully 1804, Skaneateles 1804, Salina 1807 and Camillus in 1810. By 1859, a listing in the Onondaga County Directory shows 68 post offices in Onondaga County. Many of these 68 post offices bore the names of communities that are long forgotten today. It wasn't until 1820 that a post office was established in Syracuse. One had come to Salina, a short distance north, which was eventually part of Syracuse, in 1811.

Within present Onondaga County there were sometimes confusing changes in post office locations. When the Town of Elbridge was still a part of the Town of Camillus, the Camillus Post Office was located in what is now the Village of Elbridge. When the Town of Elbridge was removed from the Town of Camillus

The steamboat "Walter McMullen" was built in Baldwinsville in 1889 as an excursion boat. It was used on the Erie Canal to transport mail, passengers and freight between Jordan and Syracuse. Courtesy of Richard Palmer.

in 1815, the Camillus Post Office was relocated to the Village of Camillus and the old post office became the Elbridge Post Office.

Starting work on the Erie Canal in 1817, water power for manufacturing from our rivers and streams, an abundance of natural resources and Onondaga's central location in the state, all attracted more and more people to Onondaga County. The 1824 NY State Gazetteer lists 29 post offices in Onondaga County and shows a population of 41,467. Thriving little communities were popping up all around the county.

A letter from the Post Office Department in Washington, taken from the OHA archives, in response to a query by Syracuse Postmaster Patrick H. Agan in 1880, states that many records of the Post Office Department were destroyed in an 1836 fire. It goes on to say on July 14, 1825 they advertised for bids on a route from Onondaga by Syracuse, Salina, Liverpool, Baldwinsville, Oswego Falls and Granby to Oswego once a week and that in 1828 that service was increased to three trips a week and in 1837 increased still again to six trips a week using four horse coaches.

Most of the towns in Onondaga had fairly rapid growth in the early 1800s as settlers arrived from Eastern New York, New England and Europe. This growth brought the need for additional post offices as

new communities were formed. After the mid 1800s a number of the towns in Onondaga County, without growing industries, started losing population along with their local post office. Spafford Hollow is one of these examples.

There were several other reasons beside population shift that changed post office locations or caused them to be closed. A new road sometimes moved the stagecoach routes and the post office location. The path through the countryside chosen by a railway company or the route of a canal often was the reason that the post office location or its name was changed. The railroad came through Apulia Station (Summit Station) in 1854, bringing growth and a post office in 1861. Apulia Station is still active today but Apulia, not on a railroad, received earlier growth and a post office in 1825 but was closed in 1944.

Presidential elections have had a tremendous impact upon the location and name of the post office as well as who was the postmaster. President Andrew Jackson, in 1829, elevated the office of the Postmaster General to a Cabinet level position, which continued until 1971 when congress made the US Post Office System an independent agency. When ever the political party of the United States President changed, thousands of new postmasters who had supported the party of the newly elected president were appointed while a similar number of the losing party lost their jobs. One of hundreds of examples was in the Town of Lysander. Noah Payne Jr. had been appointed postmaster for Dunhamville on April 4, 1832. He had been able to have the post office named after him in 1834 but lost the position to Nelson C. Dunham in 1836. When James K. Polk was elected in 1845, Nelson Dunham was not only out of a job but the post office's name was changed to Polkville and moved one mile west from Little Utica to Jacksonville.

Usually a change in the President's political party didn't require that the post office be moved to another community but just next door or across the street to a building owned by a person belonging to the new political party in power. The post office would usually be located in a corner of the store near the front door. In a situation where there were two competing stores in a community the one whose owner was postmaster enjoyed the extra traffic the post office brought to his business. The village of Tully is an example of such moves with at least six post office locations. In some communities the post office location moved back and forth between two locations several times as the political party of Presidents changed.

An article in the June 20, 1849 *Onondaga Standard* demonstrates the great importance of each Presidential election to postmasters in Onondaga County and throughout the entire country.

"The "No Party" guillotine in Operation in Onondaga"

About two weeks ago Congressman Gott returned from Washington in excellent spirits - the result of his mission here were announced in last Friday's Journal. The removal of 18 Democratic Postmasters in this county and the substitution of as many whigs in their places. With the changes announced before, this must make nearly a clean sweep of Democratic postmasters in the county." (The article goes on to list the 18 villages and the names of the new postmasters.)

The location of a village next to a larger faster growing city often resulted in the closing of their post office with mail coming from the city. The communities of Fairmount, Geddes and Lakeland were all adjacent to Syracuse but no longer have post offices and their mail comes to Syracuse.

Occasionally, when a postmaster in a small community died or retired there was no one in the community

that had an appropriate building to house the post office. At times there was no one willing to accept the appointment and the post office for that community closed. The residents then had to choose a neighboring community as their mailing address.

Some post offices received a new name without any change in postmaster or post office location. Inconsistent geographic names were recognized as a serious problem and in 1890, President Benjamin Harrison created the United States Board of Geographic Names to bring uniformity to the names of places. The Post Office Department was recognized as a major source of this geographic name confusion. The Post Office System changed the names and the spelling of many post offices after the Board's report was issued.

There are numerous examples of these name changes in Onondaga County. The DeWitt Post Office was formed in 1835 but in 1895 the Postal System changed the name to Dewitt and in 1905 changed the name back to DeWitt. It is likely that the DeWitt residents didn't like the name change and complained. This type of name change occurred throughout the country. About ten years later, with thousands of people complaining, the Postal System gave permission to have the names back to the original names.

Rural Free Delivery (RFD) has been one of the most important service accomplishments, for Onondaga County as well as most of the United States, by the Postal Service during its existence. Rural delivery of mail had been advocated, from time to time since 1863, when some city dwellers had begun receiving mail delivery. The Post Office first experimented with rural delivery in Jefferson County, West Virginia on October 1, 1891 to determine the viability of RFD. There were five routes each covering ten miles. It showed possibilities of success so experimentation continued. Initially this service was limited to selected routes in a few states. Being totally new, there was much for the Post Office to learn before they could provide RFD service throughout the country. In addition, many people were opposed to RFD because of the great number of small post offices that would be closed. These post offices were quite often the location in the community where neighbors met and shared local news. Nationally, after RFD had nicely begun, there was an attempt by fourth class post offices to band together to try to persuade the next incoming congress that RFD was detrimental rather than beneficial.

Rural Free Delivery was finally authorized by Congress and became a permanent part of the Postal

System on July 1, 1902. Now most rural residents, like city residents, were able to pick up their mail at home. In 1890, about 65% of the population of the United States lived in rural areas. John Wanamaker, Postmaster General at the time, stated that it made more sense to have one person deliver the mail than to have 50 customers each travel to a post office. Studies over a period of 12 years had been successful and RFD finally became a permanent service.

RFD came to the Onondaga County post office in Baldwinsville during June of 1898. After only a little over a year the evidence of success that was demonstrated in the Baldwinsville and other early RFD communities showed that its value outweighed its limitations. In Baldwinsville there was unexpected opposition from liquor sellers who found that the rural residents came into the village less often, diminishing the sale of their liquor. However, most of the recipients of RFD were loud in their praise for the service. The RFD experimental communities were surrounded by dozens of farm families that found it a burden to have to travel to a post office whenever they wanted to mail a letter or pick up their mail. It saved them a great deal of time traveling to and from the post office. Postal patrons who had been served by the smaller outlying post offices also found they with RFD they were receiving their newspapers earlier in the day.

Initially a variety of mail receptacles were used; everything from tin pails to potato crates. Very soon the postal authorities asked manufacturers to design standardized boxes, designed according to prescribed specifications, and required these boxes be installed in order to receive rural mail delivery. Gradually mailbox specifications were adopted and farmers were requested to put up mail boxes along the side of the road on whichever side they preferred. Residents on short roads were asked to place their boxes at the main road intersections. The carriers had a supply of postal cards and stamps with them to use for patrons that had raised the mailbox signal for the carrier to stop.

RFD became a very important service for rural Americans in numerous ways. The rural carriers sold stamps, money orders, and registered letters. In effect they became mobile post offices that came almost to the door of rural residents. Their travel on thousands of miles of unimproved roads accelerated the movement for better roads in rural areas. Stories from RFD carriers and rural residents, of the deplorable conditions of many rural roads brought action by local authorities in improving rural roads.

RFD, as feared by small town merchants, gradually took away some of their business. Rural customers ordered items from catalog companies such as Sears, Roebuck and Company with delivery to their door by their RFD carrier. However, farm groups like the National Grange were strong advocates of RFD.

There were, as always with something new and different, many complaints, some of which could be rectified by the Post Office Department and others hardly worth considering. The *Camillus Citizen* of January 28, 1910 carried a reader's complaint that the RFD carrier should spend 20 shillings ($2.50) for another horse so he could deliver the mail more promptly. In almost any Onondaga County community newspaper letters to the editor with complaints regarding late delivery or absence of delivery of mail, especially during bad winter storms where the terrain was hilly, were common. People in warm houses often had little idea of the difficult conditions faced by their rural delivery carrier.

Wisely, the Postal Service continued to try new ideas in a few small sections of the country before a new program was fully established. On April 14, 1949, a bus-like vehicle, similar to but replacing mail sorting railroad cars, began traveling between Binghamton and Syracuse servicing 22 communities. A person on the bus sorted the mail as the bus traveled from community to community. Another similar vehicle traveled west from Syracuse. In 1954 the highway mail bus service between Syracuse and Binghamton and between Syracuse and Rochester was turned over to private contractors. Post office employees continued to operate the buses and sort the mail but the equipment is to be owned and maintained by the successful bidders. The highway mail bus service began in 1949 as a means of speeding the mail to small communities which suffered from curtailed railway service but wasn't fully implemented until some years later.

Another significant era in postal history ended in November 1969 with the end of the railway post office on trains going and coming thru Syracuse. The railway post office system dated back to 1862 when it was first tested and was the mainstay of intercity post office service for about a century. Postal clerks on railway cars raced against time as they sorted the mail between cities to have it ready to drop off as the train pulled into the next station or mail bag drop off point. At times bags of mail were retrieved from the station hook and dropped to the ground while the train was traveling nearly 60 miles an hour. Railroads still carried some mail after the end of the railway post office system but no longer was it sorted on the trains.

Gradually, however, first motor vehicles and then airplanes replaced the railroads for the transportation of mail. In May 1938 airplane pilots from 36 Upstate New York communities celebrated the 20th anniversary of the first air mail flight by carrying mail from their post offices to Syracuse. The Syracuse postmaster set up a special post office in the Amboy Airport administration building where the mail was sorted and then dispatched on the regular planes of the American Airlines. Adding to the celebration, two squadrons of army planes en route to Dayton, Ohio, one of 10 planes and the other with 15, flew over the city and airport later that morning. Airplane flights, at that time, were still a novelty to most Americans, making this a really big day at the Amboy Syracuse Airport.

ZIP code delivery had its beginning in 1963. Each postoffice was assigned one or more five-digit numbers with Syracuse receiving 132 as the first three digits for each of its various post office stations and branches. The prefix of 130 or 131 was given to the 124 outlying post offices in which Syracuse was the sectional center. The assignment of numbers, left unused numbers between the ones used to allow for future growth in the area. The use of ZIP Codes was designed for faster service and lower costs for the Postal Service. They paved the way for efficient, fast and effective sorting and transporting mail from the sender to the recipient.

Three of the ZIP codes assigned to sections of the city demonstrate the human side of the Postal Service. The Syracuse University Campus has the ZIP 13244. The last two digits of 44 are the same numbers the famous Syracuse football athletes, Ernie Davis and Jim Brown, had on their uniforms. The post office station on University Ave. in Marshall Square carries the ZIP 13235, the last two digits being the numbers basketball coach Jim Boeheim had on his basketball uniform when he was an undergraduate at Syracuse. Destiny Mall, formerly named Carousel, opened in 1990 and the ZIP for the stores in that mall is 13290, the last two digits denoting the year it opened.

Beginning in 1966, door-to-door mail deliveries for new apartments and suburban developments came to an end in an attempt by the Postal Service to control costs. Suburban residents who had been receiving their mail at the door were not affected. Groups of roadside boxes in new subdivisions and the grouping of mailboxes in apartment lobbies became required for new developments. Four years later the Postal Service announced that many residents in 21 Onondaga County communities that had been without home delivery could now receive it. Persons living between one quarter and one half mile from the post office, in these communities, could file a request for home delivery. Previously they had to go to the post office to pick up their mail and they could continue to do so if they wished. It was accomplished by adding stops to existing rural routes and adding new rural routes where needed. It is likely that there were thousands of postal customers who felt that they were being discriminated against by not receiving mail as there were many post office customers on suburban routes receiving mail who lived closer to a post office.

In 1975 the Postal Service was paying a total of $380,828 annually as rent for 33 post offices and 15 sub-stations in Onondaga County. Of that figure $131,676 was for the Northern Lights annex. Crowded conditions and annual rent were two of the factors that motivated the Postal Service to purchase and make plans for building the Taft Road facility. When the Postal Service reorganized in 1971 the decision was made to rent post office facilities of less than 5,000 square feet and to buy any facility larger than that. The post office rentals for communities outside the city varied in cost from $720 in Delphi Falls to $15,482 for Liverpool.

The decision whether to lease or own post offices has not appreciably changed since 1975 in Onondaga County. Currently, in 2017, a little over half of the post offices are leased and only a few are more than 5,000 square feet. Of the properties owned only about four are less than 5,000 square feet.

Post offices, past and present, of each of Onondaga Counties towns and the city of Syracuse, are covered in the following chapters.

Post Offices in the Town of Camillus

The Town of Camillus was originally Township No. 5 of the Military Tract provided for veterans of the Revolutionary War. It was surveyed into 100 lots of approximately 600 acres each. Ninety-four were for veterans and six for gospel and school purposes. In 1829, the land to form the Towns of Elbridge and Van Buren was removed from Camillus. Five years later a portion of the Town of Onondaga was added to Camillus making it the size it is today. [1]

The first settler in the town was Isaac Lindsay who arrived in 1790. In 1792 his three brothers, James, William and Elijah settled in the town. The first post office in the town was established in 1810 in what is now Elbridge but then was part of Camillus,. [2]

The post offices that have existed in the Town of Camillus are listed in alphabetical order. The list is based on information derived from sources that are believed to be reliable.

Amboy

Established:	February 24, 1886
First Postmaster:	Delavan L. Hay
Discontinued:	November 11, 1889
Re-established:	December 23, 1889
Discontinued:	February 15, 1899
Service from **Belle Isle**	

Amboy is located on Nine Mile Creek in the northwestern quadrant of the Town of Camillus along Route 173 between Fairmount and Warners. The water power from the stream brought the community a variety of industries. By 1826 it had a flour mill, a tannery, three sawmills, a stove mill, a cooperage and a cider mill.[3] It was about a mile from the Erie Canal and grew slowly after the canal opened in 1825.

Belle Isle

Established:	February 28, 1827
First Postmaster:	Truman Skinner
Discontinued:	May 15, 1905
Service from **Camillus**	

Belle Isle was a small hamlet located along the Erie Canal about a mile west of Amboy. It's post office was established two years after the Erie Canal was opened because of the additional settlers and businesses that the canal attracted.

Camillus 13031

Established:	April 9, 1810
First Postmaster:	Truman Adams

On August 8, 1815 it became the **Elbridge** Post Office with Truman Adams still serving as postmaster. On the same date a new **Camillus** Post Office was formed which is still active today serving an area with approximately 15,000 residents.

Nine Mile Creek, passing through the village of Camillus, furnished water power for a variety of industries including two flour mills. An Erie Canal feeder line was dug from about a mile north to the village, which brought growth by providing convenient access to markets. By 1860 Camillus had a population of 552.

The current post office is located at 120 Kasson Road, about a mile east of the village, was constructed by the Postal Service in 1987. The postal carriers serving the Camillus area work out of the Solvay Station.

---

1 Bruce, Dwight H., *Onondaga's Centennial*, p. 659
2 Bruce, Dwight H., *Onondaga's Centennial*, p. 660, 665
3 Bruce, Dwight H., *Onondaga's Centennial*, p. 670, 671

Fair Mount

(previously Tyler)

Established: December 23, 1845
First Postmaster: Wheeler Truesdale

The United States Postal Service was using new guidelines in naming post offices and on September 4,1895 changed its name to **Fairmount**.
Discontinued: December 30, 1899
Service from **Syracuse**

In 1838 the construction of the Syracuse and Auburn Railroad increased the growth of Fairmount and created the need for a post office which arrived a few years later. The growth of Fairmount withdrew business from both Amboy and Wellington.[4]

---

4 Bruce, Dwight H., Onondaga's Centennial, p. 680

Lakeland

Established: February 16, 1887
First Postmaster: John T. Clapp
Discontinued: October 31, 1903
Service from **Syracuse**

Lakeland lies along the south portion of the western side of Onondaga Lake. The post office very likely was in the Town of Camillus but may have been in the Town of Geddes. When The level of Onondaga Lake was lowered several feet, in conjunction with the construction of the Erie and Oswego Canals, a large area of land along the lake's western border came into existence that had previously been under water. Resort hotels began to arise in the northern portion of the drained area. The Smith & Powell Stock Farm and Nursery pastured cattle and grew nursery stock on the southern area of this land. Their operation encompassed over 1,500 acres and they sold cattle and nursery plants not only in the

Camillus Post Office at the southwest corner of Genesee and Mechanic Streets. Picture courtesy of the Onondaga Historical Association.

United States but in other parts of the world as well. It is likely that the large volume of business from the farm created the need for the Lakeland Post Office. About 100 acres of the farm on the southern edge of Lakeland was sold in the late 1880s, as the site for the New York State Fair. Because of the gradual decline of Smith & Powell, the establishment of the post office in nearby Solvay, the beginning of Rural Free Delivery and the proximity to Syracuse, the Lakeland Post Office was discontinued in 1903.

Tyler

Established: February 21, 1843
First Postmaster: Wheeler Truesdale
Name changed to **Fair Mount** December 23, 1845

Wellington

Established: March 5, 1828
First Postmaster: Harvey Roberts
Discontinued: April 1, 1852

Wellington was in western Camillus on the Genesee Turnpike. In addition to its post office it boasted a store, two taverns and shops. It was located at a crossroads in a farming area and on a major stagecoach route. The success of the Syracuse and Auburn Railroad decreased stagecoach travel and the need for a post office in this community.

Camillus Post Office at 120 Kasson Road, Camillus NY 13031-9998. This building containing 12,014 square feet and sitting on a two acre site was constructed in 1990 and is owned by the US Postal Service.

CHAPTER 7

Post Offices in the Town of Cicero

The Town of Cicero was formed in 1807 from part of the Town of Lysander. It lost about one-half of its size when the Town of Clay was formed in 1827.

Currently the **Bridgeport Post Office** is in the Town of Cicero although during most of its existence it has been located across Chittenango Creek in the Town of Sullivan in Madison County. Bridgeport's present post office was constructed in 1988 in the Town of Cicero. Currently the post office serves three rural routes and has postal boxes for its local residents.

The post offices that have existed in the Town of Cicero are listed in alphabetical order. The list is based on information derived from sources that are believed to be reliable.

Brewerton 13029

Established: January 23, 1828
First Postmaster: Wells Crumb
Today it serves a population of about 7,000

Brewerton straddles the Oneida River at the outlet of Oneida Lake and was frequently occupied by Native Americans over thousands of years. Its location was strategic, during the French and Indian Wars, for military control to defend the passage from Albany to the Port of Oswego on Lake Ontario. As a result the British constructed a fort at this location in 1759. It was 30 years later, in 1789 after the end of the Revolutionary War, that settlers arrived to trade for furs with the Native Americans.

A post office was established at Cicero in 1821 and in 1822 a post office was established in the hamlet of Loomis Corners, later named Central Square, which was in Oswego County. Residents of the Brewerton area used these two post offices until one was established in Brewerton on January 23, 1828 with Wells Crumb as its first postmaster. Mr. Crumb was a hotel keeper and the post office was in his hotel at the corner of State (Now

Rt. 11) and Bennett Streets. Interestingly, Crumb's Hotel had been erected two years earlier on the former site of a two story log hotel built in 1791 by Patrick MaGee.

The decision to have the post office on the south side of the Oneida River was likely made because the bulk of the population of Brewerton lived on the Onondaga County side of the river. As postmasters changed, the post office often moved to a new location near the center of town.

Thanks to a clipping at the Onondaga Historical Association we have the following notice which appeared April 8, 1861 in the Syracuse Journal:

> *Postmaster at Brewerton. At a meeting of the public citizens of the village of Brewerton, to take into consideration the appointment of a Postmaster in said village, it was voted to take a formal vote to nominate a Postmaster: - Reuben Sadler received 37 votes; Carlos T. Greenleaf, 70. Whereupon Carlos T. Greenleaf was declared nominated. Charles J. Henry, Chairman, T.T. Wilton, Secretary*

Until 1886, the postmaster had been a Republican because the Postmaster General was appointed by the President and even local postmaster appointments were political. With the election of Grover Cleveland who was a Democrat, Walter W. Dority was appointed postmaster and the post office was moved to his store on the corner of State Street and Young Road.

During the term of James W. Larkin lock boxes were installed for the first time. Sometime while Nina McKinney was postmaster the post office was moved from the barber shop building at the corner of State and Railroad (Library) Streets to the Waterbury Drug Store building across the street. It remained there until July 30, 1962 when a new post office was opened. This post office was replaced by a new post office building on Bartell Road in 1988.

NOTE: *Most of the Brewerton Post Office information was furnished by Chris Huxable with material from the book, 'Brewerton, New York, USA' by Kaherine J. Barclay*

Cicero 13039

Established: April 7, 1821
First Postmaster: Isaac Cody
Today the Clay/Cicero Post Office serves a population of over 17,000 with 22 rural routes and boxes at the post office.

Cicero, previously Cicero Corners, and prior to that Cody's Corners, received a post office on April 7, 1821. The population for the entire town, which at that time included what later became the Town of Clay, was less than 1,300 with almost all of the land still covered with forests. Three years earlier, in 1818, Isaac Cody had purchased a building with one and one-half acres of land for the sum of $90. When he was appointed postmaster the post office was located in one corner of that same building where he operated a tavern. The building became a part of King's Hotel, which was demolished in 1965. It was located on the west side of Route 11 in the center of the village where an IGA was later constructed.

At the time the Cicero Post Office was formed mail was delivered once a week by a man riding a horse. A stage company was formed in 1825, which carried mail from Syracuse, following what is now Route 11, and delivered mail to all the post offices along the way. Later a local stage company that operated between Syracuse and Cicero brought the mail. This stage company was in operation until the Syracuse Northern Trolly line opened on August 27, 1908.

Cicero's mail continued to be delivered by this trolly line until truck service brought the mail beginning on January 1, 1932. Over the years the post office has been located on all four of the corners created by the intersection of State Routes 11 and 31. New post office appointments were commonly made when a United States President of the opposing political party was elected. Usually the post office was housed in a store owned by the storekeeper who supported the winning political party.

For many years farmers and other residents in rural areas had urged that a mail delivery service be created. Because this was before the day of motor vehicles, rural residents often had to walk or travel by horse more than a mile to pick up their mail. Since there was a railway station in Clay, the Postal System decided to form a rural route from Clay instead of Cicero. Rural Delivery

Route 1 came into existence in the area on October 1, 1903 with George W. Moore appointed as the first regular carrier. The delivery vehicle was by horse and wagon except in the winter when a horse pulled a cutter to glide over the snow.

On May 31, 1961 a new post office for Cicero opened on the site of the 128 year old Universalist Church which had been torn down in October 1960. The new building was built by the Onondaga Wholesale Grocery Company and leased for 10 years to the Federal Government. It contained about 1,500 square feet of interior space, up to date lighting, a loading dock and a paved parking lot. It was a drastically different post office building than the previous post offices which were normally a small portion of another building and changed location every few years.

In 1991 a new Clay/Cicero Post Office was opened on the north side of Route 31 at the western edge of the village of Cicero and the Cicero Post Office was officially discontinued.

NOTE: *Most of the information concerning the Cicero Post Office came from Cicero Through the Years' written by Lona Flynn in 1976.*

Cicero Centre

Established: July 12, 1852
First Postmaster: Silvester Ball
Discontinued: April 19, 1854
Re-established: February 7, 1890
First Postmaster: Irving Welch
Name changed **Cicero Center** in December 1893
Discontinued: October 14, 1903
Service from **Clay**

Cicero Centre was located in the eastern part of the Town on what is now NY Route 31.

East Cicero

Established: April 18, 1832
First Postmaster: Ashley Rathbun
Discontinued: November 4, 1834

The likely location for the East Cicero Post Office was in the eastern part of the Town near where the Cicero Centre Post Office was located at a later date. In 1832 there was so little volume at East Cicero that the postmaster received only $1.62 for his years work. With this volume of business it is not surprising that the post office soon closed.

NOTE: *Much of the information about the post offices of the Town of Cicero was courtesy of Ray Schader, Loomis Pardee and Chris Huxtable.*

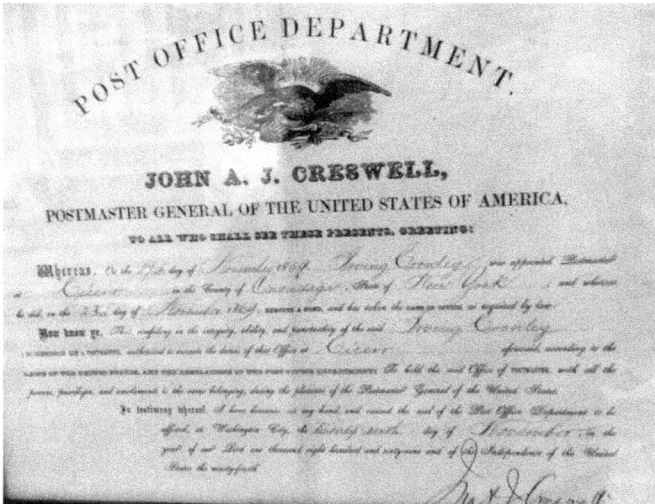

Appointment of Irving Conley as Cicero Postmaster on November 17, 1869 by John A.J. Creswell, Postmaster General.

Earlier Brewerton Post Office, located on State St. (Now Route 11) Photo courtesy of Chris Huxable.

Cicero Post Office when it was in the Cicero Food Mart. Photo courtesy of Ray Schader, Town of Cicero Historian.

Earlier Cicero Post office and Food Mart . Photo furnished by Town of Cicero Historian Ray Schader.

Cicero Post Office when it was next to Cadd Plant's store. Photo courtesy of Ray Schader, Town of Cicero Historian.

The former Cicero Post Office constructed in 1961 on the site of the old Universalist Church. It was located on the west side of Route 11 in the center of the village of Cicero. Photo from 'Cicero Through the Years' by Lona Flyn.

The Bridgeport Post Office at 7901 Bridgeport Minoa Road, Bridgeport NY 13030-9998 is 2,355 square feet and sits on a little over one-half acre. It was constructed in 1988 and is owned by the US Postal Service.

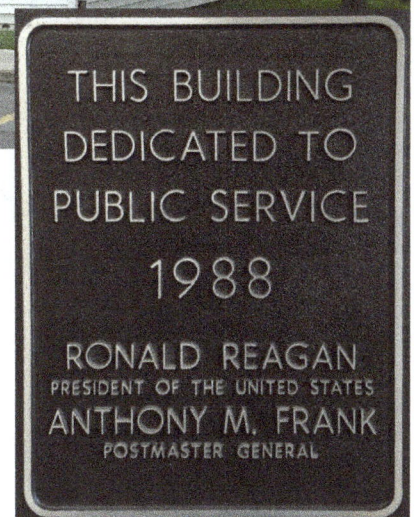

THIS BUILDING
DEDICATED TO
PUBLIC SERVICE
1988

RONALD REAGAN
PRESIDENT OF THE UNITED STATES
ANTHONY M. FRANK
POSTMASTER GENERAL

Bronze sign in Bridgeport Post Office commemorating its 1988 dedication.

The Clay/Cicero Post Office at 5601 State Route 31, Clay NY 13041-9998. The building containing 13,272 square feet and is on a site of a little over three acres. It is leased by the US Postal Service and opened in 1991.

The Brewerton Post Office is at 5560 Bartel Road, Brewerton NY 13029-9998. It is leased by the US Postal Service, contains 4,022 square feet and sits on a site of an acre and one-half. It opened in September 1995.

CHAPTER 8

Post Offices in the Town of Clay

Clay was originally a portion of the Township of Lysander and later a part of Cicero when Cicero was split off from Lysander in 1807. The Town of Clay was formed in 1827 from the western portion of the Town of Cicero.

Belgium

Established: May 19, 1892
First Postmaster: William E. Teall
Previously named Clay Post Office but service discontinued for about a decade
Discontinued: December 31, 1914
Service from **Liverpool**

Belgium is located on Route 31 where it crosses the Seneca River, adjacent to the Town of Lysander. The West Cicero Post Office was established near there in 1825 when Clay was still a part of Cicero. A toll bridge across the Seneca was under construction at the time the West Cicero Post Office was established. By 1848 there were 28 dwellings, a population of 160, three dry goods stores, four grocery stores, two hotels, three blacksmith shops, a tailor, a shoe shop and a manufacturing business that produced the famous 'Oriental Balm Pill,' which employed 30 to 40 people. The majority of these people and businesses were on the Clay side of the river.[1]

A new toll free bridge replaced the old toll bridge at Belgium in 1843. Subsequently the village was often referred to as New Bridge. The post office was located in one of the stores in the hamlet.

Cigarville

Established: December 29, 1871
First Postmaster: Jacob W. Coughtry
Name changed to Clay: May 2, 1903

Cigarville, now known as Clay, was located in Lot 39 on the Syracuse and Northern Railroad. Tobacco growing had become an important agricultural business in Clay in the 1860s and cigar making had become a substantial industry. Soon the name of the local post office took the name of the community's main industry. The post office was located in what is now a part of the Clay Historic Park.

Clay 13041

Established: May 1, 1827[2]
First Postmaster: Nathaniel Teall

It previously had been named the West Cicero Post Office. Its name was changed from West Cicero to Clay when the Town of Clay was split off from Cicero. The Clay Post Office was discontinued May 19, 1892 when it name was changed to Belgium but the name of Clay Post Office again came into being on May 2, 1903 when Cigarville's name was changed to Clay. The Clay Post Office was combined with the Cicero Post Office to become the Clay/Cicero Post Office in January 1991 when a new post office building was constructed at 5601State Route 31. It currently serves an area with over 10,000 residents and has 22 rural routes that provide service to outlying residents of Clay, Cicero and Brewerton.

Euclid

Established: April 14, 1828
First Postmaster: Andrew Johnson
Discontinued: December 30, 1940
Service by the **Clay** Post Office

For many years Euclid was known as Clay Corners. Around 1850, in addition to the post office, Euclid has several mercantile stores, harness makers, shoemakers, wagon makers, blacksmiths, a tailor and two hotels. [3]

---

1 Clayton, Professor W.W., *History of Onondaga County*, 1878, p. 334-345

2 Clark, Joshua V.H., *Onondaga, Volume II*, 1849, p 191
3 Bruce, Dwight H., *Onondaga's Centennial*, 1896 p.831

Latimer

Established: March 21, 1889
First Postmaster: Royal J. Houghton
Name changed to Three River Point March 3, 1892

North Syracuse

Established: August 5, 1887
First Postmaster: William H. Collins
Previously was named Plank Road

It continued to serve as a post office until March 1, 1955 when its patrons began to be served as a branch of the Syracuse Post Office.

North Syracuse was known as Centerville to outsiders, for a number of years, but the locals often referred to it as 'Podunk'.[4] It is located on Lot 79 in Clay and Lot 80 in the Town of Cicero.

Plank Road

Established: March 17, 1846
First Postmaster: James Wallen
Name changed to North Syracuse on August 5, 1887

In 1846, a plank road from Salina (now Syracuse) to Central Square was constructed. It was the first plank road of its kind in the country and achieved substantial notoriety. The plank road received a great deal of use in its initial years but the planks rapidly deteriorated and became costly to maintain. As the road's importance decreased, the name of the post office was changed to North Syracuse on August 5, 1887.

Three River Point

Established: April 3, 1852
First postmaster: Joseph W. Williams
Discontinued: January 5, 1865
Reestablished: March 3, 1892
Discontinued: December 1895
Postal System changed the name to Threeriver Point December 1895
Discontinued: March 31, 1898
Service by Phoenix in Oswego County
Reestablished as Three Rivers May 11, 1899
Discontinued: September 30, 1904
Service by Clay

---

4 Ibid, p.833

Three Rivers

Established: May 11, 1899
First Postmaster: Frederick H. Barnum
Discontinued: September 30, 1904
Service by **Clay**

The Postal System decided to simplify post office names in the late 1800s so in 1895 they changed the name of Three Rivers Point to Threeriver Point. The locals, like numerous other locations across the country, didn't like the new name so in a few years it was changed to Three Rivers, which was more agreeable to the people served by that post office.

Located where the Oneida and Seneca Rivers meet to form the Oswego River, it was a location where mail could be conveniently dropped off. As a result there were some people on land routes, like Baldwinsville merchant Otis Bigelow, who picked up their mail at a Three Rivers tavern.

West Cicero

Established: June 20, 1825
First Postmaster: Nathan Teall
Name discontinued May 21, 1827

Its name became Clay Post Office on May 1, 1827 when the Town of Clay was split from the Town of Cicero. A historical marker states that it was located at the corner of Routes 57 and 31 in what is now commonly known as Moyer's Corners. It was likely, however, that it was located to the west of what was called Teall Corners, now called Moyer's Corners.

In the early part of the 19th century post offices were usually located in a tavern or general store. Pearl Palmer, in the *Historical Review of the Town of Lysander, Part 35,* states that 'a rectangular frame building with small panes of glass is standing on the north side of the road on the summit of the hill about midway between Belgium and Moyer's Corners. This was the old Teall Tavern erected originally by the Teall brothers at the Corners.' Nathan Teall is buried in the Myrtle Grove Cemetery about a mile west of Belgium in the Town of Lysander.

Interestingly, it is likely the post office was in the same location since Nathan Teall continued as postmaster after the name change. In *Sweet's New Atlas of Onondaga County* by Homer D.L. Sweet, printed in 1874, he shows the Clay Post Office of that date, in the hamlet of Belgium. The residence of G.W. Teall is also in Belgium. The Teall name continues when William M.

Teall becomes a Clay postmaster in 1884 and Albert E. Teall becomes the postmaster in 1890.

Pearl Palmer in her book[5] also states, "with the establishment of stagecoach lines, mail for Belgium was brought from Onondaga Hill. At a later date the post office was kept in a large yellow house on the northwest corner just east of the bridge at Belgium. Here lived Melissa Danforth and her husband who was postmaster at that time." (Note: Information regarding postmasters at Clay are unavailable between 1924 and 1955.)

Woodard

Established: December 29, 1871
First Postmaster: Allen B. Kinne
Discontinued: June 30, 1903
Service by **Liverpool**

The opening of the Syracuse Northern Railroad in November 1871 provided the impetus for the development of Woodard and the establishment of a Post Office in that community. Later the addition of a railroad branch to Phoenix formed a 'Y' in Woodard increasing business and residential growth in the area.

Young

Established: December 29, 1871
First Postmaster: John G. Young
Discontinued: April 1891
Service by **Cigarville**

The Young Post Office was located on the Caughdenoy Road, north of Euclid, in the home of one of the Young family.

NOTE: *The help of Dorothy Heller, Town of Clay Historian, is most appreciated.*

---

5   Palmer, Pearl, *Historical Review of the Town of Lysander*, A series of articles published between 1941 & 1946 by the ONON-Town Publishing Co., Inc. in the Baldwinsville Messenger.

Mail traveling by stagecoach

Plank Road Post Office (North Syracuse Public Library), South Main Street and Shaver Avenue, Village of North Syracuse, circa 1825
The Plank Road Post Office was also the residence of its postmaster, Joseph Palmer. The building was altered for use as the North Syracuse Public Library in 1933.

Onondaga Historical Marker at the northeast corner of the intersection of Routes 31 and 57

NATHAN TEALL
FIRST POSTMASTER
WEST CICERO 1825
CHANGED TO
CLAY 1828
ONONDAGA HISTORICAL ASSOCIATION
1979

Clay Postmaster Margaret K. Schneider emptying the outside mail box as she prepares to open the Clay Post Office. From the February 28, 1960 Syracuse Post Standard Pictorial courtesy of Town of Clay Historian Dorothy Heller.

Postmistriss Margaret K. Schneider, Sean Keating, regional Post Office director, and Congressman James M. Hanley were on hand for the dedication of the Clay Post Office on Rt. 31 on July 23, 1966. Photo from Margaret Schneider.

Building in Clay that held the last Clay Post Office prior to the new Cicero-Clay Post Office constructed in 1991.

The Clay/Cicero Post Office at 5601 State Route 31, Clay NY 13041-9998. The building containing 13,272 square feet and is on a site of a little over three acres. It is leased by the US Postal Service and opened in 1991.

CHAPTER 9

Post Offices in the Town of DeWitt

DeWitt, formed in 1835, originally was a part of the Town of Manlius, which was formed from a portion of the Central New York Military Tract. The Town of DeWitt was named for Moses DeWitt a Major in the militia and a prominent early settler in the town. During the past 70 years the town has grown rapidly with both residential and business development. Interstate 481 crosses the center of the town and intersects Interstate 690 on its east and Interstate 90 on the north. There are currently five ZIP codes used for residents of the town.

Collamer

Established: December 17, 1849
First Postmaster: Henry E. Pierce
Discontinued: July 31, 1902
Service by **East Syracuse**

Collamer, which was formerly named Britton's Settlement, is located in the northeast part of the town on Route 298. It was sometimes also referred to as Brittonfield. When a post office came to the area in 1849 it was called Collamer in honor of Jacob Collamer who was United States Postmaster General at the time. Jacob Collamer had a short tenure as Postmaster General. He was appointed on March 8, 1849 and replaced on July 23, 1850 when the new President, Millard Filmore appointed Nathan K. Hall. Rural Free Delivery came into existence at the time the post office was discontinued so it is quite likely that mail was delivered to the homes of the former patrons of the Collamer Post Office by an RFD carrier from East Syracuse.

DeWitt

Established: April 9, 1835
First Postmaster: George S. Loomis
Name changed to Dewitt in December 1895
Name changed again to DeWitt in December 1905
Discontinued: February 28, 1955
Service by branch of **Syracuse**

DeWitt is approximately where Erie Boulevard connects with East Genesee Street. The community was first called Youngsville, named for John Young who had six sons and three daughters who settled in the area.[1] It later was named Orville. The name of the post office was changed from Orville to Dewitt when the Town of Dewitt was formed in 1835.

Information from DeWitt historian, Garland Blanch, places one location of the Dewitt Post Office in the Fabring General Store on E. Genesee St. at the intersection of Jamesville Road. Another location was across the street at about 4322 E. Genesee St. As United States presidents of opposing parties were elected, it was common for postmasters to be changed and local post offices to move to a new location. It is likely that the DeWitt Post Office had half a dozen different locations over its lifetime.

DeWitt Centre

Established: February 7, 1872
First Postmaster: Stephen Headson
Name changed to Dewitt Center in December 1895
Discontinued: April 15, 1899
Service by **Syracuse**

DeWitt Centre was located approximately where Thompson Road and Erie Boulevard meet. It was near Hedson's Landing along the Erie Canal. There was a slight change in the spelling of its name in 1895 and was discontinued in 1899. Its mail then came through the

---

1   Bruce, Dwight H., *Onondaga's Centennial*, page 1020

Syracuse Post Office and it is likely that the residents received their mail by an RFD carrier out of Syracuse.

East Syracuse 13057

Established: May 15, 1876
First Postmaster: Alvah Burnham

East Syracuse, earlier called Messina, grew rapidly when the New York Central and its railroad yards came to the area. The Village of East Syracuse web site states:

In the 1870's, the main line of the New York Central Railroad was built through the northern part of Messina, and the DeWitt Rail yards complex, one of the busiest in the world in its day, stretched from Messina five miles east to Minoa.

During most of the nineteenth century the larger part of the hamlet was south of the railroad yards, but as the population grew with rail workers, housing expanded to the north. In the 1960's, Interstate 690 was built through the southern part of the Village between the railroad and Erie Blvd, which was built over part of the old canal. Now only a small portion of the original settlement south of the railroad remains, including about 100 of the Village's 1,400 dwelling units.

Eastwood

Established: April 14, 1890
First Postmaster: Byron Midler
Discontinued: December 19, 1892
Service by Syracuse
Re-established: June 19, 1893 as a branch of Syracuse
Became a Syracuse Station on August 6, 1926

Eastwood was originally a village, and as a suburb of Syracuse was named for its location east of and adjacent to Syracuse. In 1928 the Eastwood neighborhood was part of the last round of annexations by the City of Syracuse. The main corridor for the Eastwood Community is James Street. As was customary for numerous small villages adjacent to Syracuse, Eastwood, like Salina and Geddes became a part of its larger neighbor.

Jamesville 13078

Established: September 2, 1811
First Postmaster: Thomas Rose

Jamesville, which was originally called Sinai, is located on the southern edge of the Town of DeWitt near the towns of LaFayette and Pompey. The water power available from Butternut Creek brought early industry

and steady growth to Jamesville soon creating the need for a post office. In addition to the usual commercial businesses a large industry in the mining of stone, lime and plaster using the area's natural resources developed.

An article from the March 25, 1861 newspaper *Journal* in the files of the Onondaga Historical Association provides an insight into the method of selecting postmasters at that time:

> At a caucus of the Republicans receiving their mail at the Jamesville Post Office, held on Saturday evening, Mr. Samuel Hill was nominated for postmaster receiving 54 of the 100 votes cast. Mr Hill is an old and respected citizen and well deserves the compliment.

Abraham Lincoln, a Republican, had been elected as president and just been sworn in so the postmaster of the United States. James Buchanan, his predecessor was a Democrat so all across the United States including Jamesville most of the Democrat Postmasters were replaced by Republicans.

The Jamesville Post Office has been in a number of locations including the Quinlan, Pfeiffer and Burke buildings. A new post office was constructed in 1965 in the Jamesville Town Square shopping center. The building, which had 2,664 square feet, was privately owned and leased to the Postal Service for a ten year period with four consecutive five-year options.

A newspaper article, from the OHA files which appeared in an unnamed local newspaper on February 13, 1978 (probably the *Post Standard*), describes the size of the Jamesville Post Office at that time:

> About 3,000 homes on over nearly 150 miles of routes in the Towns of LaFayette, DeWitt, Manlius, Pompey and Onondaga depend upon the Jamesville Post Office for mail delivery. About 300 other residents and business firms have chosen to receive their mail in post office boxes.

> There are four full-time and four substitute carriers for Jamesville, some who have served as long as 25 years. They make the daily rounds by car beginning at 7:30 a.m., returning by 2:30 p.m. So well acquainted are Jamesville postal workers with their customers that mail can often be delivered without a street address, by name only.

> The four clerks working the counter are equally familiar with area residents. A person would have a pretty hard time picking up mail if he said he was somebody he wasn't according to the postmaster.

At the time of the article William Hopkins had been the Jamesville postmaster for 18 years and had been elected Vice President of the National Association of Postmasters. He was headed to Washington to urge the passage of a bill that would block the closing of small post offices and maintain the existing postal services. Postmasters and post office patrons have struggled many years to retain their post offices which have been an extremely important part of life in smaller communities.

At the present time the Jamesville Post Office has about 700 boxes for the use of local residents and six rural routes. Jay Hotaling is the Officer-in-Charge, sometimes referred to as Operations Manager.

Messina Springs

Established: February 18, 1850
First Postmaster: Miles Benham
Discontinued: June 9, 1859

Messina Springs, named for its three natural sulfur springs flowing from the ground, was located slightly north of the intersection of James Street and Thompson Road. It was a small community, northwest of Messina (now East Syracuse), which was settled in the early 19th century around these mineral springs. James Street was then a main east-west road from Syracuse to Messina and Manlius Center, and Thompson Road was a main north-south thoroughfare.

Reputed to have healing powers, these springs attracted a large clientele, culminating in the late 19th century with a spa, hotel, casino and race track. A fire consumed the hotel and casino around 1913. All that remains of this community is a tiny cemetery on James Street just west of Thompson Road.

Orville

Established: November 11, 1815
First Postmaster: Isaac Osgood
Discontinued: April 9, 1835
Service by **DeWitt**
George S. Loomis, postmaster at Orville, became DeWitt's first postmaster

Orville was first called Youngsville, named after John Young came to the area with his large family in the late 1700s. His children also settled there making it natural for neighbors to call the settlement Youngsville. When the post office was established in 1815, it was named Orville and later, when the Town of DeWitt was formed from 36 lots of the Town of Manlius, the post office took the name of the new Town of DeWitt.

NOTE: *Much of the information concerning the DeWitt Post Offices was through the courtesy of Blanch Garland, Town of DeWitt Historian.*

Early photo of the DeWitt Post Office. Courtesy of the Onondaga Historical Association.

Jamesville Post Office on the west side of South Street looking north to Main Street. Courtesy of the Onondaga Historical Association.

The East Syracuse Post Office is located at 404 West Manlius Street, East Syracuse, NY 13057-9998. It is owned by the US Postal Service, contains 6,672 square feet and sits on a 12,447 square foot site. It opened in 1961.

The DeWitt Post Office is located at 6581 Kinne Rd., Syracuse, NY 13214-9998. It is owned by the US Postal Service, contains 9210 square feet and sits on a 53,205 square foot site. It opened in 1973.

The Jamesville Post Office is at 6499 East Seneca Turnpike, Jamesville NY 13078-9998. It is leased by the US Postal Service, contains 3,414 square feet, sits on a three acre site and was opened in 1965.

CHAPTER 10

Post Offices in the Town of Elbridge

The Town of Elbridge was formed in 1829 from a part of the Town of Camillus. The post offices in both Elbridge and Jordan were established before the Town of Elbridge was established. Previous to the formation of these two post offices, the settlers in these areas had been serviced by the Camillus Post Office, which was located in the hamlet of Elbridge and had been established in 1810.

Elbridge 13060

Established: August 8, 1815
First Postmaster: Truman Adams
Mail had previously been sent to Camillus
Currently serves a population of about 2,800

Records of the National Archives and Records Service in Washington, DC state that the Elbridge Post Office was originally named Camillus and its name was changed to Elbridge on August 8, 1815. The post office had several different locations in the Village of Elbridge before it was moved to its present location at 106 South Street. This was a new building built to Postal System specifications whereas the previous locations had been in a portion of another building operated as a store or an Inn.

The Elbridge Post Office made the national news in the early 1900s when a clerk in the post office by the name of Jessie Roberta Kinney was singled out as a glaring example of the unfairness of the 'political spoils system'. Beginning in 1829, President Jackson recognized the potential value of patronage and invited William T. Barry, the existing Postmaster General, to sit as a member of the President's Cabinet. This appointment became a precedent that continued until the reorganization of the Postal System in 1971. Postal System patronage permitted the political party in power to make thousands of postmaster and rural carrier appointments. This system provided many political workers, thousands of votes and millions of dollars for the appointing political party.

Jessica had served the Elbridge community very well as a clerk in its post office. When the postmaster, who actually did very little work in the post office and like many other postmasters at the time who hired a clerk to do most of the work, died, politics and political back room decisions deprived her a job. Her story, written by a former Harvard University President appeared in a national magazine. It made Jessica a figure of martyrdom to members of a movement trying to reform the civil service for federal employees. Jessica lost her position and worked as a store clerk in Syracuse but eventually was employed as a clerk in the post office at Cape Vincent. In 1970, the United States Congress finally voted to remove the Postmaster General from the President's Cabinet reducing the politics in postmaster appointments.

Archive records show Star Routes and Rural Routes out of the Elbridge Post Office in 1911. (Star Routes were those serviced by the low bidder for a route operated by a person who was not an employee of the post office.) At this period of time Star Route carrier Mel Carpenter not only carried the mail but also carried passengers from the train station at Hart Lot to Elbridge with his horse and buggy.

The horse and buggy was the standard form of transport used by mail carriers for many years. Allen Jones was the last carrier with horse and buggy, giving horses up for an automobile in 1921. Claude and Fred Ashby, Star Route Carriers also made mailbox deliveries on route to the Hart Lot and Jordan Train Stations where they picked up pouches of mail on a scheduled basis.

In 1957 the Highway Postal Bus was introduced in Elbridge. This was a large bus, with separate sections, so the mail could be sorted while the bus was traveling. This bus was scheduled from Syracuse to Binghamton and return daily. The bus made stops at individual post offices delivering and picking up mail along its way. This method of service gave way to Star Route Truck Service operated by low bidders who were not Postal Service employees.

Currently there are two rural routes out of the Elbridge Post Office. One of them, established about 15 years ago serves a number of businesses.

Half Way

Established: June 23, 1868
First Postmaster: William A. Martin
Name changed to **Halfway** from December 1895 to July 15, 1903
Discontinued: July 15, 1903 with service from Elbridge (probably became RFD)

The Auburn and Syracuse Railroad gave rise to the Half Way postoffice, Half Way being equal distance from both Auburn and Syracuse.

Hart Lot
(Located at Skaneateles Junction)

Established: January 15, 1850
First Postmaster: Elisha P. Cornell
Name changed to **Hartlot** in December 1895 to December 1905
Name changed back to **Hart Lo**t in December 1905
Discontinued: January 22, 1982

The Auburn and Syracuse railroad gave rise to the Hart Lot postoffice, Hart Lot being named from Josiah Hart, an early owner. It is better known as Skaneateles Junction. A short railroad connected it with the village of Skaneateles. There were coal and lumber yards, a store and small inns there.

Jack's Reef

Established: January 21, 1832
First Postmaster: Zera Shepard
Name changed to **Jack Reef** November 21, 1893
Name changed to **Jackreef** December 1895
Discontinued: February 14, 1901
Service from **Memphis**

Jack's Reef is a small hamlet located on the Seneca River where the towns of Lysander and Elbridge come together. A postoffice was established at Peru, nearly four miles east of Jordan. A Peru, NY post office had been established in 1798 in Clinton County making the name unavailable for use here. Since the hamlet of Jack's

Rift's was only a mile to the North and that name was available it is the likely reason that name was chosen. The Post Office Department apparently preferred it be named Jack's Reef rather than Jack's Rifts, named for Jack an African-American who lived on the Seneca River at that location and was noted for catching and selling fish. Even today the local people refer to the hamlet with both names. Actually it should be Jack's Rifts since the post office by the name of Jack's Reef was over a mile away in the hamlet of Peru.

Jordan 13080

Established: March 23, 1824
First Postmaster: Seneca Hale
Currently serves a population of about 3,600

The middle section of the Erie Canal opened through Jordan in 1820 with the completion of its full length in 1825. The canal brought numerous small industries to Jordan along with people to work in them. As the population increased a post office was needed. Like most post offices in their early years, the Jordan Post Office moved several times, often when a new post-master was appointed. Usually the post office occupied the front corner of a building that housed a store or an inn. Often postal customers had to climb several steps to enter the post office, quite a different situation from today when most post office entrances are at sidewalk level.

Prior to the days of Rural Free Delivery (RFD), in the early 1900s, people outside the village had to make a trip to the post office from up to several miles away to pick up their mail. When RFD came into existence it cut down on the traffic in and out of the village since the RFD carrier now brought mail to the rural residents six days a week.

Currently there are two rural routes out of the Jordan Post Office with one of them extending into Cayuga County. Changes often come slowly to the Postal System but in 1952 when the price of a penny postcard, which had been one cent since 1873, was raised to two cents the Jordan Post Office was caught by surprise with an inventory of 1,800 outdated postcards.

A new post office was constructed on Mechanic Street in 1968 as part of a larger building to house a supermarket. Three houses were purchased and the area was cleared to produce this central location.

Windfall

Established: January 14, 1840
First Postmaster: David Preston
Discontinued: September 29, 1851
Windfall later became known as Half Way

The Windfall Post Office was established in 1840, two years after the Syracuse and Auburn Railroad passed through the community. During the railroad's first year of operation stagecoach type cars were pulled on rails by horses. Steam powered locomotives were put into operation on the railroad for the first on June 14, 1839.

Quite likely the area residents thought the new railroad coming to their community was a piece of good luck or 'windfall' and may have chosen that name for their post office. Since the post office was discontinued in 1851 there was no post office until 1868 until one reopened in the same area with the new name Half Way.

NOTE: *Much of the information concerning the post offices of the Town of Elbridge was obtained through the courtesy of John Horner Town of Elbridge and Village of Jordan historian.*

This building on South Street was an earlier location of the Elbridge Post Office. Photo courtesy of John Horner, Town of Elbridge Historian.

The right corner of this building was the location of the Jordan Post Office prior to the building of the present structure at 9 Mechanic Street. Photo courtesy of John Horner, Town of Elbridge Historian.

The Elbridge Post Office at 106 South Street, Elbridge NY 13060-9998 is 2,052 square feet and sits on a quarter-acre site. It is leased by the US postal Service and was constructed in 1962.

The Jordan Post Office is 2,332 square feet and sits on a site of over one-half acre. It is leased by the US Postal Service and was constructed in 1968.

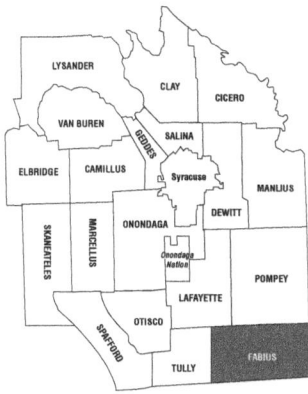

CHAPTER 11

Post Offices in the Town of Fabius

The township of Fabius was number 15 in the Military Tract. When Onondaga County was established in 1794, Fabius included nearly all of the towns of Cuyler and Truxton which are now part of Cortland County. With the formation of Cortland County in 1808 Fabius was left with the northern 50 lots in Military lot 15.[1]

A post office, named Fabius, was established in Truxton in 1800, from which most of the Fabius settlers were served during the time when Truxton was still part of Fabius. At the time Cortland County was formed, the post office named Fabius was discontinued for eight years.

The Skaneateles-Hamilton Turnpike, incorporated in 1806 and completed several years later, had a tremendous influence on where people settled in the Town of Fabius and where post offices were later established. It crossed the town from east to west permanently influencing all local industries, settled communities and where post offices were to be located.

From *Fabius, Past and Present* written in 1939 comes the story that, in the early days, mail was so scarce that one postmaster is said to have carried the mail in his top hat and to have delivered it when he saw the addressee at a meeting.

Apulia

Established: December 27, 1825
First Postmaster: Stephen Miles
Discontinued: June 30, 1944
Service from **Apulia Station**

Apulia, located to the east of Apulia Station, lost prominence when the Syracuse and Binghamton Railroad passed a little to the west. Business gradually gravitated to Summit Station (Apulia Station) because of the ease of shipping and receiving by railroad.

Apulia Station 13020

Established: June 16, 1898
First Postmaster: Frank June
Mail had previously been addressed to **Summit Station** however the post office name was changed to Apulia Station on June 16, 1898
Currently serves a population of about 150 with Post Office boxes

The arrival of the Syracuse and Binghamton Railroad in 1854 brought the community of Summit Station into existence. It became the shipping point for the town of Fabius as well as eastern Tully. Among the manufacturers bringing prominence to the hamlet was a large chair factory.[2]

A father and son combination were postmasters at Apulia Station for over 50 years. Charles R. Briggs was appointed postmaster in 1904 and operated the post office in his general store that sold a great variety of food and general needs to the residents in and around Apulia Station. Charles had purchased the store in 1891 so it was natural that when he became postmaster the post office would be in his store. He served as postmaster until his death in 1925 when his son Walter E. Briggs became postmaster and operated the post office out of the same store until 1962.

The railroad that was constructed through Apulia Station in 1854 brought growth to the community. In the railroad's early days the trains' engines burned wood to make steam to power the trains. Two hotels were constructed in Summit Station; the Summit House to house travelers and the Summit House to house travelers and the woodcutters necessary to provide fuel for the hungry engines of the trains.

---

1 Bruce, Dwight W. *Onondaga's Centennial* p. 866

2 Bruce, Dwight W. *Onondaga's Centennial* p. 886-7

Fabius 13063
(Formerly known as Franklinville)

Established: October 1, 1800 when Cortland County was part of Onondaga Co.

First Postmaster: Stephen Hedges

Discontinued as **Fabius** Post Office on April 8, 1808 when Cortland County was established

Established in Onondaga County: November 1, 1816

First Postmaster: Jonathon Stanley
(Kay and Smith, *NY Postal History*)

Re-established: May 7, 1821

First Postmaster: Isaac Powers
(from Photostats of Official Post Office Documents by Fred L. Scholl in 1954)

Currently serves a population of about 1,900 with two rural routes and post office boxes.

Fabius was once known as both Franklinville and Fabius Center. It is located at the intersection of the Skaneateles and Hamilton east-west highway (Route 80) and Route 91 from the north. At an early date it became the commercial center of the Town of Fabius. Although originally a farming community, manufacturing soon became a major factor in its growth. There were several tanneries, a shoe manufacturer, a foundry a manufacture of horse powered threshing machines, a mower factory and a carriage factory.[3]

The first post office was established in the Bush store, for years known as Hamilton's. It moved to several places in town according to whether the President of the United States was a Republican or Democrat. Locations were at the different stores as well as at Clarence Kennedy's on Main Street.[4]

About 1830 William G. Fargo of Watervale, at the age of 13, was employed by Daniel Butts, a mail contractor, to carry the mail on horseback twice a week from Pompey Hill by way of Watervale, Manlius, Oran, Delphi, Fabius and Apulia and back to Pompey Hill – a circuit of about 40 miles. He became interested in express offices as they opened in the west. By 1850 he and Henry Wells had organized the well known Wells Fargo Express Co.[5]

In 1904 when Rural Free Delivery was initiated, James Powers became the first mail carrier in the town. To make his deliveries he kept four horses, traveled twenty-four and one-half miles a day for the annual pay of $720. He delivered the mail for 13 years and was followed by Walter Schoonmaer who was succeeded by Carl Clough and then Erwin Hills in 1927. Erwin kept horses for 10 more years to cover part of the route when roads were inaccessible in the winter.

A February 19, 1946 news article shows how postmasters were appointed before Civil Service. It states, "Roger John Ryan, 37 year old war veteran who operates a soda fountain in this village, was notified today that the Senate has confirmed his nomination. Hence Carl H. Hamilton, Republican who has been postmaster for a decade, will turn the office over to his Democrat successor. This will also mean the moving of the office from Hamilton's grocery store to Postmaster Ryan's confectionary store. Ryan gets $1,900 a year as postmaster." (Author's note: The date and facts in this article are suspicious as Franklin Roosevelt, a democrat had been President from 1933 until Harry Truman, also a democrat, succeeded him, and Truman was still President in 1946. The article is worthy from the standpoint it describes the appointment process for postmasters throughout the country.)

The post office is in a leased building that has postal boxes for local residents and two rural routes.

Summit Station

Established: August 17, 1861

First Postmaster: John J. Blaney

Name changed to **Apulia Station** June 16, 1898

NOTE: *Information about the post offices and pictures furnished by J. Roy Dodge, Peter Schlicht, Town of Fabius Historian, and the Fabius Historical Association are most appreciated.*

---

3 Bruce, Dwight W. *Onondaga's Centennial* p. 886
4 *Fabius, Past and Present*, 1939, pp. 39-40
5 *Fabius, Past and Present*, 1939, p. 40

The post office in Apulia, NY in the early 1900s. Farm families came to town on farm wagons pulled by horses to trade their farm grown items for food and to pick up any mail that might have arrived at the post office. The Apulia Post Office closed in 1946.

This is a photo of the Briggs store in Apulia Station, taken in the early 1900s, which also housed the post office. In the 1970s the post office was located in a trailer prior to the new post office construction. Notice the train tracks crossing the street, which is now Route 80. There was a mailbag hook down the rail a bit so a train could come rumbling through the village and leave or pick up the mail without stopping.

For many years prior to 1946, the Fabius Post Office was located in Hamilton's store. This photo was probably taken in the late 1920s when the automobile was gradually replacing horses.

Fabius Post Office, on the right, in Ryan's store. In 1946 the post office was moved from Hamilton's grocery store to this location. Roger John Ryan served as postmaster until 1972.

This is also a photo of the Briggs store in Apulia Station, which became the post office in 1904 when Charles R. Briggs was named postmaster. After Charles death it continued as the post office when his son Walter E. Briggs was named postmaster. Walter served as postmaster until 1962. (Photo from a June 1949 Post Standard article taken from the files of the Onondaga Historical Association.)

The Fabius Post Office was one time located in the residence on the right owned by Mrs. Fellows.

Apulia Post Office when it was located in C.W. Ellis' residence and store.

Walter E. Briggs, Apulia Station Postmaster, serving a customer in his combination general store and post office. The postmaster's window, surrounded by patrons postal boxes was common to most small town post offices in the 1900s. (Photo from a June 1949 Post-Standard article taken from the files of the Onondaga Historical Association.)

The Apulia Station Post Office at 979 Apulia Road, Apulia Station NY 13020-9998 is 888 square feet in area and sits on an approximately a quarter of an acre. The property is owned by the US Postal Service and the post office was built in 1982.

The Fabius Post Office is at 1306 Keeney Road, Fabius NY 13063-9998, is 1,450 square feet and sits on a lot of 17, 560 Square feet. It was constructed in 1975 and is leased by the US Postal Service.

CHAPTER 12

Post Offices in the Town of Geddes

G eddes was the last town in the county to be formed when on March 18, 1848 it was removed from the portion of the Town of Salina lying west of Onondaga Lake.[1] It was named after James Geddes who came here to live in 1794 and formed a company to produce salt. Later he was instrumental in surveying for the Erie Canal and selecting its route through the state.

Until the level of Onondaga Lake was lowered in 1822, it was swampy along much of the southern and southwestern areas along Onondaga Lake. Lowering the lake was beneficial for both Syracuse and Geddes as well as essential in preparation for the construction of the Oswego Canal.

Geddes

Established: February 25, 1819 with David
                    W. Hollister as the First Postmaster according
                    to *NY Postal History* by Kay & Smith, or
                    November 25, 1828 with Elijah W. Curtis as
                    the First Postmaster according to *Photostats
                    of Official Post Office Documents* by Fred L.
                    Scholl in 1954
Discontinued: June 1, 1888
Service from **Syracuse**

In 1807, James Geddes made the first map of the village of Geddes when he laid out 20 lots on each side of Genesee Street. It became an incorporated village in 1832. In 1836 the village was located two miles west of the village of Syracuse, at the head of Onondaga Lake and on the Erie Canal. It was growing rapidly with a variety of industries, a salt spring and about 50 dwellings. In 1887 the Village of Geddes was annexed to the City of Syracuse and the following year its post office was discontinued with mail coming from the Syracuse Post Office. The population of the Village of Geddes at that time was almost 7,000.

Solvay

Established: March 4, 1889
First Postmaster: Samuel S. DeWitt
Discontinued: June 30, 1899 or June 21, 1899
Service from **Station of Syracuse**
Service from **Branch of Syracuse** July 1, 1908

The purchase of the Gere farm, during the summer of 1881, for the production of soda changed the face of the land adjacent to the southwestern shore of Onondaga Lake. The little community was originally called Geddesburgh in honor of James Geddes. After 1881, the village grew rapidly when the construction of buildings began for the production of soda using a method invented by the Solvay brothers in Belgium, named the 'Solvay Process'. The village was incorporated with the name Solvay in 1885 at the suggestion of Samuel DeWitt its first postmaster.

One of the reasons for the location of the Solvay process near Syracuse was the availability of two major ingredients: limestone and salt. Additional reasons for the choice of its site were the proximity to railroads, the Erie Canal flowing through the Gere property, land along Onondaga Lake to dispose of waste and a readily available supply of water. The growth of Solvay created the need for a post office which opened in 1889. Previously residents of Solvay had received their mail from Geddes, Camillus or Belle Isle.

In 1899 the Solvay Post Office became a post office station of Syracuse. By 1903 the mail came from Syracuse three times a day on a trolley of the Solvay Line. The trolleys on the Solvay Line were running as far as the notable 'stone pile' where the limestone from the Split Rock stone quarry was stored until needed in soda manufacturing. Interestingly, the site of the old 'stone pile', is the location of the present Solvay post office building.

Since the Solvay Post Office was established it has had several different locations. For several years it was

---

1 Bruce, Dwight H., *Onondaga's Centennial*, p. 1037

59

in the original Solvay town hall at the corner of Milton Avenue and Bridge Street. After World War I it was housed in several different buildings in East Solvay; on Hall Avenue, Lamont Avenue, Freeman Avenue and Milton Avenue. A special building was constructed in the 1950s for a post office at 1613 Milton Avenue. The present post office building was constructed in 1963 at 1801 Milton Avenue. It is a spacious building on a site encompassing more than an acre.[2]

Styles Station

Established: September 11, 1871
First Postmaster: Jacob D. Jewell
Name changed to **Stiles Station** November 19, 1874
Discontinued: June 15, 1901
Service from **Baldwinsville**

Stiles Station, located in the Town of Geddes close to the Town Van Buren line, was a stop on the Syracuse and Oswego Railroad where VanVleck Road crossed the tracks. The hamlet received its name because it was at the point where it crossed the farm of H.C. Stiles.

When the Styles Post Office was established in 1871 it was located in a portion of the railroad station. Jacob D. Jewell, who had acquired the Stiles farm was named its first postmaster. Freeman Blanding, a neighboring farmer who grew hops and tobacco became the second postmaster.

The west half of the station consisted of living and dining rooms. On the track side were the express room, ticket office, post office and a waiting room with two rows of seats.

A coal stove stood in the passenger section and the family bedrooms were on the upper floor. A well with a pump was to the north side of the building.

After the station had served its use as both a rail station and a post office it was moved to nearby property and used as a home. In 1966 the old station, now a home, was demolished to make way for a new highway.[3]

NOTE: *Much of the information concerning the post offices in the Town of Geddes was provided through the courtesy of Susan Millet, Town of Geddes Historian.*

---

2 Tomasetti, Mario, *Down Solvay's Memory Lane Moods & Images*, Volume 13, No. 2

3 Christopher, Anthony, *Stiles Station was Rail Depot and Post Office*, January 12, 1967

Photo of the first Solvay Post Office which was in the old Geddes town hall building at the intersection of Milton Ave. and Bridge Street in Solvay. Look closely at the sign under the flag in the middle and you will see Syracuse Post Office, Solvay Station. Photo courtesy of Susan Millet, Town of Geddes Historian.

This building became the home of the Solvay Post Office in 1950. The post office had previously been located at several different places including locations on Hall, Lamont and Freeman Avenues.

This was a two-room school house on top of the hill in Lakeland. During World War I it was also used as the camp library and camp post office. Located where the John Carno Recreation Building is today on State Fair Blvd.

MOVING THE MAIL
SOLVAY'S POSTMEN...1963

1st Row L to R, D. Ballsman, L. Bella, C. Maczonis, P. Marotta, S. Boucher, M. Gozowski
2nd Row L to R, C. Kearns, P. Notcher, A. Ranali, L. Goudy, J. Slattery, L. White, E. England, A. Volcko, T. Pastore
3rd Row L to R, H. Dabrowski, J. Smith, T. Butler, D. Keegan, H. Hilner, S. Pestillo, V. Lopez, L. Corradi, H. Dabrowski, R. McConagay, M. Kasiak, G. Zeppetello, A. Ziemba, J. Manion, F. Miller, E. Billion, A. Hooper
4th Row L to R, W. Mauser, W. Macko, J. Rea, R. Vollmer, C. Basso, C. Radecki, J. Krupka, J. Childs, S. Bordynski

A 1963 photograph of the Solvay Post Office employees. Photo from Solvay's Post Office in 'Down Solvay's Memory Lane Moods & Images' volume 13, No.2 by Mario Tomasetti.

Solvay Branch of the Post Offices at 1801 Milton Avenue, Syracuse NY 13209-9211. The property consisting of an acre and one-half with a 15,650 square foot building is owned by the US Postal Service and was constructed in 1989.

CHAPTER 13

Post Offices in the Town of LaFayette

The Town of LaFayette was formed in 1825 from 32 lots of the original military township of Pompey, which was No. 10 in the Military Tract and from the land purchased by New York State from the Onondaga Indian Reservation that was removed from the Town of Onondaga. The first settler, John Wilcox, came in 1791 to what was then Pompey but later a part of LaFayette. The town was named in honor of the French General Marquis de LaFayette who had been a close friend and of great aid to General George Washington during the Revolutionary War.[1]

Although the Tully Valley Post Office is listed in the post offices of Tully it was, during most of its years, located over the town border in LaFayette since the postmasters, who often had the post office in their homes, lived in LaFayette. Most of the residents in the northern part of LaFayette have been served by the Jamesville Post Office.[2]

Cardiff
(Previously was **Christian Hollow**)

Established:	January 15, 1830
First Postmaster:	John Spencer
Discontinued:	June 15, 1915
Service from: **LaFayette**	

Cardiff, which was originally called Christian Hollow, received its post office in 1828. Two years later its name was changed to Cardiff. It lies about two miles west of the village of LaFayette. About 1870 the post office was moved to the rear of R.F. Park's General Store and in 1915, when no one seemed interested in maintaining a post office in Cardiff, it was discontinued. The 27 families that had been receiving their mail at the Cardiff Post Office began having their mail delivered to their homes by a Rural Free Delivery carrier out of LaFayette.[3]

Christian Hollow

Established:	February 5, 1828
First Postmaster:	Salmon S. Merriman
Name changed to **Cardiff** January 15, 1830	

Collingwood
(Previously was **Linn**)

Established:	April 22, 1865
First Postmaster:	Luther Cole
Discontinued:	September 30, 1903
Service from: **LaFayette**	

Collingwood was originally called Sherman Hollow and later Linn before the name was changed to Collingwood. No one seems to know why the name was changed from Linn to Collingwood. It is located about two miles southeast of the village of LaFayette. In the 1860s and early 1870s, when Avery R. Palmer was postmaster, the post office was maintained in conjunction with his mills. He was succeeded by his son, Jirah D. Palmer, who maintained the post office in his home until the post office was discontinued. During the period when Jirah Palmer was postmaster, Milo Dean met the train each day at the Onativia station (east of LaFayette) and carried the mail more than a mile on his back to the Collingwood Post Office.[4]

LaFayette 13084
(Previously was **Pompey West Hill**)

Established:	May 6, 1825
First Postmaster:	Johnson Hall
From December 1895 to December 1905 was **Lafayette**	

---

1 Bruce, Dwight H., *Onondaga's Centennial*, p. 961, 970
2 Dodge, J. Roy, Article of October 20, 1966 in the *Tully Independent*
3 Dodge, J. Roy, Article of October 20, 1966 in the *Tully Independent*
4 Dodge, J. Roy, Article of October 20, 1966 in the *Tully Independent*

Name spelling changed back to **LaFayette** in December 1905
Serves a population of about 4,400 today with rural routes and post office boxes.

Until a post office was established in Pompey West Hill in 1816, later named LaFayette, residents had the difficult trip all the way up to Pompey Hill to obtain their mail. Since postmasters were generally determined by the political party of the United States President, LaFayette had an unusually large number of changes in postmasters from 1838 to 1866. None of the eleven postmasters, during this period, held the office for more than four years. During most of these years the post office was in the store originally owned by Asahel Smith, later operated by Johnson Hall the first postmaster. Charles Baker, who was appointed postmaster in 1866, served under all five Republican administrations up to the presidency of Grover Cleveland in 1885. Asahel R. Palmer was named postmaster at that time. He moved the post office to his store in the Odd Fellows Hall. Under the following several postmasters the post office had several different locations in the village.

In 1923 the post office was raised from 4th class level to 3rd class. At the same time Willis C. Newell constructed a building west of the Odd Fellows Hall, later known as the Rozelle building. This building was constructed especially for use as a post office. With the 1933 change of administration in Washington the building Newell constructed was not made available so the Millette building was rented for the post office. This building served as the post office until it moved into a portion of a new building constructed in the LaFayette Plaza in the early 1970s.[5]

With the nationwide beginning of Rural Free Delivery (RFD) in 1896, the delivery of mail to residents

of rural communities brought about significant change to 1,000s of rural communities throughout the country. Many small post offices closed, and today the names of many of these communities are no longer recognized. In LaFayette two RFD routes were established, one in 1903 serving the eastern area of the town and the other in 1904 serving the western area. In the early years the RFD carriers generally used a horse, pulling either a buggy or a sleigh, depending upon the weather. Later as roads became improved the horse gave way to the automobile on these RFD routes.

As post office consolidation continues today, post offices are becoming larger and more centralized. No longer are their carrier routes leaving from the LaFayette but postal patrons in the LaFayette area are being served by carriers out of the Tully office. Currently there are about 300 boxes in the LaFayette Post Office serving the community.

Linn

Established: September 27, 1852
First Postmaster: Reuben Byran Jr.
Discontinued: January 14, 1865
Re-established: February 23, 1865
Name changed to **Collingwood** April 22, 1865

Pompey West Hill

Established: November 1, 1816
First Postmaster: Asahel Smith
Name changed to **LaFayette** May 6, 1825

NOTE: *Much of the material regarding the post offices of the Town of LaFayette was provided through the courtesy of J. Roy Dodge.*

---

5 Dodge, J. Roy, Article of October 27, 1966 in the *Tully Independent*

Keith Hungerford, mail carrier, and Dr. Charles Gilette (on porch), LaFayette Postmaster in 1913. The post office is located west of The Lane in LaFayette village. Photo from Crossroads Town, a Photo-Biography of the Town of LaFayette 1979. by J. Roy Dodge

Clayton S. Baker, LaFayette Rural Mail carrier from 1904-1917. Photo courtesy of J. Roy Dodge

Clayton S. Baker, LaFayette Rural Mail carrier from 1904-1917. Photo courtesy of J. Roy Dodge.

Jirah D. Palmer's Collingwood Mills where the Collingwood Post Office was located, in the room on the right, between 1868 to 1903. Jirah Palmer was its only postmaster. Photo courtesy of J.Roy Dodge.

La Fayette Post Office prior to the addition of the small concrete block building on the left of the main building replacing the older structure in 1923 shown here. Courtesy of OHA

LaFayette Post Office, in concrete block wing on the left, 1923-1933. The post office was constructed by Republican Party leader, W.C. Newell but when postmaster position was awarded to a democrat he refused to rent it to 'any democrat'!

The LaFayette Post Office is at 2507 US Route 11, LaFayette NY 13084-9998 has 2,574 square feet and sits on a lot of 5,590 square feet. It is leased by the US Postal Service and was built in 1971.

CHAPTER 14

Post Offices in the Town of Lysander

The Town of Lysander was one of the Townships in the Military Tract reserved for certain veterans of the Revolutionary War and was one of the original towns in Onondaga County when it was established in 1794. The township had originally been comprised of one hundred lots of approximately 600 acres each. When Onondaga County was formed the town of Lysander was given the Military Townships of both Hannibal and Cicero but became much smaller when the Town of Hannibal was removed in 1806 and when in 1807 the land which comprises Cicero and Clay was also removed. Thirty-three lots were also removed to form the Town of Granby of Oswego County in 1816.

Baldwinsville 13027

Established: January 8, 1815
First Postmaster: Jonas C. Baldwin
Serves a population of over 32,000

If a village by the name of Columbia hadn't already been established in New York State, when the village fathers applied for a post office in 1815, those of us living in Baldwinsville today would be living in Columbia. Dr. Jonas Baldwin chose the name Columbia for the little settlement he was establishing on the north side of the Seneca River, across from McHarrie's landing, but was turned down by the postal authorities because they felt that two villages in the state with the same name would be confusing. As an alternative the local residents decided to submit the name Baldwinsville which was subsequently approved by the Postal System.

It is likely that the new Baldwinsville Post Office was located in a building owned by Dr. Baldwin. It was common practice then and still is the custom today in some of the smaller rural communities, that the person appointed postmaster furnish the building for the post office. Usually the postmaster owned a store or tavern in which a small area not far from the building's entrance could be set aside for use as the post office.

Baldwinsville was one of the first communities in the United States to provide Rural Free Delivery (RFD) to rural areas. In 1896 the Post Office Department began delivering mail to rural Americans as an experiment. This service was limited to selected routes in a few states. Being totally new, there was much for the Post Office to learn before they could provide RFD service throughout the country. In addition, many people were opposed to RFD because of the great number of small post offices that would be closed.

RFD came to Baldwinsville in June of 1898. Four rural carriers were appointed at an annual salary of $300 and each carrier had to furnish his own transportation. Two rode their bicycles to deliver the mail and the other two walked, often receiving rides from neighbors along their routes. They were Lyman Pelton, Mark Wilson, Richard Platt and Grant Adsit. At 8:45 in the morning, six days a week, each of these carriers left the Baldwinsville Post Office to make their deliveries which they completed between 12 and 2. As time passed most carriers used a horse and buggy or a sleigh in the winter to deliver the mail. A carrier who started delivering mail around 1900 and spent more than 20 years delivering RFD was likely to have made his deliveries by walking, bicycle, buggy, cutter and finally automobile. He was certainly an individual who was capable of withstanding nature's elements of wind, rain, snow, sleet and almost impassable roads.

Initially there was a great deal of opposition to RFD, especially from the Van Buren Post Office which was located only a short distance from Baldwinsville. There was also unexpected opposition from liquor sellers who found that the rural residents came into the village less frequently, diminishing the sale of their liquor. Most of the recipients of RFD, however, were loud in their praise for the service. The Baldwinsville area was surrounded by hundreds of farm families that found it a burden to have to travel to a post office whenever they wanted to mail a letter or pick up their mail. It saved them a great deal of time traveling to and from the post office. Postal patrons who had been served by the smaller outlying post offices also found they were receiving their newspapers earlier in the day.

RFD also provided a pleasant surprise for the Postal System with an increase in business. Accurate records were maintained by each of the carriers. During the first full month of RFD the four carriers delivered 1,318 letters, 187 postal cards, 5,519 newspapers and circulars and 56 packages while collecting 590 letters, 54 postal cards, 22 newspapers and circulars and 17 packages. Thirteen months later the total for the month had almost doubled. A few months after the RFD service was started, the amount of post office work done by these carriers had increased so substantially that their $300 yearly salaries were raised to $400.

Nationally there was an attempt by fourth class post offices, Baldwinsville was a third class post office, to band together to try to persuade the next congress that RFD was detrimental rather than beneficial. The evidence of success that was demonstrated in Baldwinsville and other early RFD communities showed that its value outweighed its limitations.

When RFD was in its early learning phase the mailboxes used took a variety of forms including pails and wooden boxes set along the side of the road at the end of driveways. Gradually mailbox specifications were adopted and farmers were requested to put up mail boxes along the side of the road on whichever side they preferred. Residents on short roads were asked to place their boxes at the main road intersections. The carriers had a supply of postal cards and stamps with them to use for patrons that had raised the mailbox signal for the carrier to stop.

An article from the OHA files that was printed in the Baldwinsville Messenger on January 22, 1959 provides a glimpse of the changes that had occurred in the 60 years that passed since the Baldwinsville Post Office began its RFD program. One change is that there is no more RFD but had become RD, Rural Delivery without the F for Free. The RFD service was never free as customers always paid for their stamps as they do now. Probably the word "Free" was originally used to make the new service more palatable to postal customers.

The population in and around Baldwinsville had increased dramatically over the 60 year period,

especially between 1949 and 1959 when the revenues of the Baldwinsville Post Office doubled. The increase in volume moved it up to a First Class Post Office. The routes had increased in length measuring from 35 to 53 miles each, a bit difficult for a letter carrier on foot or with horse and buggy. In 1959 the carriers arrived at 7:00 a.m. six days a week, sorted and loaded their mail, started delivering by 9:00, usually returned to the post office by 1:00 and completed their work by 2:00. During difficult weather conditions they finished their work later in the day.

As just mentioned in an earlier paragraph there were four rural routes, and in 1959 there were still four rural routes but the carriers were no longer driving a horse or riding a bicycle but delivering their mail with an automobile. In 1899, Route 3 served 25 farms in the Cold Springs area but in 1959 the Route 3 carrier delivered to 535 boxes in a smaller geographic area.

An article by Anthony Christopher published September 29, 1971 in the 'Baldwinsville Messenger' states that M.G. Frawley was appointed Baldwinsville Postmaster in 1901 by President Theodore Roosevelt. Mr. Frawley owned the Seneca House that would become the new location of the post office. When Woodrow Wilson, a democrat was elected president in 1913 he appointed W. H. Tappan as postmaster. This, as was normal when a new postmaster was named, caused the post office to move to a new location.

There was no mail delivery to residents' homes in Baldwinsville until September 15, 1908. Previous to that time it was necessary to go to the post office to send a letter or to receive your mail. If you did not pick up your mail in an appropriate period of time, uncalled for letters would be listed in the Gazette of the following week. From the corner of the small room in the Seneca House, with a single service window, two Baldwinsville residents, Wallace Adsit and W. H. Rowell, made deliveries to the residents of Baldwinsville. They had passed their Civil Service tests in order to be appointed and each man received $600 a year. They provided both a morning and afternoon delivery each weekday. There were also nine pickup boxes located at various points in the village for the convenience of residents.

In 1915, because of increased business and the crowded conditions in the Seneca House, the Post Office Department advertised for new post office quarters. It accepted the bid for the south store in the old Odd

Fellows Temple building on Oswego Street, slightly to the north and across the street from the Seneca House and leased it for a ten year period. It opened on November 15 with all new furniture and many conveniences. It was described in the November 11 newspaper as one of the most modern offices in the state.

The first post office building in Baldwinsville that was new and designed for the post office was located at 1 Charlotte Street and dedicated on November 8, 1937. It was constructed at a cost of $175,000 and served the Baldwinsville community until it was replaced by another newly constructed building on May 2, 1982 at 26 East Genesee Street.

There is a significant mural in the Baldwinsville Post Office; significant in both size, five feet by sixteen feet, and importance. It was commissioned in 1938, when the Baldwinsville Post Office was at 1 Charlotte Street. The post office had been constructed two years earlier as a Works Progress Administration Project (WPA) but the mural was funded a Department of Treasury agency titled "The Section of Fine Arts". This agency was formed to provide work for artists and bring art to the people.

The painting is titled 'Gateway to the West' and was painted by Paul Miller, a New York City artist. It was an appropriate painting to be displayed in Baldwinsville since it was a scene reflecting life along the Erie Canal in the 1830s, very similar to life in Baldwinsville in the 1830s along its Baldwin Canal. When a new post office was constructed in Baldwinsville in 1982, at a cost of $700,000, the mural was moved to a conspicuous location in the new building where post office patrons can enjoy it as they enter the post office. It is a vivid reminder of Baldwinsville's heritage as well as our country's heritage since the Erie Canal was influential in the opening and the development of the middle and western part of our country.

Cynthia L. Foley, Baldwinsville Postmaster, stated that in 2017 the total post office staff has increased to 48 employees with 11 Rural Routes and 11 village and suburban routes. The Baldwinsville Post Office delivers about 52,000 letters each day. Every morning they arrive by truck from the Taft Road Post Office Station in cages of six or seven trays. The letters arrive in delivery order, sorted by the machines at Taft Road, which eliminates most of the sorting that used to be accomplished at the Baldwinsville Post Office.

Magazines and packages do not arrive in delivery order, which requires sorting at the post office and by the deliverers. With the mail order explosion of the past decade, the delivery of packages has become an increasingly important part of the post office business. The Postal Service has agreements with Fed Ex, UPS, Amazon and other carriers for the delivery of packages to the postal patrons' doors. With these agreements the Postal Service now provides delivery of packages seven days a week. This arrangement makes it possible for the other parcel carriers to make drop shipments, leaving door to door delivery to the Postal Service.

An article by Richard Palmer in the April 7, 1999 'Baldwinsville Messenger' goes into great detail about the crowded conditions at the Baldwinsville Post Office, the lack of parking space for customers, the difficulty for customers to exit the parking lot onto East Genesee Street and the search for a new and larger site. Interestingly, the post office, 17 years later, has not visibly changed even though the population served by the Baldwinsville Post Office has increased substantially.

The significant change in the methods used by the Postal Service in handling the mail, like the letters being arranged in delivery order at the Taft Road Station, have made a big difference in the number of Baldwinsville Post Office staff needed to handle the mail. Without question, electronic mail use by customers and decreased cost for long distance phone service have also been factors in decreasing the average customer's need for postal service.

Dunhamville

Established: April 4, 1832
First Postmaster: Noah Payn Jr.
Name changed to **Paynville** July 23, 1834 (now known as Little Utica)
Name changed to **Polkville** August 18, 1845

In the 1800s it was not uncommon for the person applying for a post office in a newly established community to use his name for the community. It is likely that Noah Payn requested that the community be called Paynville rather than Dunhamville. The name was short lived since the name of the post office was changed 11 years later to Polkville and moved a mile west to Jacksonville when James K. Polk became President.

Lamson's

Established: August 25, 1849
First Postmaster: John H. Lamson
Name changed to **Lamson** July 25, 1894
Discontinued: June 30, 1941
Service from **Phoenix** in Oswego County

The Syracuse & Oswego Railroad was constructed in 1848 and passed through both Baldwinsville and Lamson. Until the railroad came into existence mail was normally transported by stagecoach or wagon. Transportation of mail by railroad was less expensive and more dependable so villages that were on a railroad were more likely to have post offices than those without a railroad. Since the railroad also brought people and business to a village, a post office was established about a year later where the railroad crossed the highway from Lysander to Phoenix. The post office, as quite often was the case, took the name of the community's first postmaster who was John Lamson.

Little Utica

(Previously **Payneville**)

First established: October 3, 1849
First Postmaster: Loren Dunham
Discontinued: September 28, 1853
Reestablished: September 16, 1863
First Postmaster: Albert Harrington
Discontinued: March 15, 1907
Service from **Baldwinsville**

Little Utica, which is located near the northern edge of the Town of Lysander on Lamson Road between the hamlets of Lysander and West Phoenix, has had an unusual post office history.

Had you lived in the area served by a post office in what is now Little Utica between 1832 and 1863 you had good reason to act a little confused. The post office at that location had six name changes in a 30 year period! From 1832 to 1834 it was Dunhamville, from 1834 to 1845 Paynville, from 1845 to 1849 Polkville in neighboring Jacksonville, from 1849 to 1853 Little Utica, from 1853 to 1863 Polkville in neighboring Jacksonville again and from 1863 to 1907 it was named Little Utica, which name it still carries but now is a Baldwinsville address.

Politics and the Spoils System were the reason for most of the name changes. Whatever political party won the presidential election decided who the postmaster would be and often what name the community's post office would have. During the period from 1832 to 1864 the political party of the President changed often. If both political parties' residents of a community wanted the same name for their community only the postmaster and the post office location changed but if there was disagreement between them as to what the name of the community should be the members of the winning party chose the name.

Lysander

Established: September 9, 1811
First Postmaster: Chauncey Betts
Discontinued: May 1993
Service from **Baldwinsville**

The hamlet of Lysander, originally called Betts Corners, took its name from the Town of Lysander. It is located in the northwestern part of Onondaga County. The fact that it was the first post office in the Town of Lysander may have provided the reason for its name. At the time the post office was opened, the Town of Lysander included the Town of Granby to its north. It also served residents to its west in Cayuga County, very likely providing postal service to residents within a ten mile radius. The community had a wide variety of industries including an ashery, distillery, rake manufacturer, blacksmiths, coopers, wagon shops, a tannery and a variety of other small industries. As settlers moved into other communities the importance of the hamlet of Lysander gradually decreased. Larger villages such as Baldwinsville and Syracuse had superior means of transportation and also had access to water power so the hamlet of Lysander's businesses gradually disappeared. What businesses remained serviced the farming area around it. As roads improved and the automobile came into use residents traveled to larger communities to fill their needs.

In May 1993, after 182 years of service to its residents, the Lysander Post Office closed and its residents received their mail by a rural carrier from Baldwinsville. Its last location was in the home of June M. Wilson who had served seven years as a clerk for Rose I. Litterbrant and as postmaster for 14 years. The post office had a number of other locations over the years including the home of Mary Welch on Lamson Road, west of the four-corners, and also in the general store on the northeast corner of the intersection of Lamson and Plainville Roads.

Paynville

(now the hamlet is known as Little Utica)

Established: July 23, 1834
First Postmaster: Noah Payne Jr.
Name changed to **Polkville** and moved a mile west to Jacksonville August 18, 1845

In the 1800s a new post office took the name of the first postmaster. Paynville was named after Noah Payne. Its name was changed to Polkville in 1845 when James K. Polk, a democrat, was elected President.

Plainville 13137

Established: February 20, 1826
First Postmaster: William Wilson
Service for Postal Boxes

Shortly after 1800 one of the first settlers to arrive at what is now Plainville was William Wilson. He purchased a good sized parcel of land and settled at the intersection of what are now Plainville Road and Route 370. The little settlement became known as Wilson's Corners.

There was a hollow tree a mile or two south of Wilson's Corners where a passing traveler going West could leave messages or mail, for residents of the area. Mail left there would have been picked up at the Onondaga Hollow Post Office, about 20 miles southeast of Wilson's Corners, which was established in 1795. As people passed the hollow tree they checked to see if there was mail or messages inside and if they were going near where the addressee lived they would take it to him. A letter might sit there for a week or more until the right person came by.

Wilson's Corners and the area around it were away from any main roads so the area grew quite slowly. As the number of settlers in the area increased, the need for a post office became evident. William Wilson, who lived at the intersection of the two roads, was the local preacher and a prominent citizen became his neighbors' choice to be the postmaster for the new post office.

The local citizens decided they would like to have their new post office named Farmersville. An application was sent to the U.S. Post Office but they were told the name Farmersville already existed in New York and suggested the name Plainville instead. This was accepted by the local people and on February 20, 1826 the Plainville Post Office was established with William Wilson named postmaster.

There is no record as to where the post office was located but more than likely it was in William Wilson's home. Wilson was the postmaster for only a little over a year when Sylvester Stoddard was appointed on April 9, 1827. Perhaps Stoddard had a general store or tavern in Plainville where it was more convenient for the residents. If he had such a business it would have been beneficial to him because it would bring extra business.

The following information is from the author's memory.

"Over the next century there were about a dozen different postmasters in Plainville. The first one I remember was Earl Woodruff who had a general store on the northwest corner of the Plainville four-corners. My guess is that Mr. Woodruff became postmaster in the 1920s. He continued to be postmaster until around 1950.

My family's farm was located about one-half mile South of Plainville and in the early 1900s received Rural Free Delivery out of the Memphis Post Office. My dad and grandfather started growing turkeys in the 1920s and since the farm was near Plainville they decided to name it Plainville Turkey Farm. Memphis was about seven miles away so my family rented a post office box at the Plainville Post Office to have their business mail come there. As a result we went to the Plainville Post Office several times a week to pick up our mail and often to buy something in the store. The Memphis RFD continued to deliver the newspaper and some personal mail to our mailbox in front of the house.

Since my great-great grandfather settled on the farm in 1835, about 70 years before there was a Rural Free Delivery Route, he had a box at the post office all of those years. The family may have continued to keep the box at the Plainville Post Office. Several generations of the family attended both the school and church in Plainville making it easy to pick up the mail without making a special trip.

My memories, from childhood, of the Plainville Post Office are as follows. The building was a large two story structure that had previously been a hotel. There was a gas pump near one corner of an open front porch and a kerosene pump on the other corner of the porch. A big sign across the front of the store read, 'Red & White Chain Stores'. Under this sign was a smaller oval sign that read, 'Plainville Post Office'. There were two steps, almost as wide as the porch leading up to the deck where a bench and two arm chairs seemed to invite people to come up, sit a while and talk with their neighbors. The visual message was effective because very often several people were sitting and enjoying some gossip or talking about the prospects of this year's tobacco crop. On a warm summer evening the overflow of sitters seated themselves on the steps.

Inside the store were aisles of items necessary for rural residents that do not have access to a larger store without traveling several miles. Just inside the front door on the right was the little post office containing less than 100 boxes. The boxes had a glass face so a customer could see if there was mail and not bother the postmaster if he was in another part of the store. When business was quiet, the postmaster was usually sitting in his chair behind the postal boxes ready to wait on a customer.

Next to the post office boxes was the candy counter containing all sorts of treats, some that only cost a penny. I must admit the candy counter was far more enticing than the post office boxes. On the rear wall of the store were deer heads, a moose head and even a bear that had made a visit to the taxidermist.

The post office was the focal point of the community. Everybody went there to check if they had mail or to buy a needed item. Anything that happened in the community quickly was shared at the post office and soon everyone was informed. If a community member died the postmaster collected donations for a basket of flowers. When someone was sick the word quickly traveled and soon volunteers pitched in to help in any way they could. A neighbor often picked up the mail for a person that might have difficulty reaching the post office. When the post office was at the store there was the opportunity to lend a hand to someone in need and share a little community news or gossip.

Eventually Mr. Woodruff sold the store, resigned as postmaster and retired. The post office moved across the street to Robert's Garage. This location didn't lend itself effectively as a community meeting place since no longer was there store traffic and a place to sit and talk. Most of the people were quickly in and out to pick up their mail. Later the post office moved around the corner to the residence of Edith Pickard Forsythe who had grown up in the house diagonally across the street from the store.

Mrs. Forsythe served as postmaster from 1955 to 1976 and continued to provide the friendly, efficient service to which the post office box holders were accustomed. Later the Postal Service purchased a post office site a few hundred feet further south on Plainville Road to use as a post office. Another life long Plainville resident, Virginia Pecore Billings, served as postmaster at that location from 1976 to 1992, also providing fine service for the area residents. The Postal Service placed a mobile home for use as the post office on the site and later constructed a permanent building. Mrs. Billings was followed by Shirley Stock, who had worked as a substitute during Mrs. Billings tenure. Mrs. Stock served as Officer-in-charge for about seven months before Carey Sevier was named postmaster. Mrs. Stock service ended 167 years of Plainville Post Office service provided by a Plainville resident.

Ms. Sevier served as postmaster for a little over three years and was followed by three different Officers-in-Charge during the following three years. On July 4, 1998 Carole Conlan was named postmaster and she provided excellent service from 1998 to 2012. Another Plainville resident, Robin Bridenbaker, was named Officer-in-Charge in 2012 but the Plainville Post Office was converted to a remotely managed post office on March 9, 2013 under the direction of the postmaster of the Cato Post Office.

I can speak of only the years from the 1930's to 2013 when I moved to Baldwinsville but I can confidently say that the Plainville postal employees during that period of time served the local Plainville residents very well. They were also a credit to the United States Postal System."

Polkville

(Previously **Dunhamville** and **Paynville**)

Established: August 18, 1845
First Postmaster: Hugh McKiernan
Discontinued: October 3, 1849
Reestablished: September 28, 1853
Discontinued: September 16, 1863
It received the name **Little Utica**

Polkville became the name for the Paynville Post Office when James K. Polk, a democrat, was elected President in 1845. Its name was changed to Little Utica when Polk was defeated by Zachary Taylor, a whig, and then it was changed back to Polkville when Polk was elected President for the second time. After Abraham Lincoln, a republican, was elected President its name again became Little Utica.

NOTE: *Much of the information concerning the post offices in Lysander was through the courtesy of Bonnie Kisselstein, Town of Lysander Historian, and Sue McManus of McHarrie's Legacy. Material also came from several papers written by Anthony Christopher in columns that appeared in the Baldwinsville Messenger from 1960 to 1975.*

Both of these letters are written on a sheet of paper folded into its own envelope to save postage. The lower one was mailed from Schuylerville NY (near Vermont) to an uncertain destination (note address) as William Ward and family had recently traveled over 150 miles by ox drawn sleigh to this area. The letter would have been picked up by William Ward, within a month or two when he came to town, and postage paid at that time. The upper letter was written a few years later to a known address. Letters received by the author's grandfather.

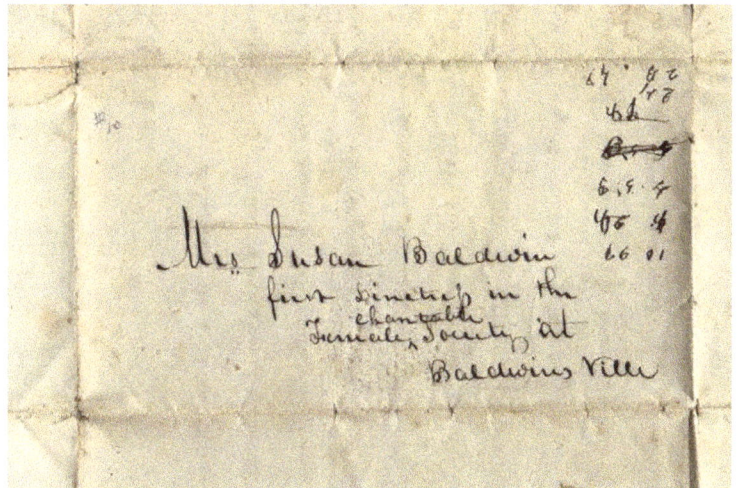

An 1827 stampless letter from Stephen Baldwin, son of Baldwinsville's founder Jonas Baldwin, to Susan Baldwin. Photo from the files of McHarrie's Legacy and the courtesy of Sue McManus.

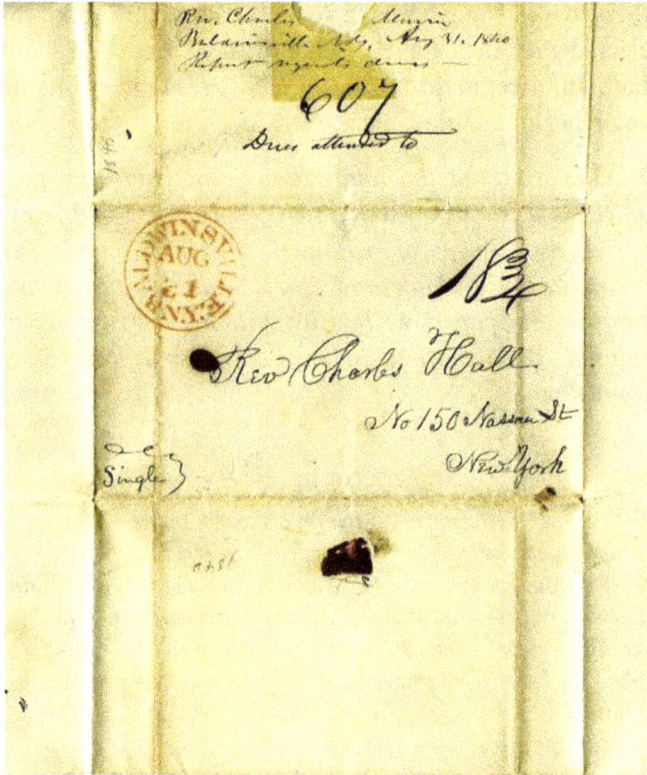

Baldwinsville cancellation on an 1840 letter. Note that the
envelope is the folded letter and the remains of the wax where
it was sealed. Photo from the files of McHarrie's Legacy and
the courtesy of Sue McManus.

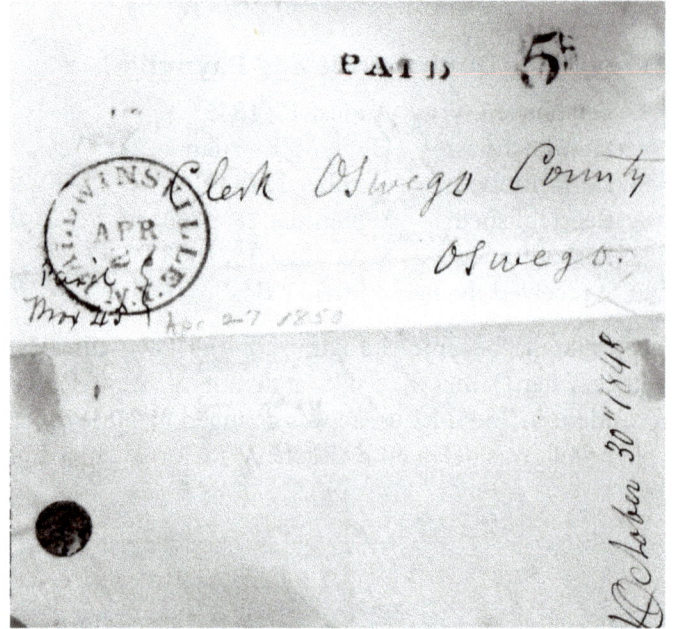

Envelope mailed in Baldwinsville 1848. Note that the postage
of five cents was paid by the sender and that stamps were not
used at this time.

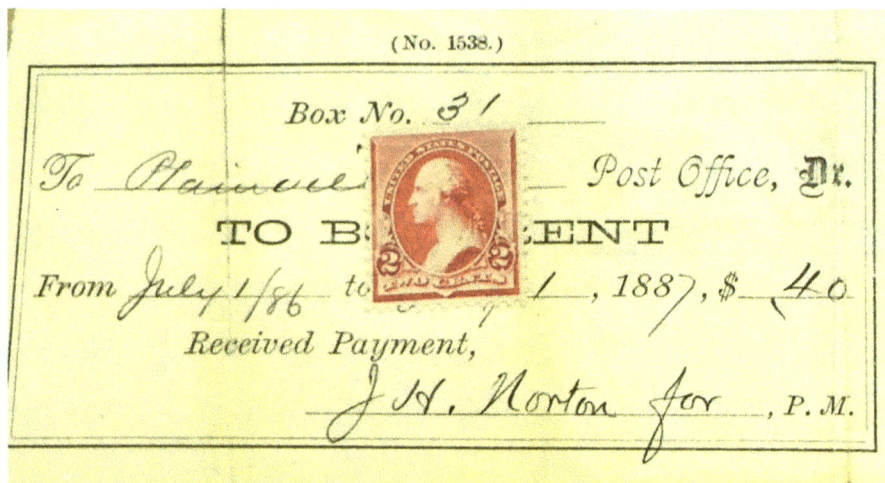

Receipt for Box rental at Plainville Post Office in 1886. Note that a half-year box
rental was forty cents.

Grant Adsit was one of the four original Baldwinsville RFD carriers in 1898 and delivered the mail to rural residents for many years. Photo from the files of McHarrie's Legacy and the courtesy of Sue McManus.

Baldwinsville Post Office in the Seneca House on the northwest corner of West Genesee and Oswego Streets. The post office sign shows just above the omnibus in front of the hotel. Photo from the files of McHarrie's Legacy and the courtesy of Sue McManus.

Omnibus wagon in front of Post Office in the Third Baldwinsville Seneca House. Circa 1890. Photo from the files of McHarrie's Legacy and the courtesy of Sue McManus.

The right side of Oddfellows Hall on the east side of Oswego Street was one of the locations of the Baldwinsville Post Office. Records tell of its move there in 1915 and it was located there in this photo. Photo from the files of McHarrie's Legacy and the courtesy of Sue McManus.

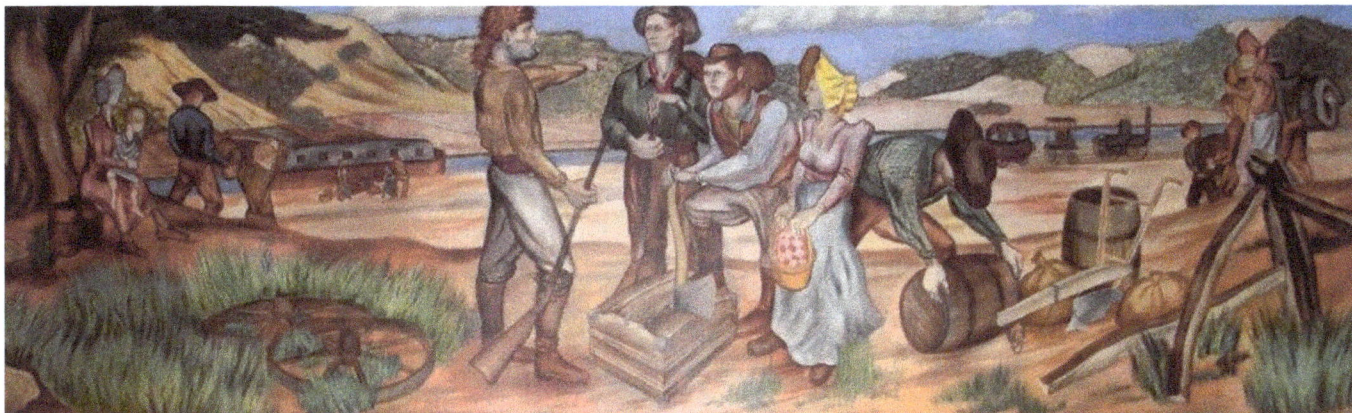

This mural, measuring five feet by sixteen feet, was commissioned in 1938 for display in the Baldwinsville Post Office on Charlotte Street. When the new post office was constructed on East Genesee Street in 1982 it was moved there and is now on the wall over the postal boxes. The painting is titled 'Gateway to the West' and was painted by Paul Miller, a New York City artist.

Hamlet of Lysander's last post office on the south side of Lamson Road in the home of Postmaster June M. Wilson. Picture taken a few years after it closed. The area's customers were provided service out of Baldwinsville.

Plainville Post Office in the home of Edyth Forsythe, on South Street from 1955 to 1976.

In the early 1980s the Plainville Post Office was located in a trailer on South Street when no other suitable location was available.

The Plainville Post Office at 8,000 Plainville Road, Plainville NY 13137-9998 is 638 square feet in size and is on a half-acre site. It is owned by the US Postal Service and was constructed in 1988.

Baldwinsville Post Office on Charlotte Street prior to moving to the new building on East Genesee Street in 1982.

Postal clerks windows in the Baldwinsville Post Office when it was on Charlotte Street. The building now houses two dentists.

The Baldwinsville Postoffice at 26 East Genesee Street, Baldwinsville NY 13027-9998 sits on a 47,479 square foot site with a building of 9,540 square feet. It is owned by the US Postal Service and was constructed in 1982.

Baldwinsville Postoffice customer postal boxes with five foot by sixteen foot mural of life along the Erie Canal in the 1830s by artist Paul Weller. This mural was painted in 1938 and moved from the post office on Charlotte Street to this post office when it was constructed in 1982.

The customer service counter in the Baldwinsville Post Office.

CHAPTER 15

Post Offices in the Town of Manlius

The Town of Manlius was No. 7 of the 25 original townships that made up the Military Tract which was designated for veterans of the Revolutionary War. It, like the others, was divided into 100 lots of approximately 600 acres each. One of the original lots was transferred to Cicero and other lots were removed to form Onondaga, Salina and finally DeWitt, in 1835, leaving the Town of Manlius with its current size.[1]

A partial quote from a Spafford's 1824 Gazetteer provides a description of the Town at that time:

"In this town are an abundance of mill seats, on Limestone, Chitteningo and Butternut creeks, and a great number of mills. ... The inhabitants are immigrant Yankees, or German and Dutch, from the Mohawk River, industrious and prosperous. ... There are four post offices and five 'villages' known by local names. Manlius, a Post-Borough, (or incorporated village), is situated on Limestone Creek at the junction of three or four turnpikes. It contains 100 dwellings, and about 200 buildings of all kinds, 3 churches, ... a Masonic Lodge, a printing office, a cotton factory and has a great deal of hydraulic, mechanical and trading business. The Post-Village of Fayetteville, 2 miles N. of Manlius, on the N. branch of the Seneca Turnpike, has 25 houses. The Post-Village of Orville, 5 miles N.W. of Manlius, on the same turnpike, has about 20 houses, a church and a side cut to the Erie Canal. Eagleville, one and a half mile E. of Manlius, near the E. line, has about 20 houses. The Post-Village of Jamesville, 5 miles W. of Manlius is on Butternut Creek and has mills and about 35 houses."[2]

Settlers came to to Manlius in the late 1700s creating the need for a post office in the hamlet of Manlius. The Post Office was established in 1800 and served settlers

from several miles in all directions. Mail was picked up at the post office until around 1900 when Rural Free Delivery (RFD) and home delivery in the larger villages was available. Because of this each resident was able to make his own choice as to which post office to use. This choice often corresponded with the trading location or family connection rather than strictly geographical. This is a practice that still continues today when for various reasons a person or business chooses to rent a post office box and pick up their mail at the post office of their choice rather than to have it delivered.

Elkhorn

Established:	April 26, 1890
First Postmaster:	Cortland A. Snook
Discontinued:	July 31, 1895 (Kay & Smith)
	July 12 (Scholl)
Service from **Fayetteville**	

Elkhorn was a small settlement with undefined edges. High Bridge is an approximate location but the land has been substantially altered by road construction. A number of homes were demolished by Route 92 construction and improvements. Years ago there were two churches and a schoolhouse in the community. The churches are gone but the stone schoolhouse is still a visible landmark from Route 92.

Fayetteville 13066

Established:	April 10, 1818
First Postmaster:	John W. Hyde
Currently serves a population of over 12,000	

Fayetteville, in its early settlement days, was called The Corners or Manlius Corners. It held this name until the establishment of its post office in 1818. A tavern was established in 1801 and a store in 1802.[3] In 1818, when the post office was established, most post offices were

---

1 Bruce, Dwight H., *Onondaga's Centennial* p. 768
2 Spafford H.G., *Gazetteer of the State of New York* 1824, p. 304

3 Bruce, Dwight H., *Onondaga's Centennial* p. 790

located in stores. There is no proof available but it is logical that this post office was in the store constructed by John Delamater, about 1808, on the east side of South Manlius Street between the 500 block of East Genesee Street and Salt Springs Road.

The village grew rapidly and by 1860 the population was 1,859. The water power from Limestone Creek and a feeder canal from the Erie Canal brought two flour mills, three sawmills, a pearl barley mill, a paper mill and three lime and plaster mills.[4]

In 1926, residents of Fayetteville had the pleasure of home delivery of their mail. Until then they had to pick up their mail at the post office unless they lived outside the village on an RFD route where home delivery had commenced in 1902. Until 1950, when once a day delivery began, the mail had been delivered two times a day.

A February 5, 1926 article in the *Fayetteville Bulletin* stated about one-half of the Fayetteville residents received their mail by carriers. Mail was not delivered on the sides of streets without sidewalks. Collection boxes were placed at several locations in the village so patrons did not have to travel to the post office to mail a letter.

The Fayetteville Post Office had a number of different locations in the village usually on one side or in the front corner of a store. The post office location in 1841, when Dr. Curtiss J. Hurd was postmaster, was in the Mead & Co. variety store in the west portion of its double-front store at 100 Limestone Plaza. When Henry Ecker was postmaster from 1861 to 1878, the post office was located in his clothing store in the Beard business block on the south side of Limestone Plaza. In 1879 the post office was located in the Gaynor building at 103 Brooklea Drive. This was the first time that the post office was not located with another business. After Arthur C. Agan became postmaster the post office was moved from 103 Brooklea Drive to 106 Brooklea Drive where the National Bank of Fayetteville had earlier been located.

In 1888 Howard H. Edwards was appointed postmaster by his old boyhood friend President Grover Cleveland, who had spent his boyhood days in Fayetteville. The Fayetteville Deputy Postmaster, William Austin had also been a boyhood friend of President Cleveland.

During Arthur C. Agan's tenure as postmaster, beginning on February 6, 1910, he ran a Sunday mail

service which was discontinued a year later following the general closing of post offices on Sunday.

Post offices throughout the country were often broken into during the dark of night by thieves looking for money and stamps. In April 1905 the Fayetteville Post Office was their target. The thieves blew open the safe and escaped with a total of $726.38 in cash and stamps. Another robbery attempt in 1912 was unsuccessful. Their attempt to blow open the safe was a failure but the noise did awaken nearby residents, too late to catch the thieves in the act. The safe was badly damaged and took the locksmith shop employees three hours to break open the safe with sledgehammers and chisels.

To be appointed postmaster it was usually necessary to be a member of the same political party as the President of the United States. Mr. Edwards happened to be chairman of the Manlius Democratic Town Committee and his successor, Frank C. Boynton, also appointed by President Cleveland but during his second term, amazingly was chairman of the Manlius Republican town committee.

Rural Free Delivery (RFD) arrived for the rural residents near Fayetteville in 1902. It had started, in other areas of the country six years earlier but took a number of years to fully implemented across the country. One of the deterrents was poor condition of the roads in many parts of the country. A side effect of RFD was it accelerated the improvement of rural roads. Many communities with a small post office opposed RFD because of the loss of their local post office because their mail then came from a larger post office that provided the RFD service.

Judson A. Snook and Leo D. Worden became the first RFD carriers out of the Fayetteville Post Office. They even delivered the mail to their customers on Christmas Day. It is likely that during the early years they used horse and buggy during snow free days but reverted to horse and sleigh during much of the winter. In 1915, Snook earned $1,092 and Judson $1,188 for their year's work delivering the mail. They had to furnish their own horse and vehicle and feed and care for the horse as part of their pay.

Beginning in 1934 the Fayetteville and Manius Post Offices closed at 1:00 p.m. on Saturdays in line with the government's policy to give the employees a shorter work week.

Commencing December 28, 1939 the Fayetteville Post Office shared its post office space with a United States Armed Services recruiting officer on Thursday of each week. During the war, parcels were limited in

---

4 French, J.H.,1860 *Gazetteer of the State of New York*, p. 484

size because of the shortage of shipping space. During World War II, citizens were urged to ship packages to service personnel for Christmas in October. By October 24, 1944, 1,561 packages had been sent out of the Fayetteville Post Office to service people. With fewer than 400 local folks in the service it appeared that the residents of Fayetteville were doing all they could to give comfort to their service personnel.

A new 2,700 square foot post office, which cost $18,000, was opened at 112 Brooklea Drive on February 1, 1952. It served the village until August 27, 1978 when it was replaced. Sometime earlier, because of the increased volume of parcel post mail, it had been necessary to construct a parcel post building in the parking lot next to the post office. In 1978, when the new post office opened, the services were consolidated into one building.

In 1975 the Postal System purchased a one acre site for a new post office at 599 East Genesee Street for $70,000. Three years later, on August 28, 1978, the new post office opened for business.

Over its 198 year history, hundreds of dedicated Fayetteville Post Office employees have provided outstanding service for Fayetteville and its vicinity residents.

NOTE: *Much of the material concerning the Fayetteville Post Office came from a manuscript entitled,* A History of the Fayetteville Post Office *by Kathy Crowell, Ann Moore and Nancy Schiffhauer. The manuscript, housed in the Fayetteville Public Library, provides a wealth of information regarding Fayetteville's post offices and postmasters as well as history of the US Postal Service.*

Hartsville (now Mycenae)

Established: March 1, 1826
First Postmaster: Henry H. Potter
Discontinued: June 26, 1852

Hurlgate

(perhaps located next to the tollgate on the Salina and Bridgeport Plank Rd.)

Established: June 2, 1855
First Postmaster: William C. Shute
Discontinued: April 8, 1856

Hurlgate was a settlement in the northeast corner of the Town of Manlius near Schepp's Corners (earlier called Hurlburt Corners). One Hurlburt *family* lived next to the toll gate on the Salina to Bridgeport Plank Road, now generally Route 298. The post office was in existence less than one year. William C. Shute, the first and only postmaster, was a farmer.

Kirkville 13082

Established: May 13, 1824
First Postmaster: Robert Cunningham (*per New York Postal History*)
Name changed to **Kirkville Station** September 7, 1898
Changed back to **Kirkville** September 1, 1899
Serves a population of about 5,000 today

The opening of the Erie Canal brought about the hamlet of Kirkville. A tavern was opened with houses and buildings gradually clustering in the area. Edward Kirkland settled on a farm northwest of the hamlet and in 1824 became its first postmaster. Both the settlement and post office were named for Mr. Kirkland.[5] The post office was on the banks of the original 1825 Erie Canal. The 1972 Kirkville Post Office was about a mile south, on the banks of the relocated 1850 Erie Canal, now used as a state park.

An article in the OHA archives, from the February 22, 1978 Eagle-Bulletin, DeWitt News-Times, relates information about the Kirkville Post Office. Currently the post office is at 6365 Kirkville Road but in 1978 it was located along the banks of the Erie Canal in what was once the Sweeting and Mosher Dry Goods Store, which did a brisk business during the Erie Canal Days. Other locations for the post office have been in Bill Moore's store and later Plopper's store on Main St. near Pools Brook Road. At the time of the article Daisy Myers had worked for the Kirkville Post Office 24 years, the last seven as postmaster. She remembers the days when the mail came by train. The train slowed down when passing through the village and picked up the mail from a hook adjacent to the tracks. The mail for the post office was tossed from the train and carted from there to the post office in a wheelbarrow. There were no walking carriers in 1978 but the 13082 zip for Kirkville was the address for postal customers in an 80 square mile territory that extended from Bridgeport to Fayetteville and from Minoa to the Town of Sullivan in Madison County.

The minutes from the Manlius Town Board meeting of March 2, 1917 relate a problem the Kirkville Post Office was experiencing with freight trains standing

5   Clark, Joshua V.H., *Onondaga*, 1849 volume II, p.219

on the tracks by the post office blocking the road and preventing the mail carrier from fulfilling his duties. The mail carrier at times found it necessary to wait as much as two hours for the train to move or had to take another road which added extra miles. The town board passed a resolution directing the Manlius supervisor to communicate with the railroad, explain the problem and give the railroad opportunity to correct the problem.

Kirkville Station

Established: September 7, 1898
First Postmaster: Herbert H. Brown
Discontinued: September 1, 1899 becoming
Kirkville again

Manlius 13104

Established: November 26, 1800
First Postmaster: Luther Bingham
Servers a population of over 15,000 today

The hamlet of Manlius was originally called 'Liberty Square'. The post office was established in 1800 but because the residents did not like the name it soon became called Manlius Square.[6] The first post office was in the home of its postmaster Luthur Bingham. For some unknown reason the village was given the name 'Derne' in 1806 when it contained 30 houses. Perhaps it had something to do with the name of the first newspaper published in Onondaga County named 'Derme' which was published in the village.[7]

By 1860 its population had reached 934. The water power provided by Limestone Creek brought commercial industries to the village and included two carriage shops, two flour mills, an axe factory, two foundries and a paper mill.[8]

Eagle Village, which was older than either Manlius or Fayetteville, had no water power, so it grew slowly never having the population to support a post office. Residents of Eagle Village had to travel to a nearby post office to pick up their mail until Rural Free Delivery (RFD) came into existence around 1900. Many of the RFD carriers became an important part in the lives of the people they served.

An article by Adeline Hopkins published on July 1, 1976 in the *Eagle-Bulletin, DeWitt News-Times* tells about Alfred B. Cross, nicknamed 'Ack' by all that knew

him, who delivered the mail with horse and buggy or sleigh in the winter, to residents in the Eagle Village area. Ack lived in Eagle Village and early each morning would drive his horse to Manlius to pick up the mail he would later deliver to the Eagle Village area. Normally the top of his cutter was down and he piled the mail on the side of his seat and under the seat as well as on the buggy floor. In good weather it took him almost all day to deliver the mail and even longer when making his way through snow drifts in the winter. People with a letter to mail, put their pennies in the mailbox to have Ack apply a stamp. Sometimes he had to dig the pennies out of snow that had blown into the mailbox, freezing his fingers in the process. He was so dedicated to serving his postal customers that when side roads were impassible because of the snow he would leave his sleigh on the main road (Route 173) and walk across the fields to deliver the mail. Ack was always cheerful and friendly and although he wasn't allowed to have passengers while delivering the mail, once the mail was delivered he always offered a ride to anyone traveling in his direction.

An article by Kathy Johnson published April 12, 1978 n the Eagle-Bulletin, DeWitt News-Times provides some of the locations of the Manlius Post Office over the years, the changes in volume of mail and the areas served. Currently and also at the time of this article the post office was at 110 Wesley Street and previously in what was known as the Fowler block. When Guy Hobbs, the postmaster in 1978, started working for the Manlius Post Office in 1947 they served 600 rural homes and provided street delivery to 400 homes. In 1978 the Manlius Post Office served 3,500 homes. In 1978, the area, with the Manlius zip code of 13104 covered an area with 164 miles of road in the Towns of Manlius, Fabius, Pompey and Cazenovia. Mr. Hobbs noted that the mail for Manlius came by railroad, until railroad service declined, then by a highway bus, which was a modification of the train service and in 1978 by a truck owned by a private operator.

Manlius Centre

Established: March 20, 1824
First Postmaster: Alfred Palmer
Name changed to Manlius Center in December 1893
Discontinued: July 31, 1906
Service from Kirkville

---

6 Bruce, Dwight H., *Onondaga's Centennial* p. 775
7 Bruce, Dwight H., *Onondaga's Centennial* p. 777
8 French, J.H.,1860 *Gazetteer of the State of New York*, p. 484

Manlius Center is a small settlement near where the road to Oneida Lake (now Route 257 and Minoa Road) crosses the Erie Canal. The main buildings in the hamlet were two stores on the northeast and the northwest corners of the bridge plus a hotel on the south side of the canal. In 1860 there were about 40 houses in the community.

Manlius Station

Established: June 21, 1855
First Postmaster: Peter J. Terpening
Name changed to **Minoa** August 16, 1895

The opening of the Syracuse and Utica Railroad in 1839 brought growth to the village and created the need for a post office which was established in 1855.

Minoa 13116

(Previously Manlius Station)

Established: August 16, 1895
First Postmaster: Ephraim E. Woodward
Serves a population of about 3,500 today

A March 8, 1978 article in the Eagle-Bulletin, DeWitt News-Times, from the OHA archives provides a glimpse of the Minoa Post office at that time. Before 1963, Minoa residents had no street delivery of mail. In 1968 it had two postmen who walked eight or nine miles a day with each one delivering 1,300 to 1,400 pieces of mail daily. Previous to 1963 the residents came to the post office each day to pick up their mail. For many years the post office was located in the old Minoa Methodist Church on East Avenue. Later a new post office was built at 115 North Main Street. At the time this article was written all who received mail addressed to Minoa 13116 actually lived in the village of Minoa. Since Minoa had no rural delivery routes mail to houses just outside of the village carried a Kirkville, East Syracuse or Fayetteville address.

Mycenae

(in the same area where Hartsville had previously been located)

Established: April 4, 1889
First Postmaster: Jay G. Dewey
Discontinued: March 31, 1903
Service from **Kirkville**

Mycenae is located in the eastern part of the town at the meeting point of Route 5 and Route 290, about a mile from Madison County.

North Manlius

Established: December 31, 1851
First Postmaster: Cyrus P. Camp
Discontinued: April 30, 1914
Service from **Kirkville**

North Manlius was located in the northern part of the town, adjacent to Chittenango Creek and about a mile south of the Town of Cicero.

NOTE: *Much of the information regarding the Town of Manlius Post Offices was obtained through the courtesy of Barbara S. Rivette, Town Historian.*

W.C. Moore's store and Kirkville Post Office. Courtesy of Barbara Rivette, Manlius Town Historian.

View of 100-102 Brooklea Drive looking east. Harbottle & Co. and the Post Office were located in the southern portion of this double-front brick building. The connecting stores at the far right did not then exist. Courtesy of the Fayetteville Free Library.

Post Office on Seneca Street in Manlius from History of Fayetteville -Manlius Area by Anguish

Post Office in the Fowler building in the Village of Manlius from the book Growing Up in Manlius Village in the 30s and 40s by Sue Goodfellow

Manlius Post Office on Seneca Street, west of Wesley Street. Courtesy of Barbara Rivette, Manlius Town Historian.

Fayetteville Post Office at 112 Brooklea Drive from February 1, 1952 to August 27, 1978. Courtesy of the Fayetteville Free Library.

Kirkville Post Office from 1957 to November 11, 1980 when the building burned. Courtesy of Barbara Rivette, Manlius Town Historian.

Manlius Post Office on the west side of Wesley Street in 1988. Photo courtesy of Barbara Rivette, Manlius Town Historian.

The Manlius Post Office is at 110 Wesley Street, Manlius NY 13104-9998. It is owned by the US Postal Service, was constructed in 1989, is 8,048 square feet and is on a lot of approximately one acre.

The Fayetteville Post Office is at 599 East Genesee Street, Fayetteville NY 13066-9998. It is owned by the US Postal Service, was constructed in 1978, is 6,013 square feet and on a lot slightly more than an acre.

The Kirkville Post Office is at 6365 North Kirkville Road, Kirkville, NY 13082-9998. It is leased by the US Postal Service, was constructed in 1982, has 2,076 square feet and is on an acre lot.

The Minoa Post Office is at 115 North Main Street, Minoa NY 13116-9998. It is leased by the US Postal Service, was constructed in 1973, has 1,910 square feet and is on a 13,860 square foot lot.

CHAPTER 16

Post Offices in the Town of Marcellus

Marcellus was the original Township number 9 in the Military Tract designated for veterans of the Revolutionary War and was comprised of 100 lots of about 620 acres. It originally included what is now Skaneateles, the northern part of Spafford and the northwest two-thirds of Otisco. In 1794, the year that both the County of Onondaga and Town of Marcellus were formed, the first permanent settlers came to what is now the Town of Marcellus. The first post office in the town came into existence three years later.[1] The post offices of the town follow in alphabetical order.

Clintonville

Established: January 8, 1818
First Postmaster: Manassah Eaton
Name changed to **South Marcellus** February 1, 1832

Clintonville was located about four miles south of Marcellus in Lot 46. The families of Bowen and Cody located at Clintonville in 1794. Joseph Cody built and kept the first tavern at Clintonville in 1806. Manassah Eaton opened a store in Clintonville in 1815 and became its first postmaster three years later.[2]

Elliston

Established: February 22, 1849
First Postmaster: Furman B. North
Name changed to **Thorn Hill** August 24, 1853

Elliston was located a little south of Marietta in Lot 61 near the Spafford town line and later was called Thorn Hill.

---

1 Bruce, Dwight W. *Onondaga's Centennial* p. 631
2 Bruce, Dwight W. *Onondaga's Centennial* p. 634

Empire

Established: May 20, 1898
First Postmaster: Norman B. Sheppard
Discontinued: December 14, 1898
To: **Rose Hill**

The Empire Post Office was in existence for less than a year. One authority gives its location in the Town of Marcellus. Another authority states that it is two and one-half miles south of Rose Hill on Skaneateles Lake, which would likely place it in the Town of Spafford.

Marcellus 13108

Established: April 17, 1797
First Postmaster: Dr. Jesse Munger
Serves a population of over 6,000

Dwight H. Bruce in *Onondaga's Centennial* on page 635 states that Dr. Elnathan Beach opened the first store in Marcellus and became its first postmaster in 1799. He was also appointed that year as Onondaga County Sheriff. Until 1799 the village of Marcellus was known as Nine Mile Creek but soon after the establishment of the post office it became Marcellus.

Marcellus Falls

Established: September 24, 1840
First Postmaster: Salmon B. Norton
Discontinued: December 30, 1965
To: **Marcellus**

Settlement of Marcellus Falls began in 1806. It was originally called Union Village. The power from the water in Nine Mile Creek brought numerous industries to the area. By 1823 there were 19 mills and one furnace along Nine Mile Creek.[3]

---

3 Bruce, Dwight W. *Onondaga's Centennial* p. 641

Marietta 13110

Established: March 8, 1832
First Postmaster: Thaddeus Thompson
Serves a population of about 2,300 with two rural routes and post office boxes.

Like in many small communities throughout the state, the Marietta Post Office has moved many times. When John Hicks was postmaster in the 1880s he moved it to the store that his father had built. Later when Frank Rathbun was postmaster he moved it to his grist mill. Still later it moved back to the store and eventually it was in a small stone building that had earlier been a shoe repair shop. Ripley's *Believe it or Not* featured the Marietta Post Office, when it was in this small stone building, as the smallest post office with a rural route. Later the post office moved back to the store again. In 1985 the Postal Service moved into a new post office in Marietta. There are currently two rural routes served by this post office in addition to post office boxes for local customers.

Rhodes

(Initially in Town of Marcellus but became part of Skaneateles after 1830)

Established: February 23, 1828
First Postmaster: John Adams
Discontinued: August 15, 1843

When the Rhodes Post Office was established in 1828, it was located at what was later known as Shepard Settlement at that time part of Marcellus. In 1830, when the Town of Skaneateles was formed the post office continued under the name Rhodes until it was discontinued in 1843. John Adams, its first and only postmaster, purchased his farm in 1804 and the post office was located in his home on the farm.

Rose Hill

Established: October 24, 1890
First Postmaster: Frank B. Mills
Discontinued: October 7, 1899
Name changed to Rosehill from December 1895 to January 31, 1900
Name changed back to Rose Hill February 1, 1900
Discontinued: June 30, 1957
To: **Marietta**

Frank B. Mills, who was the first postmaster, started a seed farm in the late 1800s. He was very successful and sold seeds, most of which were mailed, over a wide area of the country. Because of his great need for postal service the Rose Hill Post Office was opened and became the post office with the second highest volume in Onondaga County.[4]

The Postal System made an effort to simplify post office names in the 1890s. One of their changes was to combine two words in a name into one. This is why Rose Hill was changed to Rosehill. Many of the post office patrons in Rose Hill and other post offices where the names were changed were unhappy with the change so the Postal Service relented and changed the name back to Rose Hill.

An article in the July 8, 1893 Marcellus Observer, from the OHA archives, states the salary of the Syracuse postmaster has been increased from $3,500. to $3,600. and that the pay of the postmasters of Skaneateles and Rose Hill at $1,700. are the same. Even though the Skaneateles Post Office was much larger, the business of F. B. Mills seed business made more money for the Post Office Department.

Shamrock

Established: December 15, 1890
First Postmaster: Charles M. Goodspeed
Discontinued: September 30, 1899
Service from **Thorn Hill**

The hamlet of Shamrock along with the Shamrock Post Office were located about four miles South Southwest of Marcellus near Thorn Hill.

---

4 Bruce, Dwight W. *Onondaga's Centennial* p. 657

South Marcellus

(formerly **Clintonville**)

Established: February 1, 1832
First Postmaster: Caleb N. Potter
Discontinued: February 14, 1855

South Marcellus was located about four miles south of Marcellus in Lot 46.

Thorn Hill

(formerly **Elliston**)

Established: August 24, 1853
First Postmaster: Obadiah Thorne
Name changed to **Rose Hill** October 24, 1890
Re-established: December 23, 1890
Spelling changed to **Thornhill** December 1895
Discontinued: October 15, 1904
Service from **Borodino**

Thorn Hill was located a little south of Marietta in Lot 61 near the Spafford town line and previously had been named Ellston. It received its name from the Thorne family. Obadiah Thorne who was a wool buyer was instrumental in establishing the post office.

NOTE: *Much of the information concerning the post offices of the Town of Marcellus was obtained through the courtesy Peg Nolan, Town of Marcellus Historian.*

Location of the Rhodes Post Office in the home of John Adams, its first postmaster, in 1828. Courtesy of the Marcellus History Museum

Post Office boxes used in the Marcellus Post Office in the mid 1800's, which was located in the Samuel Rice Tavern on Main St. Courtesy of the Marcellus Historical Society.

Postoffice boxes used in the Marcellus Falls Postoffice from the early 1900's to 1965.

This frame structure was the location of the Marcellus Post Office in 1889. Later the building served as a bank. Courtesy of Peg Nolan, Town of Marcellus historian.

This building was the site of the Marcellus Post Office, after it moved from the National Bank building, until the new post office was constructed in 1962. Courtesy of Peg Nolan, Marcellus historian.

The John C. Kennedy Store and Post Office of Marcellus Falls (zip 13109) – 1908
Present owners are Mr. and Mrs. Dennis Haney, 1993.

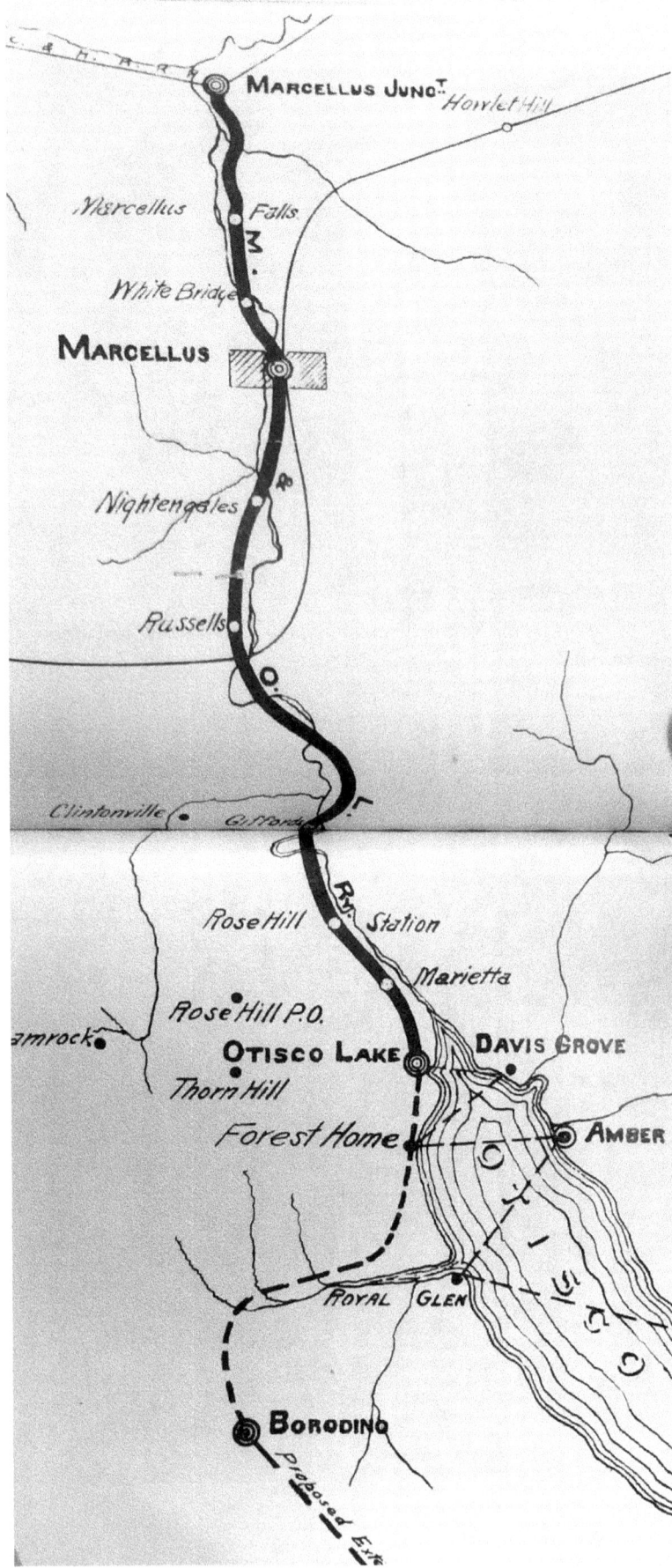

Drawing showing the geographical locations of Marcellus, Clintonville, Rose Hill, Thorn Hill, Marietta and Amber. Courtesy of the Marcellus Historical Society

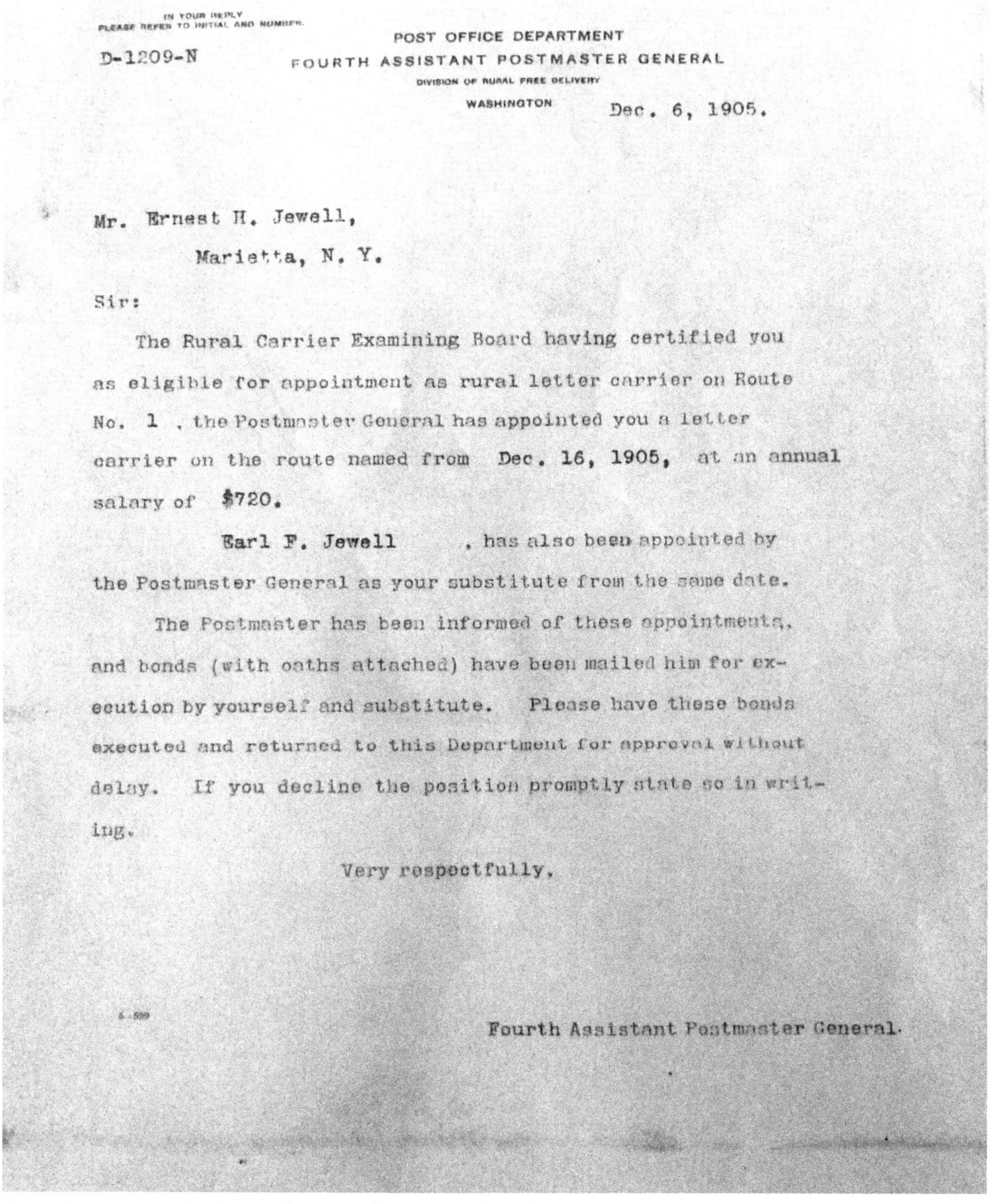

IN YOUR REPLY
PLEASE REFER TO INITIAL AND NUMBER.

D-1209-N

POST OFFICE DEPARTMENT
FOURTH ASSISTANT POSTMASTER GENERAL
DIVISION OF RURAL FREE DELIVERY
WASHINGTON   Dec. 6, 1905.

Mr. Ernest H. Jewell,

Marietta, N. Y.

Sir:

The Rural Carrier Examining Board having certified you
as eligible for appointment as rural letter carrier on Route
No. 1 , the Postmaster General has appointed you a letter
carrier on the route named from Dec. 16, 1905, at an annual
salary of $720.

Earl F. Jewell   , has also been appointed by
the Postmaster General as your substitute from the same date.

The Postmaster has been informed of these appointments,
and bonds (with oaths attached) have been mailed him for ex-
ecution by yourself and substitute. Please have these bonds
executed and returned to this Department for approval without
delay. If you decline the position promptly state so in writing.

Very respectfully,

Fourth Assistant Postmaster General.

Letter of appointment of Earl F. Jewell on December 16, 1905 as rural letter carrier at an annual wage of $720. Quite likely he had to furnish his own horse and buggy to deliver the mail as well as his time for the $720. Courtesy of Peg Nolan, Marcellus historian.

A late 1930s photo of the Marietta Post Office. In 1959 it received national recognition as the smallest post office in the United States.

Earlier location of the Marietta Post Office before the new one was constructed in 1985. Courtesy of Marcellus historian, Peg Nolan

Postal marker of Thorn Hill. Courtesy of the Marcellus History Museum

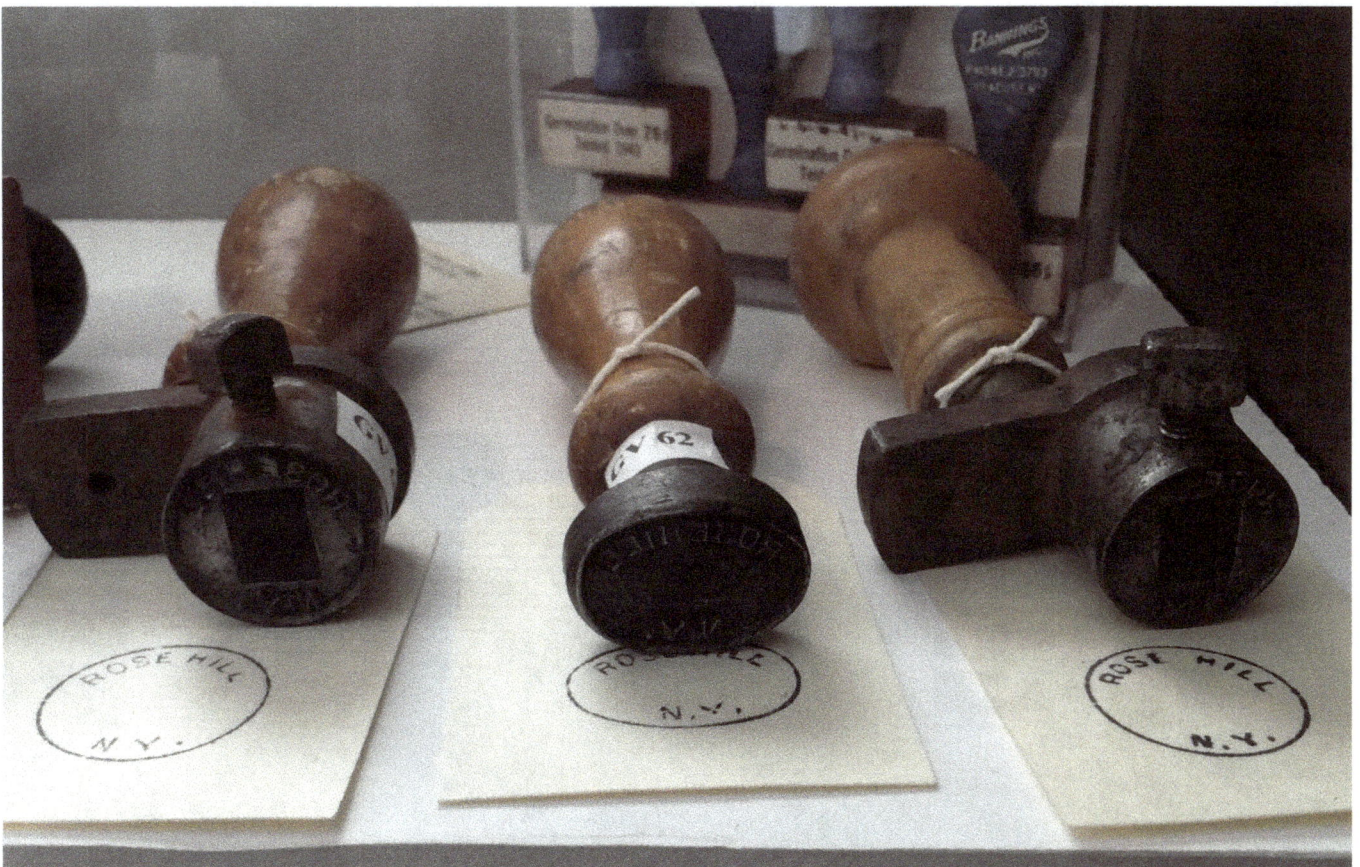

Rose Hill postal markers. Courtesy of the Marcellus History Museum

The Marcellus Post Office is at 9 East Main Street, Marcellus, NY 13108-9998. It is leased by the US Postal Service, was constructed in 1962, has 2,299 square feet of space and is on an 18,810 square foot lot.

The Marietta Post Office is at 2796 State Route 174, Marietta, NY 13110-9998. It is owned by the US Postal Service, was constructed in 1985, has 1,275 square feet of space and sits on a lot of a little over one acre.

CHAPTER 17

Post Offices in the Town of Onondaga

The Town of Onondaga was incorporated in 1798. It was created from parts of the Towns of Marcellus, Pompey and Manlius along with portions of the Onondaga and Salt Springs Reservations. In 1809 a part of Salina was removed and in 1834 a portion of Camillus.[1]

Located near the geographical center of the county and initially serving as Onondaga County's county seat brought impetus for rapid growth in population. As the town's population grew, substantial portions were annexed to the city of Syracuse to its north. A growing, mostly semi-urban population created need for more than a dozen post offices at various times in the Town's history.

Cedarville

Established: June 29, 1871
First Postmaster: Lewis Amidon
Discontinued: May 15, 1901
Service from **Marcellus**

Cedarville, originally called Terry Hollow and Oakland Mills is located in the middle-western part of the Town of Onondaga on the headwaters of Onondaga Creek. It's post office was closed in 1901 at the time Rural Free Delivery (RFD) came to the area.

East Onondaga

Founded: January 22,1883
First Postmaster: George B. Clark
Discontinued: June 1899
Service from **Syracuse**

East Onondaga Post Office became the East Onondaga branch of Syracuse. Syracuse was undergoing rapid growth in the late 1800s and was spreading out into adjacent communities.

Elmwood Park

Established: May 7, 1891
First Postmaster: Walter W. Norris
Discontinued: June 30, 1899
Became a post office station served by **Syracuse**

Elmwood Park was also absorbed into Syracuse as it rapidly expanded in the late 1800s. It was located about a mile west of Route 81 and east of Onondaga Creek approximately a mile south of present downtown Syracuse. The current Elmwood Park is the approximate location of the old post office.

Elmwood Park (Syracuse Station)

Established: July 1, 1899
Discontinued: February 1, 1900
Service from **Syracuse**

This post office was in the same location as Elmwood Park but became a Syracuse Station for less than a year before finally being absorbed into the Syracuse Post Office.

Howlet Hill

Established: May 18, 1829
First Postmaster: Wheeler Truesdale
Discontinued: October 15, 1900
Service from **Camillus**

(A notation by Richard Wright, past director of the OHA, indicates that the Howlet Hill patrons were served by a rural route from Marcellus rather than Camillus.)

Howlet Hill was named after Parley Howlett who settled there in 1797. It is located in the northwest corner of the Town of Onondaga less than two miles from Camillus. It was commonly spelled with two *t*'s but the post office name had just one *t*.

---

[1] Clayton, Professor W.W., *History of Onondaga County* p. 271

Joshua

(also called Cradleville)

Established: October 29, 1886
First Postmaster: Charles V. Webber
Discontinued: November 15, 1905
Service from **Marcellus**

Joshua was located in the south western part of the Town of Onondaga on what is now US Route 20.

Navarino

Established: February 28, 1828
First Postmaster: Alexander H. Cowles
Discontinued: March 30, 1907
Service from **Marcellus**

Navarino, first called Hall's Corners after the Hall family, is located in the southwestern part of the Town of Onondaga on what is currently US Route 20.

Nedrow 13120

Established: September 5, 1917
First Postmaster: Alfred E. Perry
Serves a population of over 2,000 today

Nedrow is located in the Town of Onondaga on the southern edge of Syracuse at 6709 South Salina Street, a little north of the Onondaga Indian Reservation. November 22, 1954 marked the first day that residents of Nedrow had their mail delivered to their door by carriers. Previously they had to pick up their mail at the Nedrow Post Office. It still has an active post office with postal boxes for some of its patrons.

Onondaga

Established: April 17, 1830
First Postmaster: Reuben West
Discontinued: December 31, 1959
It became a branch of the **Syracuse** Post Office with ZIP Code 13125.

Jane Tracy wrote the following in her 2004 letter about the Town of Onondaga Post Offices:

"The first Onondaga Post Office, then called Onondaga C.H., was situated in the Hotel Stackhouse on the corner of West Seneca Turnpike and East Avenue. Later Edward Curtis, the shoemaker, was the postmaster in the same building as his shoe repair shop. About 1908 Harry Thompson ran the post office out of his grocery store at the corner of East Avenue and West Seneca Turnpike. Leslie A. Makyes was the postmaster on the hill from 1936-1941 when he resigned and was succeeded by his wife, Mrs. Mildred S. Makyes. Mrs Makyes was an old hand at the job since she had substituted for her husband many times during his five years in office. The Onondaga Hill Post Office was located in the Makyes filling station at South Avenue and West Seneca Turnpike. Everyone had a box in the post office because there was no carrier service in the area at that time."

Onondaga C. H.

Established: February 9, 1816
First Postmaster: Nehemiah H. Earle
It was discontinued on April 17, 1830 when its name was changed to **Onondaga**.

It was called Onondaga C. H. with the C.H. as an abbreviation for Court House. Because Onondaga was where the Onondaga County Courthouse was situated the C.H. helped avoid confusion with the one a few miles north named Onondaga Hollow.[2] The courthouse was relocated to Syracuse in 1830 causing the name change to Onondaga.

Onondaga Castle

Established: September 22, 1849
First Postmaster: Albion Jackson
Discontinued: November 29, 1859
Re-established: January 23, 1860
Postmaster: Jerome J. Cook
Discontinued: September 3, 1868
Re-established: January 6, 1869
Discontinued: October 25, 1875
Re-established: November 9, 1875
Postmaster: Henry Conklin
Discontinued: February 14, 1903
Service from the East Onondaga Station of
Syracuse

(A notation by Richard Wright, former Director of the OHA, indicates that an earlier application made for this post office with Albion Jackson to be postmaster was denied by the United States Postal System on March 15, 1842.)

---

2 Clayton, Professor W.W., *History of Onondaga County* p. 277

Onondaga Castle was located at the junction of U.S. Rt. 11 and N.Y. Rt. 11A south of Nedrow. It was the home and fortified camp of the Onondaga Indians for many years and is in the Onondaga Indian Reservation. The fact that it was established and discontinued several times could be because of a lack of a post office site, a change in the politics of U.S. presidents or the need to appoint a new postmaster.

Onondaga Hollow

Established: April 1, 1795*
First Postmaster: Comfort Tyler
Discontinued: September 18, 1849
Name changed to **Onondaga Valley**

(*Joshua Clark's book of 1849, Onondaga states 1794)

Onondaga Hollow Post Office was the first United States post office in Onondaga County. It was located in Onondaga Valley about two miles east-southeast of Onondaga Hill. It was a post office of importance over a wide geographical area with mail distribution as late as 1812 to people living in the towns of Camillus, Pompey, Marcellus, Otisco, Spafford, Lysander and Manlius.[3]

Onondaga Valley

Established: September 18, 1849
First Postmaster: Arthur Pattison
Discontinued: June 21, 1899
Became a branch served by Syracuse until July 1, 1908
Became a **Syracuse** Station March 31, 1921

The post office in the Valley had numerous locations. For many years it alternated between the east and west sides of the Valley.[4] Some of the locations listed in Jane Tracy's 2004 letter about Town of Onondaga Post Offices were the house at the corner of Riverside Drive and West Seneca Turnpike, the "Wood Store" at the corner of Academy Green and West Seneca Turnpike, the John Hopper house on West Seneca Turnpike when it was under the ownership of the Rood/Madigan family, the Samuel Forman house on West Seneca Turnpike (about 1900 or after) and in Cranston's Hardware Store in the 4900 block of South Salina Street.

Rock Cut

Established: February 1, 1890
First Postmaster: George J. Hoyt
Discontinued: September 15, 1890
Service from **Syracuse**

The Rock Cut Post Office was in existence for less than a year. It was discontinued at almost the same time that the Split Rock Post Office opened so it may have been in that general area.

South Onondaga

Established: February 15, 1828
First Postmaster: Samuel Kingsley
Discontinued: February 18, 1907
Service from **Syracuse**

The village of South Onondaga is in the southern part of the Town of Onondaga which was originally part of the Onondaga Indian Reservation. Earlier it had been known as South Onondaga Hollow. It became a thriving community because of the available water power. In 1845 it had two gristmills, two sawmills and a clothing works.[5]

The post office was at one time in a building that later became a Red & White grocery store. The mail came to the village from Syracuse by stagecoach. (From a paper at the Onondaga Historical Association called *The History of South Onondaga* written by Thelma White in 1940.)

The South Onondaga Post Office was discontinued when Rural Free Delivery (RFD) came to the community in 1907. The residents were actively opposed to RFD as illustrated by a June 29, 1906 Onondaga news article in the OHA archives. It stated:

"A large signed remonstrance against Free Delivery near and through this village is being circulated, nearly everyone signing to keep the post office, and through that the stage from Navarino to Syracuse. Without that we would have no public conveyance or any way to send an errand even, and we want to keep it. W.W. Newman who is making the most effort to get it, now has free delivery in the neighborhood and we cannot see why he should be so anxious about us, who think it detrimental to our personal interests, unless it is the small commission he gets in selling U.S. mail boxes."

3 Clark, Joshua V. H., *Onondaga of Earlier and Later Times*, p. 131
4 Bruce, Dwight H., *Onondaga's Centennial* p. 859
5 Bruce, Dwight H., *Onondaga's Centennial* p. 861

Split Rock

Established: February 21, 1890
First Postmaster: Stephen H. North
Name changed to **Splitrock**: December 1895
Name changed back to **Split Rock**: December 1905
Discontinued: December 31, 1911
Service from **Syracuse**

The opening of the stone quarry at Split Rock to furnish limestone for Solvay Process in the late 1800s brought workers and businesses to supply the workers, creating the need for a post office. The post office name was changed twice because of a United States Postal System attempt to simplify names and later relenting back to the original name. A cable with buckets attached was installed in 1888 to transport the limestone from the Split Rock Quarry to the Solvay Process plant at Solvay.

West Onondaga

Established: February 5, 1851
First Postmaster: Myron Clift
Discontinued: April 10, 1862

The author has been unable to find any information as to where the West Onondaga Post Office was located. We might expect it was near the western edge of the town and in a sparsely populated area. Also, that it was not very far from another post office that could serve its area residents.

A notice appearing in an April 17, 1862 newspaper article in the Onondaga Historical Association archives states that the Postmaster General closed the post office because it was unnecessary and that the people of West Onondaga should notify their friends as to what post office they will hereafter receive their mail.

NOTE: *Much of the information regarding the Town of Onondaga Post Offices is through the courtesy of the Town of Onondaga Historian Mary Nowyj.*

NEDROW POSTOFFICE AND POSTMASTER.—Glenn R. Bailey is the Nedrow postmaster. The office has two carrier routes in Nedrow and one Rural Delivery route through the Onondaga Indian Reservation and South Onondaga. Rep. R. Walter Riehlman, now of Tully, was one of the first Nedrow postmasters, back in the 1920s.

From the October 2, 1955 Syracuse Post-Standard. Copied from the archives of the Onondaga Historical Association.

A FIRST FOR NEDROW. Kenneth Shearer, seated, mounted carrier, James Knox, foot carrier, and Glenn R. Bailey, acting postmaster, are shown today as first delivery of U.S. mail was made to Nedrow residents.

From the October 2, 1955 Syracuse Post-Standard. Copied from the archives of the Onondaga Historical Association.

The Nedrow Post Office is at 6709 South Salina Street, Nedrow, NY 13120-9998. It is leased by the US Postal Service, was constructed in 1961, has 2,835 square feet of space and sits on a lot of 14,561 square feet.

CHAPTER 18

Post Offices in the Town of Otisco

The Town of Otisco was formed in 1806 from portions of Pompey, Marcellus and Tully. The town lies in the south-central part of the county and is approximately five miles long by four miles wide. The population, during the 19th century, peaked in 1840 with 1,906 residents but then gradually decreased to 1,326 in 1890 as residents gravitated away from its rural environment to larger communities. Before the consolidation of post offices created by Rural Free Delivery, there were four post offices in Otisco; Otisco Center, Amber, Otisco Valley and Zealand.[1]

Amber

Established: April 21, 1817
First Postmaster: William V.R. Lansurgh
Discontinued: March 15, 1939
Service from **Marietta**

Amber is located in the northwestern part of Otisco about a half-mile south of the Town of Marcellus. There was a postoffice in Amber over 120 years until in 1939 when it was closed and the residents started receiving their mail through the Marietta Post Office.

Case

Established: February 17, 1898
First Postmaster: Edith L. Russell
Discontinued: November 14, 1904
Service from **LaFayette**

Case settlement is in the northeastern corner of the Town of Otisco where a number of members of the Case family lived. Maple Grove is about a half-mile further east. Some people considered them to be the same community while others thought of them as two separate hamlets.

Until a post office came to Case in 1898, the residents of the area had to travel three miles to Otisco to pick up their mail. This was normally a once a week trip where neighbors might take turns picking up the mail for each other. Residents, at that time and as we still can today, could rent a box in the post office most convenient to them. A few went to South Onondaga for their mail.

Prior to RFD the mail for Case arrived daily by stagecoach from Tully. In the early days of the stage, if the weather was such that the stage could not get through, the pay for that day only covered the actual mileage for that day. The stagecoach driver received approximately a dollar a day for the 22 mile trip.[2]

The Case Post Office was in the home of Mr. and Mrs. George Russell with Mrs. Russell serving as postmaster. When Rural Free Delivery (RFD) came to the area in 1904, the Case Post Office was closed and the mail came from LaFayette.

Otisco

Established: January 21, 1815
First Postmaster: Luther French
Name changed to Otisco Centre May 23, 1833
Name changed back to Otisco January 23, 1834
Discontinued: August 15, 1923
Service from **Tully**

Otisco village is located in the center of the Town of Otisco in lot 99. The Otisco Post Office, established in 1815, was the first post office in the town. Although the post office stayed in the same community there were several name changes for the post office. First it was Otisco, then for eight months Otisco Centre, and finally Otisco until it was discontinued in 1923 with mail for its residents coming from Tully.

Otisco Centre

Established: May 23, 1833
First Postmaster: Oliver H. Kingsley
Discontinued: January 23, 1834
Service from **Otisco**

---

1   Bruce, Dwight H., *Onondaga's Centennial*, pp. 922-931

2   Abbott, Clifford A., *The Story of Case Settlement 1800 to 1952*, p. 27

Otisco Valley

Established: May 20, 1868
First Postmaster: Hannah Webster
Discontinued: July 15, 1944
Service from **Preble** in Cortland County

Otisco Valley Post Office was located at the southern end of Otisco Lake next to the Town of Spafford. The post office was in existence for 76 years, with the mail coming from Preble, when it closed in 1944.

Zealand

Established: September 28, 1892
First Postmaster: Mrs. Augustus (Carrie) Rice
Discontinued: July 14, 1906
Service from **Marcellus**

The Zealand Post Office was located in lot 97 along the edge of Otisco Lake, south of Amber and north of Otisco Valley. It was discontinued in 1906 when the residents of the area began being served by a RFD carrier out of Marcellus.

CHAPTER 19

Post Offices in the Town of Pompey

Pompey, one of the original towns in Onondaga County, was formed in 1794. When it was formed it included what are now the towns of Fabius, Tully and land in other towns. Previously to formation of Onondaga County in 1794, Pompey was a part of the Town of Mexico in Herkimer County. Since Pompey was one of the towns where early settlers decided to live, a post office came to Pompey in 1803. A stage line was established in Pompey about the time the first post office opened and it is likely that the establishment of one influenced the formation of the other. By about 1811 the stage traveled from Utica to Onondaga twice a week carrying passengers and transporting mail.

Prior to the formation of any post office in Pompey rural residents had an informal 'letter exchange'. The old Conklin grist mill, established in 1798 and presently located in the Town of LaFayette was such a place. There were two splint baskets in the mill with one marked east and the other marked west. These were used to place or pick up letters either locally or to travel further toward the addressee. Near these was another basket for messages that might even be written on wood because of the cost and scarcity of paper. Sometimes mill customers might come to the mill only once a year and that gave them the opportunity to catch up on the news while they were waiting for their grain to be ground. The old mill had a long life and was finally torn down in the 1923.

Boxes in grist mills to hold letters were not uncommon since grist mills were usually one of the first buildings to be constructed in a community where water was available to power a mill. People came to the mill to have their grain ground for flour, often from a radius of 10 miles or more. Manoah Pratt's mills at Pratt's Falls is another early location where there were boxes to hold letters.

Customers came from all directions to have grain ground at the mill, especially from the east and west, on a primitive road cut through Pompey in 1790 or 1791. In 1803 the state granted a charter for a road from

Utica to Canandaigua, named the Seneca Turnpike. This road brought many settlers to the southern portions of Onondaga County.

J. Roy Dodge in his book 'An Historical View of Pompey Hill, NY' has put together a significant amount of information regarding early post offices and the delivery of mail.

He quotes an early newspaper item as follows:

"Within the memories of our fathers and mothers it was the receiver, not the sender, who paid the postage on a letter. The postage on one letter used to be a shilling. (twelve and one-half cents) An envelope is a comparatively new thing. It is seldom we see an epistle written on real letter paper at present. The letter was folded in a peculiar manner, the fourth page of the sheet on the exterior where the superscription was placed and then sealed with wafer or wax."

Another article, from the March 3, 1914 *Syracuse Herald* and quoted in his book, vividly describes some of the difficulties in stagecoach travel to get the passengers and the mail to their destination. The article is one of hundreds that could have been written over the first 100 years of stagecoach travel in both Pompey and throughout Onondaga County. In this article, Tom Maher, RFD carrier is transporting five passengers from Jamesville to Pompey.

"A short distance from Jamesville the blizzard struck the stage. Having traveled over the route for 13 years, Maher assured the party that the trip would be made in safety as the horses would find the way. Presently the snow began drifting across the highway, making it impossible for the driver to keep the horses on the road. Members of the party said they could not see ten yards ahead.

Suddenly both horses disappeared from the view of the driver. Maher jumped down and found both horses lying in the ditch. They were righted and the stage went on. A mile further a similar occurrence took place. This time the sleigh tipped and threw the occupants into the snowbank. As the snow broke their falls, they were unhurt except for a few bruises."

The article went on to say that the horses fell four times during the trip and that at one time the two women in the coach were pinned under the sleigh and that the men had to unhook the horses to remove the sleigh from on top of the women. Eventually the stage with its passengers and mail reached Pompey but with some very cold passengers. The two women were left at a farmhouse along the way where stimulants were administered to relieve them from their unfortunate exposure to the elements of nature.

Berwyn
(previously **Marionville**)

Established: January 4, 1893
First Postmaster: Daniel Woodford
Discontinued: October 31, 1904
Service from **Pompey**

Marionville was named for Lt. Col. Francis Marion who was a famous American soldier during the Revolutionary War. Although Marionville was not an official United States Post Office until 1878 it had an important role in the community as a 'letter exchange' at Conklin's Mills. The name was changed to Berwyn in 1893 because the name was similar to some other New York post offices and mail was often sent to the wrong location.

The name Berwyn was chosen by Cornelia Birdseye Woodford who had visited Illinois with a village with that name and had taken a strong liking to the name. The post office was initially located in a cooper shop in front of the blacksmith shop directly south of the Berwyn schoolhouse.

Delphi

Established: April 14, 1814
First Postmaster: Schuyler Van Renssalear
Name changed to **Delphi Falls** April 21, 1902

The post office boxes, before 1900, cost three cents a quarter. The boxes with locks cost ten cents a quarter. Early into the 1900s the cost of the lock boxes increased to 25 cents a quarter and the open box cost was raised to ten cents a quarter.

Delphi Falls 13051

Established: April 21, 1902
First Postmaster: James R. Fenner
Today has approximately 150 postal boxes

The local post office is an important part of any rural community and in 1997 when its long time postmaster Carolyn Houck retired, the community rose up to thwart any attempt by the postal service to close the post office. At that time the Delphi Falls Post Office yearly income was $18,000, the least amount of revenue of any post office in Onondaga County. Their efforts were successful in convincing the postal service to keep the post office open as evidenced by the fact it is still serving the community in 2016.

Marionville

Established: April 18, 1878
First Postmaster: Daniel Woodford
Name changed to **Berwyn** January 4, 1893

Oran

Established: May 23, 1818
First Postmaster: Philo Cleveland
Discontinued: May 14, 1833
Re-established: June 26, 1833
Discontinued: January 20, 1996
Service from Manlius

Oran is a small community along Route 173 about two miles south of Manlius and a few miles north of Cazenovia. The hamlet had a post office for over 175 years until it was closed in 1996 with mail for its patrons then coming from Manlius.

An article in the *Eagle-Bulletin, DeWitt News-Times* of December 11, 1975 titled '*Vanishing Landmarks?*' was an early forecast of its, and numerous other hamlets post office closures. It described the post office as having a lobby 15 feet long by 10 feet wide with a live Christmas tree in one end, cut by Postmaster Jerry Goodfellow. He also used evergreen boughs to decorate the door and fill a window box. Goodfellow estimated he handles between 200 and 500 pieces of mail a day. There were no delivery routes from the post office so all patrons picked up their mail at this little post office.

In another *Eagle-Bulletin, DeWitt News-Times* from March 7, 1979, Mr. Goodfellow is quoted as follows. "As a rural postmaster you do everything. I have gone out and pushed people out of ditches. I've comforted people who have been in accidents, before the emergency vehicles came. Anyone who goes away in Oran, I'm the guardian of their property. People always come to me and ask that I watch their house for them. I've even rounded up runaway animals. One time I had a horse tied up to the flagpole out front."

The article also mentioned that, in 1979, the post office was located in a building more than 100 years old which formerly also housed a grocery store.

The Oran Post Office, as described in the above article and like 1,000s of other small communities throughout the countryside, was a community center where patrons shared the local news and gossip with the postmaster and their neighbors. It was more than a post office but a place that provided the glue that helped bind the people of that community together.

Pompey

Established: May 2, 1803
First Postmaster: Daniel Woods
Today has 266 postal boxes

The residents of the area call the hamlet of Pompey, Pompey Hill. Until a post office arrived it was known as Butler's Hill. Apparently the postal system had other ideas because all references refer to it simply as Pompey. The Pompey Post Office has almost always served a large area of the surrounding countryside, especially during its early years, so it is actually well named.

Before the post office was formed mail came from the Onondaga Hollow Post Office, which was established in 1794 and perhaps at sometime from Manlius which was formed in 1800. In its early years mail might come once or twice a week. When the roads were deep in mud or piled high with snow and the stage couldn't travel a horseback rider might deliver the mail.

Even when travel was difficult the mail almost always reached its destination. There were, however, unscrupulous characters in the 1800s and 1900s as well as today. Articles in the October 23, 1913 editions of both the *Herald* and the *Journal* tell of a mailbag for the Pompey Post Office thrown from the train at Jamesville, as was normally done, missing and later found in a farmer's field. It had been cut open and letters were scattered around indicating that some thief had been looking for money. Syracuse postal authorities were notified and were expected to investigate.

Rural Free Delivery came into existence during the last years of the 1800s and the early 1900s. Pompey had a rural route from about 1903 to 1940. Tom Conan,

brother of postmaster Jerry Conan, was the rural carrier. When he retired in about 1940 the Pompey rural route was divided between LaFayette and Fabius. The Jerry Conan store, built in 1836, housed the Pompey Hill Post Office from June 1, 1899 with Jerry serving as postmaster from 1900 until his death in 1941, over 40 years. A new post office was constructed to serve the community in 1975.

From an article in the March 7, 1979 *Eagle-Bulletin, DeWitt News-Times*, Postmaster Betty Sullivan stated that she had seen the post office location shift from an old garage on Sweet Road, to a temporary trailer and to the present new building. She also remarked that the postmaster job, in former times, was one shared by a man and his wife with the children helping out by running the rural routes.

Pompey Centre

Established: October 10, 1831
First Postmaster: Charles G. Merrell
Name changed to Pompey Center May 8, 1893
Discontinued: July 31, 1902
Service from **Manlius**

Pompey Center is about three miles south of Oran and three miles northeast of Pompey.

Watervale

Established: December 20, 1826
First Postmaster: Ansell Judd
Discontinued: November 30, 1903
Service from **Manlius**

Watervale is located about four miles south of Manlius and four miles north of Pompey.

NOTE: *Most of the material regarding the Town of Pompey post offices was provided through the courtesy of the Town of Pompey, the Pompey Historical Association, its historian Ruth Hotaling and J. Roy Dodge.*

Jerry Conan's stone store and Tom Maher's stage ready to take one of its regular trips from Pompey to Onatavia Station (LaFayette) carrying both mail and passengers. Photo courtesy of the Pompey Historical Society

Collins General Store and Post Office in Oran during the early 1900's. Photo courtesy of the Pompey Historical Society

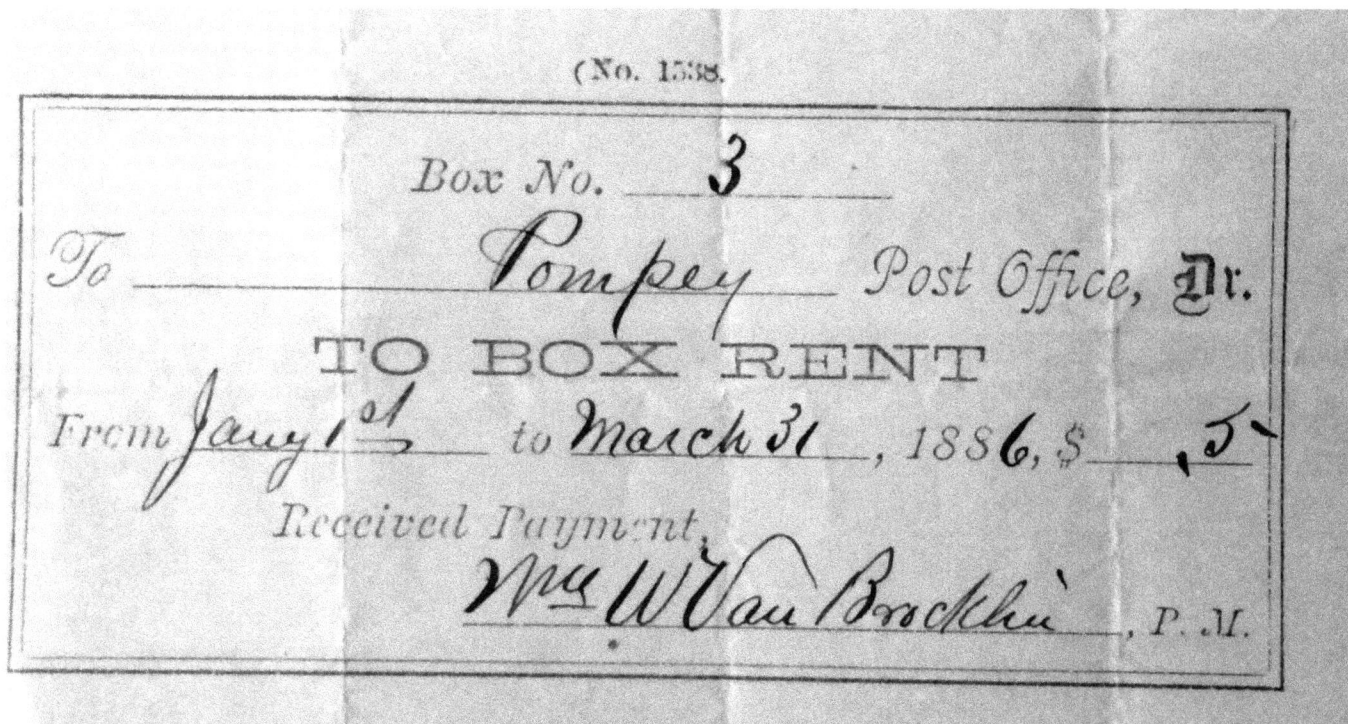

(No. 1538.

Box No. **3**

To _____ *Pompey* _____ Post Office, **Dr.**

TO BOX RENT

From *Jany 1st* to *March 31*, 1886, $ *.5*

Received Payment,

Wm W Van Brocklin, P.M.

A receipt for box rent at the Pompey Post Office for five cents in payment for January thru March 1886. Courtesy of J. Roy Dodge

ORAN POST OFFICE

Boyd's General Store and Oran Postoffice in the early 1900's. Oran is located in the northeast corner of Pompey southeast of Manlius. Photo courtesy of the Pompey Historical Society

121

Oran Post Office in late 1800's, 1942 and again in the 1970s. The political party that was in power in Washington determined who would be postmaster and always where the post office would be located until Congress transformed the Post Office Department into the United States Postal Service in1971, removing the Postmaster General from the President's Cabinet. Photo courtesy of the Pompey Historical Society

Berwyn was located about two miles south-southwest of Pompey and had previously been known as Marionville. The residence in this photo is also the post office as was very common in small rural communities through the 1800s, 1900s and still to some extent today. Photo courtesy of Carl Swift and the Pompey Historical Society

The Pompey Hill Post Office was located in this store, built in 1826, on several occasions: Horace Wheaton 1838-1843; John J. Taylor 1866-1867; plus continually from April 1873 to June 1899. The photo was taken in 1881 for James V. Butts, standing on the right, who was the postmaster a number of years. Photo courtesy of the Pompey Historical Society.

This 1916 photo of the Jerry Conan Store, built in 1836, housed the Pompey Hill Post Office after June 1, 1899. Jerry, standing in post office doorway, was postmaster from 1900 until his death in 1941. Photo courtesy of J. Roy Dodge from the Fabius Historical Society

Delphi Falls, early 1900's, plank sidewalks leading to E. Blowers' General Store and Post Office, same location now as Learnouth's market, 1976, prior to Blowers' Store, T.J. Piester had general store and post office, 1893. Courtesy of Mildred Lamb.

Berwyn was located about two miles south-southwest of Pompey and had previously been known as Marionville. The residence in this photo is also the post office as was very common in small rural communities through the 1800s, 1900s and still to some extent today. Photo courtesy of Carl Swift and the Pompey Historical Society

A photo of the general store and post office in Delphi Falls during the 1930s. Photo courtesy of Hazel Yale and the Pompey Historical Society

Pompey Post Office in the 1960s when Charles R. Whitton was postmaster. Photo courtesy of the Pompey Historical Society

125

The Delphi Falls Post Office is at 2185 Oran Delphi Road, Delphi Falls, NY 13051-9998. It is leased by the US Postal Service, was constructed before 1950 and is 610 square feet in area.

The Pompey Post Office is at 7360 Academy Street, Pompey, NY 13138-9998. It is leased by the US Postal Service, was constructed in 1975, has 1,104 square feet of space and sits on a lot of 19,442 square feet.

Post Offices in the Town of Salina

The Town of Salina was formed in 1809 from the northwest corner of the Town of Manlius and a portion of the salt reservation. In 1797 when the State took formal control of the salt springs it was required by law to lay out a portion for the manufacture of salt which was given the name Salina. A year later a village was laid out in part of this area and also given the name Salina.

Liverpool 13088

Established: September 9, 1811
First Postmaster: Henry Case
Serves a population of about 30,000

Note: *The complete list of Liverpool postmasters is in the appendix.*

In 1991, Liverpool Village Historian, Dorianne Gutierrez, wrote the following information concerning the settlement of the village and the development of its Post Office:

Settlement began in 1797 with nine log cabins on Brow and First Streets by 1808. In 1811 when the Liverpool Post Office was established there were 36 salt manufacturers that produced a total of 20,000-30,000 bushels of salt a year. When Liverpool was first settled there was very little development to its West but that changed rapidly when the Erie Canal was completed in 1825. The Oswego Canal, completed in 1829, ran where the pedestrian path along Onondaga Lake is today. These canals coupled with a rapidly growing salt industry brought rapid growth to Liverpool and its need for post office services.

It is believed that the first post office was located at 329 First Street. Later, when Francis Alvord was postmaster the post office was moved to 304 Tulip Street, which also housed his barber shop. Sometime around 1930 the Post Office was
moved to 330 First Street. The next move was to 103 Third Street in 1950. In 1962, a new post office building was constructed at 300 Cypress Street with about 9,000 square feet of space, three times the size of the previous building.

Mail came to Liverpool by stagecoach, canal or cart until the 1870s when trains passed through the village and brought the mail. Many times the train didn't even stop to pick up the mail because of a 'hook' arrangement on the side of the railroad right-of-way. A sack of mail was hung from a hook and the passing train had an arm to catch the mail bag. The train's momentum allowed the bag to slide along a rail and bring it into the train. By a similar method sacks of mail were dropped off to be picked up by a Liverpool Post Office employee and carted to the Post Office. A train might be traveling as fast as 50 m.p.h. and this system still functioned effectively.

An undated and unknown source has written in the Liverpool files about a mail messenger called 'Pete' who carried the mail from the railroad to the post office with a two-wheeled cart. He also delivered 'special delivery' letters. He was a bit of a character , careless in dress, dirty, ragged and spoke funny. It was reported that once when he delivered a special delivery letter the lady that opened the door fainted at the sight of him. When Washington heard of this an inspector arrived and ordered Pete's removal.

A payment record shows that Raynor Meloling, a Liverpool carrier received $7.50 a month when he carried the mail in 1899. Undoubtedly he had a rather short route in the village. When Rural Free Delivery came to Liverpool, in the early 1900s, the first route ran from the Will & Baumer Candle Co. to Three Rivers. Frank Gleason was the carrier and his wife was often called upon to serve in his place.

In late 1949 a new highway post office route known as the Syracuse-Oswego-Rochester was inaugurated.

The highway post offices looked like buses and were equipped like railway mail cars. In addition to the driver there was a mail clerk who delivered mail to all the community post offices along the route. Liverpool was the first stop out of Syracuse.

Liverpool has grown very rapidly since 1939 and its postal system has expanded to meet the residents' needs. An unidentified Liverpool historian wrote that in 1939 there were only two village carriers, John Clippert and Clayton Dennick, who worked a total of 14 to 18 hours a week. Total receipts in 1939 were $6,800. John Gaffney became postmaster at that time and receipts grew to $8,000 during the next two years moving Liverpool from a third class post office to second class in 1941. It was only eight years later that post office receipts had increased to over $40,000 and Liverpool became a first class post office. At the time Kenneth Andrews was installed as postmaster, in September 1991, the post office served 49,575 people, had 50 delivery routes and annual receipts of $5.7 million.

It was in 1963, when the Postal System initiated the new ZIP Code system to speed up the mail, that Liverpool received the ZIP 13088. By 1969, Liverpool was the second fastest growing post office in New York and receipts passed a million dollars. The post office served 8,576 delivery stops and over 10,000 area families in 1969. They even analyzed the average amount of time for each delivery which was only slightly more than a minute.

As early as 1997 the search was on for a new post office site but postal automation at the Syracuse area processing center on Taft Road has negated the need for a larger post office in Liverpool. In addition, the Liverpool Post Office branch at Bayberry, with the ZIP 13090-9211 leased by the Postal Service, relieves some of the demand.

Salina

Established: July 1, 1807
First Postmaster: Isaiah Bunce
Discontinued: January 27, 1848
Re-established: February 17, 1848
Discontinued: February 6, 1871
Service from **Syracuse**

Salina (Station of Syracuse)

Established: March 15, 1909

NOTE: *Information concerning Town of Salina Post Offices provided by Dorianne Gutierrez, Liverpool Historian, and from the collections at the Liverpool Village Historian's Office are most appreciated.*

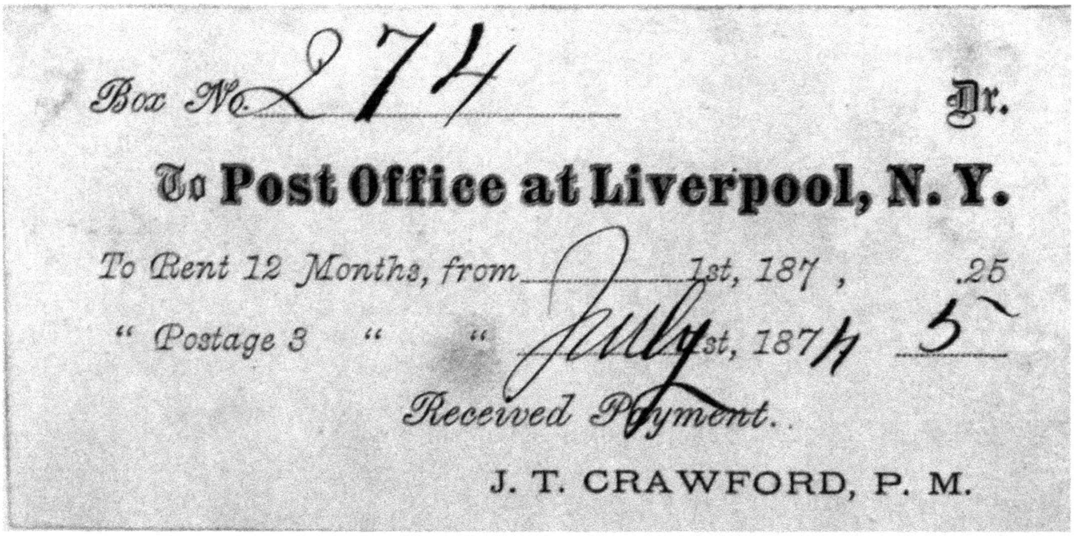

Box No 274 Dr.

To Post Office at Liverpool, N. Y.

To Rent 12 Months, from July 1st, 187 , .25

" Postage 3 " " 1st, 1874 5

Received Payment.

J. T. CRAWFORD, P. M.

Receipt of five cents for box rent at the Liverpool Post Office in the 1870s. At that time box rent for one year was 50 cents. Furnished courtesy of Liverpool Village Museum and its historian Dorianne Gutierrez.

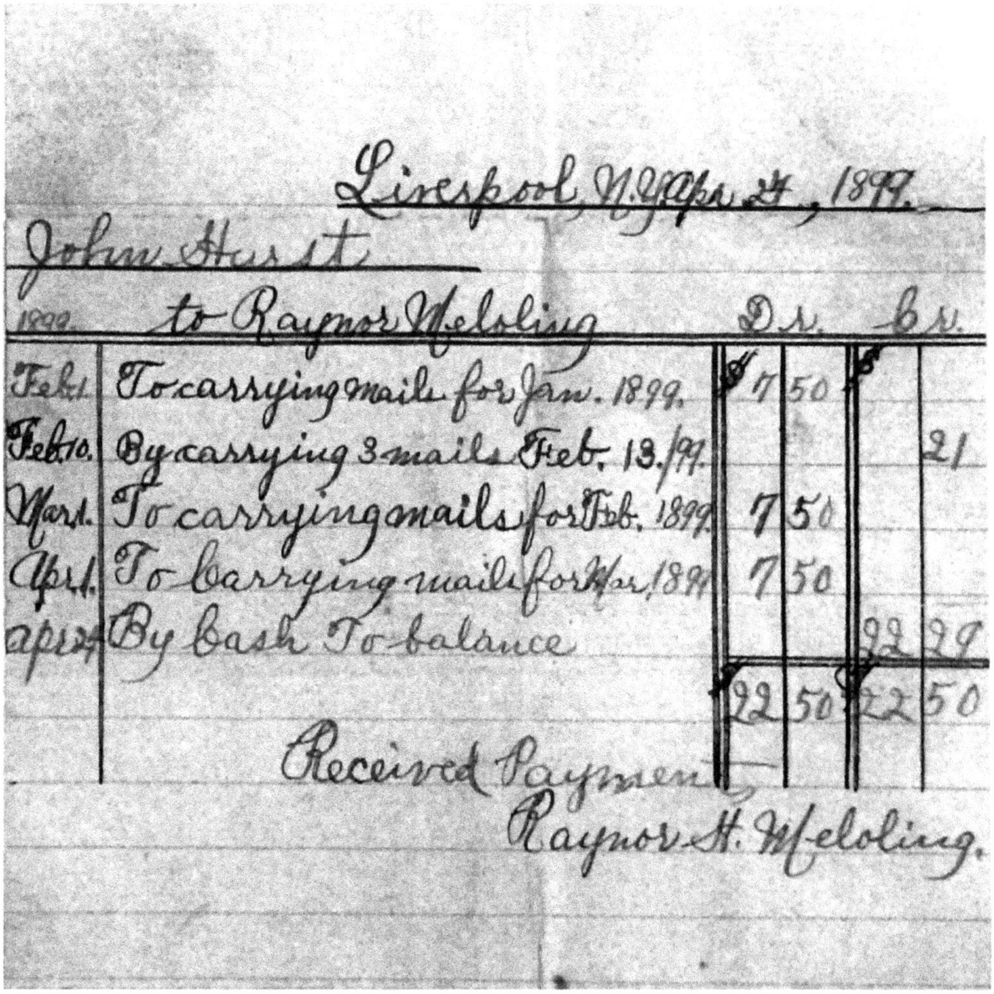

Liverpool, N.Y. Apr. 24, 1899.

John Hurst

1899	to Raynor Meloling	Dr.		Cr.	
Feb. 1.	To carrying mails for Jan. 1899.	7	50		
Feb. 10.	By carrying 3 mails Feb. 13/99.				21
Mar. 1.	To carrying mails for Feb. 1899	7	50		
Apr. 1.	To carrying mails for Mar. 1899	7	50		
Apr. 24	By cash To balance			22	29
		22	50	22	50

Received Payment

Raynor H. Meloling.

Receipt from Raynor Meloling on April 24, 1899 of $22.50 for delivering mail during February, March and April. Furnished courtesy of Liverpool Village Museum and its historian Dorianne Gutierrez.

A train spouting steam while rapidly moving as it picks up and discharges bags of mail at Liverpool is captured in this photo. Twice a day, in the morning and in the afternoon, the Rome, Watertown & Ogdensburg Railroad brought and picked up mail at Liverpool while moving rapidly through the village. A hook, obscured by the steam, has just grabbed a bag of mail that had been positioned on the crane while a full bag has hit the crane as it came flying from the train. A partial bag of mail, on the lower left has just hit the ground. The photo from a November 11, 1939 newspaper is furnished courtesy of Liverpool Village Museum and its historian Dorianne Gutierrez.

John J. Murphy, Liverpool Post Office employee, is placing a sack of outgoing mail on a crane to be picked up by a moving train as it speeds by. The momentum of the train causes the bag of mail to slide along a hook and into the mail car. The photo from a November 11, 1939 newspaper is furnished courtesy of Liverpool Village Museum and its historian Dorianne Gutierrez.

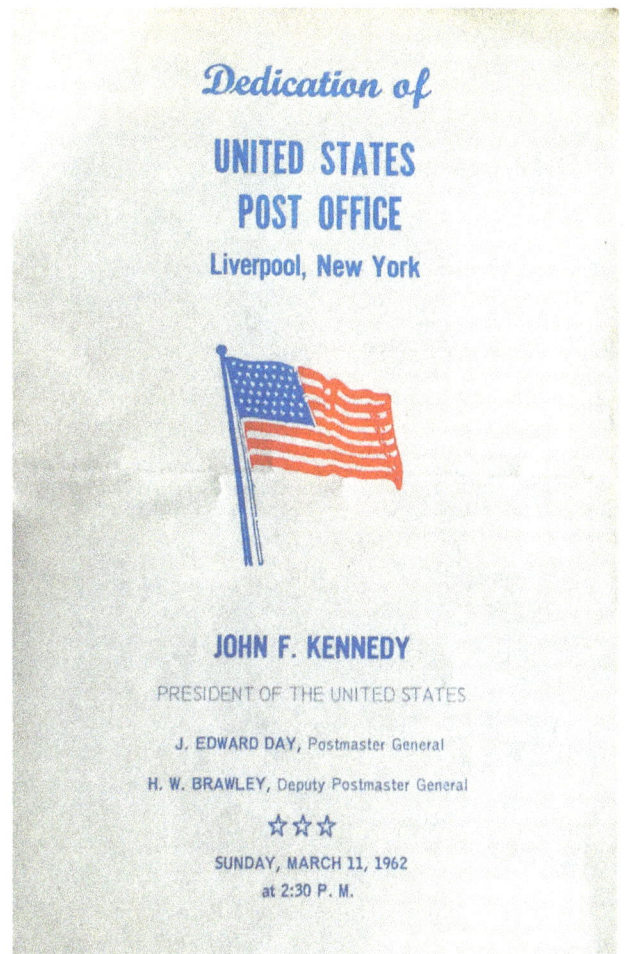

Cover of program at the dedication of the new Liverpool Post Office at 300 Cypress Street on March 11, 1962. Furnished courtesy of Liverpool Village Museum and its historian Dorianne Gutierrez.

Dedication of

UNITED STATES POST OFFICE

Liverpool, New York

JOHN F. KENNEDY

PRESIDENT OF THE UNITED STATES

J. EDWARD DAY, Postmaster General

H. W. BRAWLEY, Deputy Postmaster General

☆☆☆

SUNDAY, MARCH 11, 1962
at 2:30 P. M.

Liverpool Post Office when it was on Tulip Street.

The Bayberry branch of the Liverpool Post Office is at 7608 Oswego Road, Liverpool, NY 13090-9211. It is leased by the US Postal Service, was constructed in 1986, has 10,000 square feet and is located on a site of 28,500 square feet.

The Liverpool Post Office is at 300 Cypress Street, Liverpool, NY 13088-9998. It is leased by the US Postal Service, was constructed in 1961, has 8,600 square feet and sits on a 28,500 square foot site, augmented by another 7,500 square feet of space purchased in 2011 for employee parking.

CHAPTER 21

Post Offices in the Town of Skaneateles

The Town of Skaneateles was formed on February 26, 1830 from a portion of the Town of Marcellus which was Township number 5 in the Military Tract designated for veterans of the Revolutionary War. A portion of the Town of Spafford was also added to Skaneateles in 1840 making it the size it is today.[1]

Mandana

Established: May 21, 1828
First Postmaster: Tunis VanHoughton
Discontinued: October 31, 1901
Service from **Skaneateles**

Mandana is a few miles south of the Village of Skaneateles on the west side of Skaneateles Lake. It was an agricultural community serving the residents of the areas north, south and west for several miles. An 1852 Fagan map shows the post office at the home of S. Fowler on West Lake Road on the southern side of the hamlet. After 1868 the post office was served three times a week from Skaneateles. In 1894 the Post Office System approved a request for daily service. The Mandana Post Office was discontinued on October 31, 1901 when John Simmons, whose route included the Mandana area, became the first Rural Free Delivery (RFD) carrier out of Skaneateles.

Mr. Simmons was the carrier for the 24 mile route for 19 years. Upon his retirement he stated that while driving the route he had worn out seven horses and estimated he had traveled 140,000 miles. Mr. Simmons was recognized as being competent and careful in performing his duties, missing deliveries only in extremely severe weather.

Mottville 13119

Established: March 1, 1832
First Postmaster: Ansel Frost
Serves post office boxes

Mottville, named after Arthur Mott who owned a large woolen mill, was originally called Sodom. Power, furnished by the water flowing from the outlet of Skaneateles Lake, attracted several mills and brought settlers to work in these mills. In 1836 there were about 30 dwellings, a furnace, a grist mill, a sawmill, a tavern, a post office and the woolen mill.[2]

Numerous other industries came to Mottville over the years including the famous Mottville chair.

The Mottville Post Office has been in several locations over the years. It was in Sidney Benedict's store at 873 Crow Hill Road for much of the last half of the 1800s. It was in Evan's General Store at its current site from about 1900 to about 1938. John Quigley, who was postmaster for 25 years and retired in 1963 had the post office in Quigley Brothers grocery store a little to the west, also on Crow hill Road. Later, when another suitable location could not be found the Post Office was installed in a trailer, about a half-mile north of its present location, on Jordan Road as a temporary measure. It was in the trailer most of the 1970s and 80s until it came back to its original home where it is now.

Rural post offices have often been subject to unwanted visitors during the night and the Mottville post office has had its share of night time visitors. An article in the June 6, 1909 *Elbridge Citizen* questions if Mottville shouldn't receive the blue ribbon for having its post office looted the most times. Another article in the March 20, 1914 *Marcellus Observer* tells of the Mottville post office safe being blown open. The postmaster stated that the thief didn't get any stamps because after

---

1 Bruce, Dwight W. *Onondaga's Centennial* p. 977

---

2 Bruce, Dwight W. *Onondaga's Centennial* p. 992

two earlier experiences of the safe being blown open he didn't store his stamps there anymore.

The post office became a contract post office in about 1990, whereby the Postal Service contracts with someone to furnish a building and labor for a monthly check but is not an employee of the Postal System. Since then several different people have had the contract. A November 28, 2002 article in the *Syracuse Post Standard* pictured the post office and Stephanie Davis postal contractor in a store at 873 Crow Hill Road. It states that the post office sits on the site of the original general store and post office. Deb Holbein has had the contract for the last nine years and the post office still rests on the original site and in the original post office building that it now shares with an antique store.

Skaneateles 13152

Established: October 1, 1804
First Postmaster: William J. Vredenburgh
Serves a population of about 8,000

Although the first store opened in 1797, where the Village of Skaneateles now stands, the first post office didn't come to the village until 1804. Colonel William J. Vredenburg came to Skaneateles from New York City in 1803. He was a man of means and was not pleased to have to travel to Marcellus twice a week to pick up his mail. He wrote to Washington voicing his dis-satisfaction and requested a post office in Skaneateles. His request was approved and he was named postmaster of the new Skaneateles Post Office.[3] The first mail bags came twice a week and were opened in his home which stood on the corner of Onondaga and Genesee Streets.

In about 1805 Isaac Sherwood carried the mail on foot from Onondaga Hill to the west. Later he used a horse to carry the mail, then a wagon and finally a stagecoach. He evolved into a large stagecoach operator with mail routes scattered throughout the state. He was not only a large stagecoach operator but was also large physically in that it is said he weighed 380 pounds. We can all be suspicious that he weighed much less when he was walking many miles a day carrying the mail. One year, when he had many postal routes, he was paid $60,538 for the year by the United States Postal System. At one time, the stagecoach with its mail passed by the post office and stopped at Sherwood's Inn to pick up and discharge passengers, requiring someone to carry the mail back to the post office.

In 1804 Jason Parker and Levi Stephens had been given an exclusive contract to run a mail coach or sleigh at least twice a week along the Genesee Turnpike from Utica to Canandaigua. The trip was to take no longer than 48 hours and they were limited to a maximum of seven passengers in their stagecoach. By 1808 the mail run had become a daily run.

It is believed that the imprint of the *Skaneateles, New York* post mark was carved into a piece of round cork by the postmaster. The image was inked and stamped by hand on each letter. In 1804 a letter traveled for eight days from Skaneateles to New York City and cost from 20 to 40 cents. Actually this was quite fast when you consider that it was about 300 miles and carried by a man on foot, horseback, wagon or man powered boat all the way. Roads were often barely passible with muddy ruts or were buried in snow.

The construction of railroads was the beginning of the demise of the stagecoach.

The opening of the Syracuse and Auburn Railroad in 1838 changed the delivery of mail to Skaneateles. The mail came by railroad to Hart Lot, located a few miles North of Skaneateles, in the Town of Elbridge. From there it came to Skaneateles by a carrier under contract with the postal system.

One of those carriers was James Gallager, a farmer and store owner from Mottville. Early each morning he met the train at Skaneateles Junction (Hart Lot) and delivered the mail to the post office at 5 West Genesee Street with his horse and wagon regardless of the weather. He provided prompt service for 11 years even when he had to plow through deep snow on cold winter mornings.

Rural Free Delivery (RFD) came to the residents outside of the Village of Skaneateles on December 1, 1901 with John Simmons the first RFD carrier. His route covered 24 miles on West Lake Road, Mandana and beyond. During that first month he delivered 1,013 letters, 134 postcards, 2,503 newspapers, 214 circulars, and 123 packages. Mr. Simmons retired in 1920 after 19 years of service and 140,000 miles, many of them on horseback.

The Skaneateles Post Office, like many other post offices throughout the country, has experienced unwanted visitors during the night. For the year 1897 the U.S. Postal System reported 1,573 post office robberies. The robbery at Skaneateles came during the early morning hours of February 27, 1897 when two men entered the post office, chiseled open all the

---

3 Bruce, Dwight W. *Onondaga's Centennial* pp. 977-986

drawers and boxes, drilled a hole in the top of the safe and dropped in a stick of dynamite. The explosion blew out the post office windows and made so much noise it alerted the village's night watchman. Shots were fired by both the intruders and the watchman but in the darkness no bullets found their target. The robbers had a buggy waiting and disappeared into the night.

On May 19, 1938 there was a special celebration for the 20th anniversary of the first air mail flight in America. That morning a special plane left Skaneateles for a six minute flight to Syracuse carrying mail from the local post office.

Similar to most villages, the Skaneateles Post Office has had several locations. It's first location was in a small yellow building on the site of the present St. James church. Half of the building was a post office and store with the other half used for a church. The building was moved to another location in 1827 so that a new church could be constructed on the site. Later the post office was located in a building just west of the alley way at 32 East Genesee St. which was destroyed in the 1835 fire.

In 1874 the post office was shown on Sweet's map as being located at 58 East Genesee St. and later on Jordan St. From there it moved to 5 East Genesee where it remained until 1962. On December 10, 1962 a new post office opened at 16 West Genesee St. It's last move was in 1997 to 20 and 22 Fennell Street where two houses had been razed to provide an appropriate site.

At the time the new post office was opened in 1962, postmaster Paul Irving had a staff with three clerks, two mail carriers, three rural delivery carriers, several part time carriers and a part time custodian.

Three Skaneateles postal workers spent almost 30 years working together serving the Skaneateles community. They were Tom Garbo who started as a carrier in October 1961, Bill Pavlus who also started as a carrier in the spring of 1962 and Milan Sefka who started as a carrier in the winter of 1965. All three retired on the same day. Mr. Garbo spent his entire postal career of 31 years delivering the mail in Skaneateles, covering a 14 mile route in sunshine, rain and snow. He remembered only one day over those years when the mail was not delivered to customers. It was in 1966 when the weather was so bad that no one could move.

Mr. Sefka moved from his carrier position to distribution and later served as a window clerk where he processed mail for customers. Mr. Pavlus moved to assistant postmaster and in December 1973 became the Skaneateles postmaster. Mr. Pavlus had the enviable

record of serving a 15 year stretch without missing a day, however, all three were almost always on the job seldom using a sick day. They had rewarding careers serving residents of the Skaneateles area.

Lock boxes came to the post office in January 1963. Zip codes also came to Skaneateles in 1963 and in 1978 mail was sent to the Taft Road facility in Syracuse to be processed and canceled by machine. As new areas were gradually added for the Skaneateles Post Office to serve, the number of rural routes increased, as did the number of the postal staff.

An April 2, 2003 article in the *Skaneateles Press* by Mary Soderberg gives a little insight into the relatively current responsibilities of a mail delivery person where she tells of Ann Coleman walking 12 miles a day, for over a decade, delivering the mail to 355 Skaneateles addresses. Ann and the other mail deliverers arrived at the post office at 7 a.m. and then spent about two and one-half hours sorting and loading their mail before heading out on their routes. Ann stated that she gets to know the dogs on the route, only two had bitten her, loves the toddlers that run to the door when they hear her truck and see how the children change, year to year as they mature and go to school. She stated that she had been taught to watch for signs of possible problems when the mail has been left in a box too long. One day, when dropping the mail in a customer's box, she heard a woman crying out. With assistance from a neighbor they entered the home and obtained medical help for the woman. She had been lying on the floor for a day and one-half praying that Ann would hear her when she delivered the mail. Ann's life, like many others in the postal service, meant much more to postal patrons than simply delivering the mail.

The mail volume of post office gradually grew along with the increase in new houses around Skaneateles and a larger facility was needed by the 1990s. Parking for customers was becoming inadequate and the number of lock boxes had increased from the initial 267 to more than 600. It was difficult to find an appropriate site in the middle of the village and took several years to find a suitable solution. A new post office finally opened on July 1, 1997 that was a mirror image of the previous one but was twice as large. By the 200th anniversary of the Skaneateles Post Office in 2004, the post office had 20 employees.

On April 5, 2014 Mark Lawrence became the postmaster of Skaneateles. Former postmasters Charlie Tanner and Bill Pavlus stopped by to wish him well.

Between them they had served as postmaster of Skaneateles for over 35 years, Bill for 19 years and Charlie for 16 years. Over the course of their careers each had seen many changes in the Skaneateles community which they served.

Skaneateles Falls 13153

Established: November 24, 1874
First Postmaster: Eben Bean
Serves about 200 customers with post office boxes

Skaneateles Falls, previously known as Maryville, is located along Skaneateles Creek about a mile north of Mottville. A dam across the creek provided a good source of power because of a substantial drop in elevation as the creek flowed to the north. In the late 1800s there were several woolen mills, a paper mill, a lime

works and a large cooper shop. At that time the post office was located in P.S. Feeley's store which in addition to groceries carried dry goods, boots and shoes. In addition to Feeley's store there were three other stores in Skaneateles Falls indicating that it was a thriving community. The post office is now an adjunct of the Elbridge Post Office. There are about 180 postal boxes in the post office, which are used by local residents.

NOTE: *Most of the information concerning the post offices of the Town of Skaneateles was provided through the courtesy of Beth Batlle, Town of Skaneateles historian. The author is especially grateful for her article written on the 200th anniversary of the Skaneateles Post Office and the material furnished by the Skaneateles Historical Association.*

A circa 1871 photograph of the Mottville Post Office still in it's original building on the present site. Photo courtesy of Deb Holbein.

A circa 1910 photograph of the Mottville Post Office still in it's original building on the present site. Photo courtesy of Deb Holbein.

This building, one of the smallest post offices in the area, served as the post office in Skaneateles Falls at one time. Photo from the collection of The Skaneateles Historical of the Society.

139

An early 1900s photo of some of the staff inside the Skaneateles Post Office. Photo from the collection of the Skaneateles Historical Society

This photograph is of the Mottville Post Office when it was located in Quigley Brothers grocery store. John Quigley was the postmaster from about 1938 to 1963.

A circa 1940 photograph of the Skaneateles Falls Post Office which had earlier been Thomas Major's combination gas station, barber shop and convenience store. Photo from the collection of the Skaneateles Historical Society.

At one time, in the later 1900s, there was no building readily available to house the Mottville Post Office so the Postal Service provided a mobile home to serve as the post office for a number of years. This photograph appeared in the April 5, 1984 Neighbors West edition of the Post Standard.

The Skaneateles Post Office, which opened at 16 West Genesee St. in 1962 and served the village until the present post office opened in 1997. Photo from the collection of the Skaneateles Historical Society.

Newspaper photo of 30-year veterans, Tom Garbo, Bill Pavlus and Milan Sefka, of the Skaneateles Post Office when they retired on October 2, 1992.

The Mottville Post Office physical location is at 873 Crow Hill Road, Mottville NY 13119. It is the same building where the post office was first housed in 1828 although it has been in at least two other locations. Today the building serves two purposes: the post office and as a gift and antique shop.

The Skaneateles Post Office is at 20 Fennell Street, Skaneateles, NY 13152-9998. It is leased by the US postal Service, was constructed in 1997, has 5,000 square feet of space and sits on a lot of 7,760 square feet. Before its construction two houses had been razed to provide an appropriate location for the post office.

The Skaneateles Falls Post Office is at 4564 Jordan Road, Skaneateles Falls, NY 13153-9998. It is leased by the US Postal Service, was constructed in 1957 and is on a lot of 5,092 square feet.

CHAPTER 22

Post Offices in the Town of Spafford

The Town of Spafford is composed of portions of the Military Tract set aside for veterans of the Revolutionary War. The Town was formed in 1811 from parts of Tully, Marcellus and Sempronius. In 1840 small portions of the Town were removed and annexed to Skaneateles and Marcellus. It lies between Skaneateles Lake on the west and Otisco Lake on the east. Spafford contains more lake frontage than any other town in Onondaga County and has the highest elevation point of 1,982 feet. The first settler arrived in 1794 but the Town grew slowly and did not receive a post office until 1820.

Spafford was named in honor of Horatio Gates Spafford, who was the author of a Gazetteer of New York State and who owned a piece of land in the Town. In 1820 the population of the Town was 1,294, reaching its 19th century peak of 2,647 only 10 years later. It is an agricultural town with little industry so the population gradually dropped back to its 1820 level by the end of the century. With a small population, the post offices gradually were discontinued and the residents served by carriers from post offices in adjoining towns.

Borodino

Established: January 22, 1821
First Postmaster: Daniel Baxter
Discontinued: February 15, 1940
Service from **Skaneateles**

Borodino is located in the northern part of Spafford about a mile east of Skaneateles Lake. It, like Spafford village, was located on the main road from Skaneateles to Homer. This highway brought travelers from both north and south and provided access to markets. At one time Borodino had three stores, three taverns, three tailor shops and three blacksmiths in addition to other businesses. The construction of the Binghamton & Syracuse Railroad in 1854 materially affected villages along this Skaneateles to Homer highway by the diversion of much travel to the railroad.

A notice from the December 29, 1873 Journal in the OHA archives states that the residents of Stafford now have daily delivery of mail rather than the previous three days a week. The delivery route was from Borodino via Scott and Glen Haven to Homer. The residents still had to pick up their mail at the post office as this was still about 30 years previous to RFD.

Edgewater
(known as 5-mile Point on Skaneateles Lake)

Established: December 21, 1898
First Postmaster: William H. Harris
Discontinued: May 4, 1899
Service from **Shamrock** (in Town of Marcellus)

South Spafford

Established: May 19, 1879
First Postmaster: Samuel L. Churchill
Discontinued: January 15, 1911
Service from **Spafford**

South Spafford was located in the southern part of the Town near Cold Brook next to Cortland County.

Spafford

Established: December 21, 1820
First Postmaster: Asahel Roundy
Discontinued: April 30, 1915
Service from **Homer** (in Cortland County)

Spafford hamlet, often referred to as Spafford Corners, was about seven miles south of Borodino on the main road from Skaneateles to Homer. Asahel Roundy, Spafford's first postmaster, was Captain of the militia during the War of 1812 and one of the leading men of the Town.

The first mail came to the Town by horseback until 1827 until a wagon brought it on its travel from Homer to Jordan.

Spafford Hollow

Established: October 9, 1837
First Postmaster: William O. Farrell
Discontinued: December 29, 1843
Re-established: February 13, 1844
Discontinued: August 20, 1864

Spafford Hollow was located in Lot 23 near Tully along the Otisco Valley Road. Water power from Spafford Creek attracted a few settlers and provided power for mills.

After many years of decline in population, automobiles and improved roads are bringing more people to live in Spafford. The majestic countryside along with the amazingly beautiful Skaneateles and Otisco Lakes views are magnets that will continue to bring people to Spafford.

Borodino Store and Tavern at Borodino. Photo from the book "Spafford, Onondaga County, New York" by Captain George Knapp Collins, 1902. Reprinted by the Spafford Historical Society, 1988

Roundy's Tavern at Spafford Corners. Photo from the book "Spafford, Onondaga County, New York" by Captain George Knapp Collins, 1902. Reprinted by the Spafford Historical Society, 1988

Berry's Store at Spafford Corners. Photo from the book "Spafford, Onondaga County, New York" by Captain George Knapp Collins, 1902. Reprinted by the Spafford Historical Society, 1988

CHAPTER 23

Post Offices in the City of Syracuse

The first settler in the area that later became Syracuse was Ephraim Webster who, in 1786, built his cabin near the mouth of Onondaga Creek for the purpose of trading with the Indians. For several years he made it his headquarters before moving to Onondaga Valley.[1]

Syracuse was originally within the boundaries of the Salt Springs Reservation, and when Onondaga County was founded in 1794 it was in the Town of Manlius. In 1804 an act by the New York State Legislature authorized the surveyor-general to sell 250 acres of the reservation to provide money to improve the section of Seneca Turnpike in Onondaga County. James Geddes was appointed by the surveyor-general to lay out the tract. He made sure to include a suitable site for a mill and to exclude as much swamp land as possible. The result was an irregular site which which was later to evolve as the core of the city of Syracuse. The land was sold at auction to Abraham Walton and later became known as the Walton Tract. When Mr. Walton laid out the lots in his tract it was called South Salina, a mere off-shoot of the Town of Salina to the North.[2]

In 1805 Mr. Walton constructed a dam across Onondaga Creek where it is crossed by West Genesee Street. He built a grist mill and a year later a sawmill, which were powered by the flow of water from a pond several acres in size, created by the dam. The construction of an oil mill, a tannery and an axe factory along with an influx of settlers brought steady growth to the little village, initially called Milan. When the application for a post office was sent to the Postal Service it was discovered that there was already a Milan in the state so another name needed to be chosen and it was Corinth. When it became time to choose the final name for the post office a committee was formed to select the name. The new name was suggested by John Wilkinson,

who became the first postmaster. He suggested Syracuse because of an old poem he remembered where there was a Salina near the ancient city of Syracuse. The committee agreed to request that name for their new village and post office resulting in what has become the city named Syracuse.[3]

Syracuse 13220

Established: February 24, 1820
First Postmaster: John Wilkinson

John Wilkinson was appointed the postmaster of Syracuse on February 24, 1820 and established the post office in Amos P. Granger's store which later became the site of the Syracuse Savings Bank. Four years later it was moved to the printing office of John Durnford, the future site of the Onondaga Savings Bank. Mr Wilkinson requested the move for greater convenience of its customers. Mr Dunford resisted the move because he felt there was not enough room in his place of business for the post office. When Mr. Wilkinson arrived with the entire contents of the post office on his back, including mail, letter bags, boxes and everything else, Mr. Dunford concluded he had plenty of room to accommodate all of the requisite wants of the Syracuse Post Office.[4] Later the post office was moved to the east wing of the Syracuse House.[5]

When it became known for certain that the Erie Canal would be constructed on a route passing through Syracuse, settlers and businessmen in larger numbers were attracted to the little village of Syracuse. Actual construction of the Erie Canal began in 1817 and the middle section, which passed through Syracuse, was opened for the first boat on April 21, 1820 only two months after the post office was established. Unquestionably the fact that the Canal was coming

---

1 Bruce, Dwight H., *Onondaga's Centennial* p. 399
2 Bruce, Dwight H., *Onondaga's Centennial* p. 400

3 Bruce, Dwight H., *Onondaga's Centennial* p. 401-408
4 Clark, Joshua V.H., *Onondaga* p. 99-100
5 Bruce, Dwight H., *Onondaga's Centennial* p. 408-409

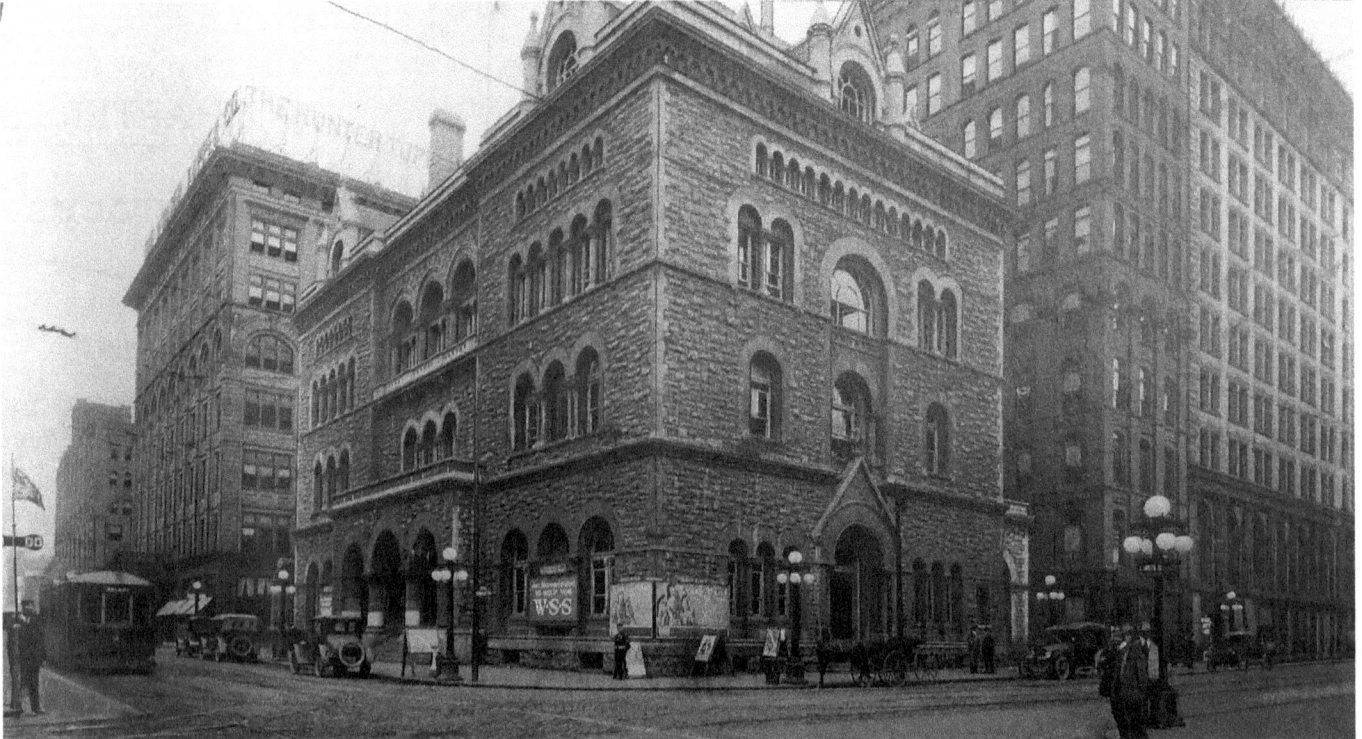

Syracuse Post Office at the northwest corner of Warren and East Fayette Streets from 1889 to 1928.

through Syracuse hastened the establishment of the post office. A visitor to Syracuse, at the time the Erie Canal opened, would have observed only two frame houses, a tavern, log cabins scattered on dry areas and slab houses for the canal laborers. The population of Syracuse was only about 250 because the large areas of swamp land created an environment for disease.[6]

When Mr. Wilkinson stepped down from his duties as postmaster, a review of his books showed that during the beginning of his service as postmaster the total receipts for a quarter of a year had been less than $10. but by the end of his service in 1840 the receipts for a quarter had reached almost $2,000.[7]

As Syracuse Postmaster, John Wilkinson, received a salary of $920.64 in 1832. At that time a Postmaster's salary was based upon their post office's volume of mail. The postmasters of Auburn, Canandaigua, Geneva and Oswego all received a larger salary indicating that in 1832 these cities were more prosperous than Syracuse. With the Erie Canal, salt and central location, it was only a few years before Syracuse surpassed these other cities in growth. Salina, which at that time was a separate village, before later becoming part of Syracuse, had about one-half as much income as Syracuse.

During the middle of the 19th century, before mail delivery to homes or businesses began, there was a 'penny postman' who delivered foreign letters and collected the postage due on them plus an extra penny for the delivery service. As late as 1834 there was only one delivery of mail to the Syracuse Post Office a day.[8]

In 1864 an order was received from the Postal Department establishing free delivery in the city of Syracuse. The city was divided into nine districts with one carrier appointed for each district. The two 'penny carriers were retained and seven additional carriers appointed. They delivered the mail twice a day in the outlying areas of the city and five times a day in the business district. The mail was collected in stores where people left their letters for carriers or at their residences as the carriers stopped to deliver their mail.[9]

When the post office moved into the new government building in 1889, the city had seen tremendous growth as evidenced by the size of the post office staff consisting of Postmaster Carroll E. Smith, Assistant Postmaster E.H. Maynard, 24 clerks and 43 carriers. The old post office officially closed on November 18, 1928 when the new post office was constructed at the corner of West Genesee and Clinton Streets. When the time

---

6 Bruce, Dwight H., *Onondaga's Centennial* p. 409
7 Bruce, Dwight H., *Memorial History of Syracuse*, 1891, p.560

8 Bruce, Dwight H., *Memorial History of Syracuse*, 1891, p.560
9 Bruce, Dwight H., *Memorial History of Syracuse*, 1891, p.561

came that the old post office building was demolished in 1949, the undertaking proved to be more difficult than expected. The stones, of Onondaga limestone, were massive and cut to fit perfectly together. Many of these stones were transported for use in a flood control dam on Route 11A, south of Syracuse, not far from where they were quarried.

In 1899 an order came from the Postmaster General to abolish the suburban post offices at Solvay, Elmwood Park, Onondaga Valley and East Onondaga and make them stations to the Syracuse Post Office. There had been no local delivery by the suburban post offices and it was anticipated by their becoming city stations they would receive the same services as the city including home delivery. Their mail was sorted in Syracuse and delivered to the stations by horseback mounted carriers. Of the new stations, Solvay, where about 3,000 people got their mail, was considered the most important. At the time of this order, there were approximately 300 postal employees in Syracuse, 160 of them being railway mail clerks. Syracuse's first substation appeared on March 16, 1909, covering the north side of Syracuse and was called Salina. Soon after, the Colvin substation was established.

In 1899 postal customers as yet were not required to have mail slots in their houses or to have mailboxes. Mail was delivered directly from the hand of the mail carrier to the hand of the recipient. This caused the carrier to have to wait several minutes until someone came to the door. This waiting was costly for the post office so a 'carrier's call' was devised of three short rapid rings to encourage faster response. Sometimes it was even necessary for the carrier to make a return trip when hopefully the customer would be home.

The 1928 move of the post office to Clinton Square brought the Syracuse Post Office, known as the Federal Building, to a section of the city that had been bustling for years. Clinton Square was named for DeWitt Clinton the major proponent of the Erie Canal. The Erie Canal passed through the center of Syracuse adjacent to what later became the south side of the post office. After the canal was closed in the early 1900s it was filled to form Erie Boulevard. Clinton Square was also at the intersection of major North-South and East-West highways and traditionally a busy market center.

In 1948 Syracuse residents throughout the city began receiving two deliveries a day. This had been made possible by the opening of the University Postal Station, six new postal routes and new routes out of Salina, Eastwood, Colvin, Solvay and Elmwood Stations. The University area had been served, for the previous 25 years, out of a Syracuse University building at University Place, on Marshall Street. Previously, twice a day deliveries had been made to only part of the city.

Later, in an effort to control expenses the twice a day delivery to homes was discontinued. Another cost saving measure is revealed by an article of March 11, 1976 in the *Post- Standard* stating that Postmaster A.J. Sarno announced that Syracuse downtown businesses will no longer receive an afternoon delivery in an attempt to cut costs and that this change is being made nationally.

Postmasters, until 1971, were determined by political appointment. An article in the April 5, 1861 Journal from the OHA archives states:

It is expected that the appointments of Post Masters for this county will be made during the ensuing week. The Post Master at this city is appointed by the President, and the others in this county are appointed by the Post Master General. (It is worth noting that at this time the President's inauguration was in March and that the Postmaster General was appointed by the President. Generally, the appointments made were persons of the same political party as the President.)

As the city of Syracuse increased in size more than one post office was needed for the city. Until 1908 the terms 'station' and 'branch' were used interchangeably. Beginning in 1908, branches were defined as a postal unit administered by a post office specifically located outside of city limits and stations were defined as a postal unit located inside city limits administered by a post office. (However the Postal Service notes that this distinction does not always hold true today.)

The first known post office branch had been established in New York City in 1837 when Syracuse was still a village. Stations were formed and independent post offices discontinued to provide free home delivery both in the city and also in rural areas when Rural Free Delivery was provided around 1900. Consolidation of post offices to provide more efficient delivery of the mail is an ongoing process that continues today.

Until 1929 horses did a good share of the mail hauling in Syracuse. Horses transported letter carriers to their districts in outlying areas, hauled mail to and from the railroad stations and provided the power for other needs of postal service. When the changeover to motorized vehicles was completed, two horse-drawn vehicles were retained for postal deliveries to the downtown congested area of Syracuse. Soon they were also replaced by motor vehicles.

It was in the early 20's that the post office received its first trucks, which were two Model T Fords. The horse and wagons had worked out of the post office at Fayette and Warren Streets and later from the Northrup Station on West Water Street. When the changeover to trucks was made in 1929, the postoffice had 25 horse-drawn wagons, nine of which were used for parcel post deliveries. The horses were rented from several Syracuse livery stables.

Records indicate that motor vehicles did some delivery of parcel post when the parcel post system first went into operation in 1913. At the end of World War I, the post office also used a few motorcycles to improve operations.

On June 1, 1928 the first air mail plane landed at Syracuse Field in Amboy. Each evening many residents of Syracuse were attracted to the airport to see the mail leave.

The Postal Service has performed some unusual tasks in the past. In the 1930's, when Social Security had its beginning, it listed every employer and employee in the city of Syracuse for the Social Security Board. In 1937 the letter carriers made an unemployment census. They reported that about 15,000 Syracuse residents were unemployed or partially unemployed at that time.

In 1954 the highway mail bus service between Syracuse and Binghamton and between Syracuse and Rochester was turned over to private contractors. Post office employees continued to operate the buses and sort the mail but the equipment was to be owned and maintained by the successful bidders. The highway mail bus service began in 1949 as a means of speeding the mail to small communities which suffered from curtailed railway service.

In 1959 the Onondaga Post Office became a branch of the Syracuse Post Office. At that time, when the Syracuse Post Office took over a post office it became a branch and could retain its name. When a post office became a Syracuse "Station" it lost its original name. At this time the Syracuse branches were Solvay, Mattydale, De Witt, North Syracuse and Onondaga. The stations were Colvin, North Salina Street, University, Elmwood and Eastwood

Later, in an effort to control expenses, the twice a day delivery to homes was discontinued. Still later, an article of March 11, 1976 in the *Post- Standard* states that Postmaster A.J. Sarno announced that Syracuse downtown businesses will no longer receive an afternoon delivery in an attempt to cut costs and that this change is being made nationally.

In the 1950s before automatic sorting of mail with ZIP codes by machines, postal distribution clerks were required to have a good memory. In Syracuse they had not only to remember the names of its 2,100 streets but they also had to know the street location to postal zones. Newly hired Syracuse postal clerks were required to go through a 30 hour training program over a period of 15 weeks. Outgoing mail clerks were also required to have good memories in order to place pieces of mail in the appropriate spot. This training program was initiated in 1960 and of the first 37 clerks going through the program only six dropped out. A clerk going through this program made fewer errors and was able to sort letters more rapidly.

Dogs have historically been viewed as a nemesis to postal carriers. In 1961 dogs bit 32 postal carriers in Syracuse, 28 of which required medical treatment. Dogs continued to plague letter carriers so in 1964 the Syracuse postal carriers were supplied with, "Halt", a new dog repellant in an aerosol spray. The spray had been test marketed in four cities in other parts of the country for several months and found to be effective. The carrier carried a can in his mail pouch or attached to his belt and if the dog attacks him he sprays it in the dogs eyes. In theory the dog retreats without a whimper and the effect wears off in a few minutes. It's success or failure might rest in which one is faster, the mail carrier or the dog.

In 1971, the Syracuse Post Office was designated as the sectional center for the processing of mail for the 20 first-class post offices in the Central New York area. All mail from these 20 communities that was not for delivery in this postal district went to the Syracuse Post Office for processing before it was sent on its way. This mail was postmarked " U.S. Postal Service NY 130". Mail for local delivery in the communities in this district carried the local postmark but was sent to Syracuse and distributed from there.

In 1975, because many customers desired a local postmark on the mail, the Postal Service partially relented. The letters from a 10 county area in the

Syracuse District could now have the Syracuse postmark rather than "U.S. Postal Service NY 130".

Following is a list of Syracuse Stations in Syracuse that was compiled by John L. Kay and Chester M. Smith titled, *New York Postal History: the Post Offices and First Postmasters from 1775 to 1980*. No attempt was made to research the history of these stations or of the newer stations established since 1980.

South Syracuse
(Colvin Station)

> Established: March 29, 1882
> First Postmaster: John C. Larkin
> Discontinued: December 13, 1889
> Service from **Syracuse**

Air Base
(Branch of Syracuse)

> Established: October 1, 1942
> Discontinued: March 15, 1944
> (from Postal Bulletins 18499 and 18705)

Clinton Square
(Branch of Syracuse)

> Established: July 25, 1977
> (from Postal Bulletin 21131)

Colvin Station
(Branch of Syracuse)

> Established: December 1, 1909
> (from Postal Bulletin 9026)

Northrup
(Station Syracuse)

> Established: January 1, 1915
> Discontinued: March 1, 1929
> (from Postal Bulletins 10606 and 14849)

Station A Syracuse

> Established: December 1888
> Discontinued: 1896

(Stations designated by a letter (A) were 'Classified Stations' that were staffed by postal employees and provided delivery services.)

Station A Syracuse
(Elmwood Park)

> Established: July 1909
> Discontinued: December 31, 1927

Teall
(Station Syracuse 13217)

> Established: September 11, 1976
> (from Postal Bulletin 21097)

Veteran's Hospital
(Station Syracuse 13201)

> Established: July 12, 1954

Syracuse Post Office, Stations and Branches in 2017

Main Post Office	5640 East Taft Road
Solvay	1801 Milton Avenue
Federal Building	100 South Clinton St.
Eastwood	2509 James Street
Teall	226 Teall Ave.
DeWitt	6581 Kinne Road
Onondaga	4912 West Seneca Turnpike
Franklin Square	401 West Division Street
Downtown	444 South Salina Street
Colvin	2200 South Salina Street
Mattydale	1900 Brewerton Road
University	720 University Ave.

The Syracuse Post Office has been in continual change since it was first established in 1820. Change will continue, new post offices will appear and the Postal Service will continue to meet the needs of the people it serves. The past 200 years have brought amazing changes to both Syracuse and the Postal Service. With change occurring faster each year it is impossible to imagine what awaits in the future.

Syracuse Post Office under construction in 1885. It took four years to construct this massive stone building.

Syracuse Post Office being constructed on the corner of Fayette and Warren Streets in 1885.

A 1908 photo of the Syracuse Post Office interior at the corner of Fayette and Warren Streets in the December 20, 1953 Post-Standard. From the archives of the Onondaga Historical Association.

Demolition of the building at the northwest corner of Fayette and Warren Streets, in 1949, that had housed the Syracuse Post Office from 1889 to 1928.

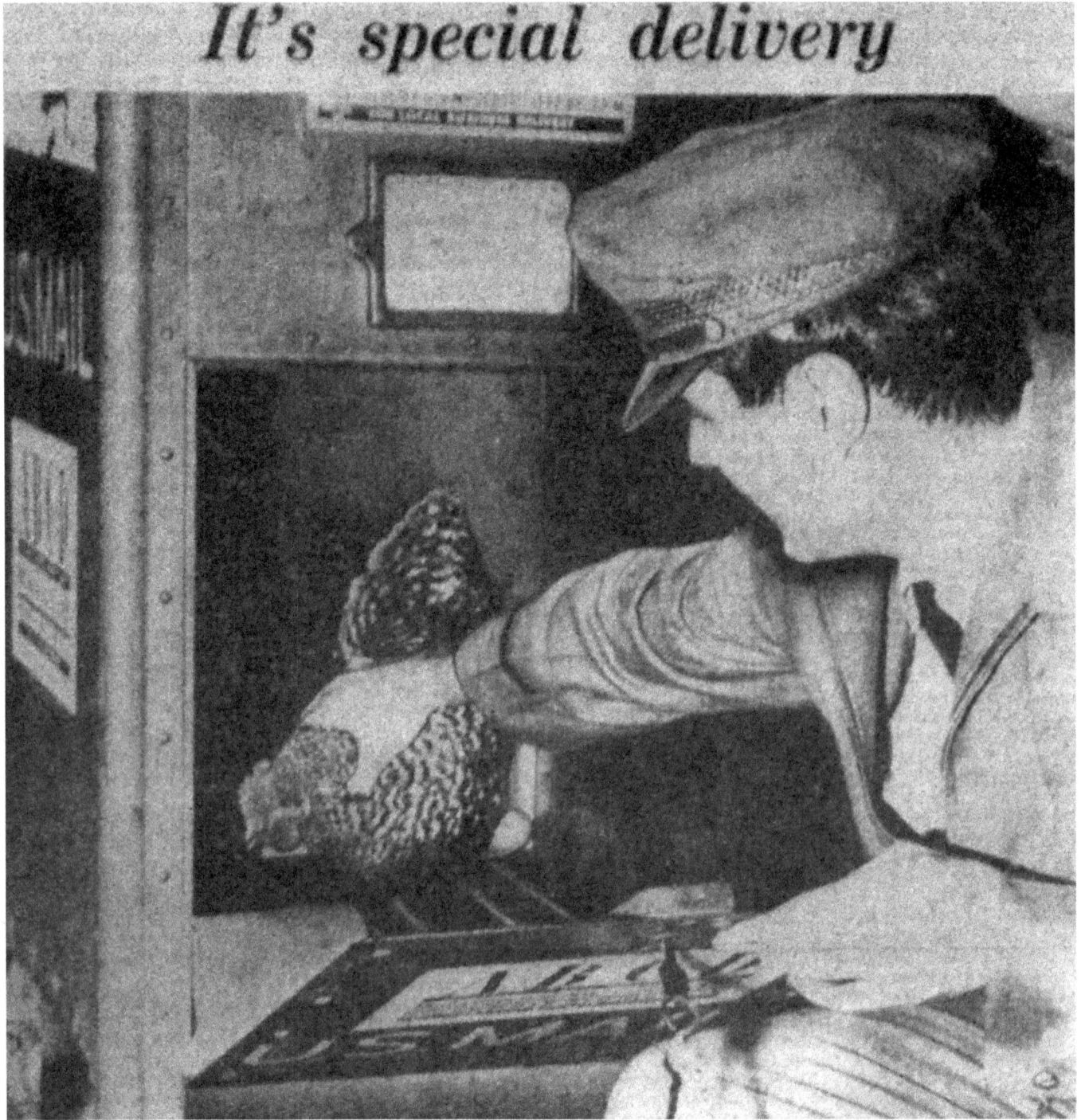

A Syracuse mail carrier received a surprise on November 26, 1966 when he opened the mail relay box at Jefferson and Salina Streets. A live chicken and a brown egg greeted him. Postal authorities had no idea how the chicken got into the box. Apparently someone confused Thanksgiving and April Fool's Day. Photo from a Hearld Journal article in the archives of the Onondaga Historical Association.

Syracuse Post Office on Clinton Square between 1928 and 1978.

Old cart to carry mail which currently sits in the lobby of the Syracuse Solvay Post Office Station.

159

April 17, 1977 article in the Post-Standard telling of the beginning of the move of the Syracuse Post Office to Taft Road after 150 years in downtown Syracuse.

Post Office Moving to N. Syracuse

By SUSAN PRESTON

As the U.S. Postal Service moves the heart of its mail processing operation into a new $12.3 million center on Taft Road this weekend, it marks the end of a 150-year-old association with downtown Syracuse.

Since 1820 when the first post office opened on Clinton Square in the General Granger Store (the present site of Syracuse Savings Bank), through six moves to other buildings, the main postal operation for Central New York always has been downtown.

But it's not with any regret that Syracuse Postmaster A.J. Sarno bids Clinton Square adieu. "It's about time Syracuse moved into a facility sophisticated enough to provide the complex services a city of this size should have," he said.

Syracuse Post Office, Main Office is at 5640 East Taft Road, Syracuse, NY 13220-9998. It is owned by the US Postal Service, was constructed in 1977, has a floor area of 256,944 square feet and is on a site of approximately 50 acres. It serves as the mail processing and distributing center, administrative office of the postal inspection field division, administrative office of the Inspector General, the United States Postal Service and as the main Syracuse Post Office. Adjacent to this property is the maintenance center and vehicle maintenance center.

The customer entrance to the Syracuse Main Post Office at 5640 East Taft Road.

Sign in front of the Syracuse Postal Complex at 5640 East Taft Road.

Syracuse Franklin Square Post Office Station at 401 West Division Street. Syracuse, NY 13218-9211. It is owned by the US Postal Service, was constructed in 1997, has 24,000 square feet and sits on a three and one-half acre site.

*Syracuse Post Office
Federal Station is at
100 South Clinton Street
Syracuse, NY 13261-9211.*

Syracuse Post Office Downtown Station is at 444 South Salina Street, Syracuse, NY 13201-9211. It is owned by the US Postal Service, was constructed in 1982 and is on a site of over half an acre.

Syracuse Post Office Colvin/Elmwood Station is at 2200 South Salina Street, Syracuse NY 13205-9211. It is leased by the US Postal Service, was constructed in 1996 and has 1,510 square feet of space.

Syracuse Post Office Onondaga Station is at 4912 West Seneca Turnpike, Syracuse, NY 13215-9211. It is owned by the US Postal Service, was constructed in 1978, has 4,970 square feet and is on a site of more than an acre.

Syracuse Post Office University Station is at 720 University Avenue, Syracuse, NY 13235-9211. It is leased by the US Postal System, was constructed in 1981and has 2,385 square feet of space. This photo shows the inside of the post office as the post office is surrounded by other businesses.

Syracuse Post Office Teall Station is at 226 Teall Avenue, Syracuse, NY 13217-9211. It is owned by the US Postal Service, was constructed in 1976, has 17,000 square feet and is on a three acre lot.

Syracuse Post Office Eastwood Station is at 2509 James Street, Syracuse, NY 13206-9211. It is leased by the US Postal Service, was constructed in 1976, and is 2,950 square feet.

Syracuse Post Office DeWitt Station is at 6581 Kinne Road, Syracuse, NY 13214-9211. It is owned by the US Postal Service, was constructed in 1973, has 9,210 square feet and is on a site of over an acre.

Syracuse Post Office Mattydale Station is at 1900 Brewerton Road, Syracuse, NY 13211-9211. It is leased by the US Postal Service, was constructed in 1982 and has 1,440 square feet.

Syracuse Post Office Solvay Station is at 1901 Milton Avenue, Syracuse, NY 13209-9211. It is owned by the US Postal Service, was constructed in 1989, has 15,650 square feet and is located on one and one-half acres.

Post Offices in the Town of Tully

The Town of Tully is a portion of the Township of Tully which was Township Number 14 in the Central New York Military Tract set aside for veterans of the Revolutionary War. The Township originally contained 100 lots of 600 acres each and was part of Onondaga County when it was established in 1794. Gradually portions of the Tully Township were removed to form parts of the towns of Otisco, Spafford, Preble and Scott. By 1815 only 26 of the original 100 lots in the Township remained to form the present Town of Tully.

The first white settler of the Town came in 1795 with additional settlers gradually coming after that date. In 1806 the Hamilton/Skaneateles Turnpike (now NY Route 80) was opened bringing an increasing number of settlers to Tully.

Assembly Park

Established: May 14, 1897
First Postmaster: David H. Cook
Discontinued: February 15, 1916
Service from **Tully**

Assembly Park is located along the southern border of Tully on the east side of Tully Lake.

Bromley

Established: November 30, 1892
First Postmaster: John W. Howard
Discontinued: May 31, 1910
Service from **Preble** (in Cortland County)

Bromley is located in what was lot 45 in the southwest corner of the Town of Tully, close to Cortland County and south of Otisco Valley. An article in an unidentified newspaper of 1933 in the Onondaga Historical Association archives states that before Bromley had a post office it was known as Bennett Hollow. Bromley's Post Office was in a red brick house that was the home its first postmaster John W. Howard. Probably the red brick house was Bromley's only post office as the second and last postmaster's name was Warren J. Howard.

Tully 13159

Established: January 1, 1804
First Postmaster: Jonathan Buell
Serves a population of about 5,000

The Village of Tully is located in the southeastern part of the Town of Tully at a major crossroads where NY Route 80 (originally the Hamilton/Skaneateles Turnpike) crosses US Route 11 and just east of where Interstate 81 crosses NY Route 80. This crossroads location brought settlers and commerce to Tully at an early date creating the need for a post office. The Tully Post Office serviced a wide area because of the lack of another nearby post office at that time. It was 16 years before the town received its second post office which was in Vesper about six miles to the northwest and 17 years before Fabius, a few miles to the east received its post office.

There have been at least six different locations of the Tully Post Office. The first location recorded was in the shopping plaza that was on the southwestern corner of the main intersection. When the shopping center was destroyed by fire the post office was moved to the Slayton Hotel located across the street at the corner of Elm and Warren Streets. The third location, from 1900 to 1910 was a few doors south in the VanBergen building on the west side of State Street. The fourth known location between 1910 and 1962 was in the Wright drug store building adjacent to where it was from 1897 to 1900 in the Slayton Hotel. Location five, from 1962 to 1999 was on Elm Street in a newly constructed shopping center. The last move was in 1999 to its present location west of the shopping center at 24 Elm Street.

The current post office building, located at 24 Elm Street, was constructed in 1999. It has approximately 500 postal boxes for the local residents and operates four rural routes in the Tully area and three rural routes in the LaFayette area.

Tully Lake Park

Established: July 23, 1890
First Postmaster: George Fenker
Re-named Tullylake Park in December 1895
Discontinued: May 15, 1905
Service from **Tully**

Tully Lake Park is located on the west side of Tully Lake and across the lake from Assembly Park. The Tully Lake Hotel was constructed in 1890. The hotel was filled with guests and unable to fill the demand so the next year plans were made for enlargement and to open 17 additional cottages. A July 20, 1890 article in the *Syracuse Herald* read:

> *It has only been three days since it became permissible to make use of this Post Office address. The hundred and more campers and cottagers on the park and in this vicinity were set rejoicing last Thursday by a letter from Representative James J. Belden to "Fred" J. West. It gave the information that the United States government had heard of this summer resort, how it was sure now to be a permanent and growing settlement. In view of this condition of things, Postmaster-General Wanamaker and his staff had made up their minds that they ought to establish a branch office here. They accordingly appointed Landlord George Tinker of the Summer Hotel for Postmaster and named the office over which he will preside, "Tully Lake Park, N.Y." (from 'A History of Tully Lake Park' p. 15)*

Tully Lake Park

(the second time for this name)

Established: July 1, 1913
First Postmaster: Ira VanAllen
Discontinued: May 31, 1914
Service from **Tully**

Tully Valley

Established: July 25, 1833
First Postmaster: Ornan King
Discontinued: April 8, 1856
Re-established: November 20, 1857
Discontinued: October 14, 1903
Service from **Tully**

J. Roy Dodge states that the Tully Valley Post Office was located in the Town of LaFayette during most years since the postmasters lived in LaFayette. He also states that the postoffice, for many years, was in the house at the intersection of roads on Lot 88 in LaFayette. The post office was in the home of Albert Benjamin during its later years. When the post office closed the residents were served by Rural Free Delivery carrier out of Tully.

Vesper

Established: April 3, 1820 (in *NY Postal History* date is April 3, 1826)
First Postmaster: William Clark
Discontinued: April 7, 1829
Re-established: February 9, 1830
Discontinued: July 31, 1916
Service from **Tully**

Vesper is located in the northwestern part of the Town of Tully near the towns of Otisco and Spafford. In the late 1700s it was known as Pudding Village but no one seems to know how it came up with this name.

NOTE: *Many thanks to Nancy Chawgo and the other historians of the Town of Tully. Also to the Town for the information and pictures of Tully that came from their book 'A Timeline History of the Town of Tully 1803 to 2008'.*

1910 photo of Wright's Drugstore and Post Office, the fourth location of the post office, on Warren St. in Tully. From the archives of the Onondaga Historical Association

Old red brick building, which a score of years ago was Bromley postoffice. Built longer ago than the oldest old timer of the vicinity remembers, this structure now is the home of James Walker, 74, and his sister, Mrs. John W. Howard, 83.

Bromley Post Office in Tully. Photo was taken in approximately 1933 by a newspaper reporter and comes from the archives of the Onondaga Historical Association.

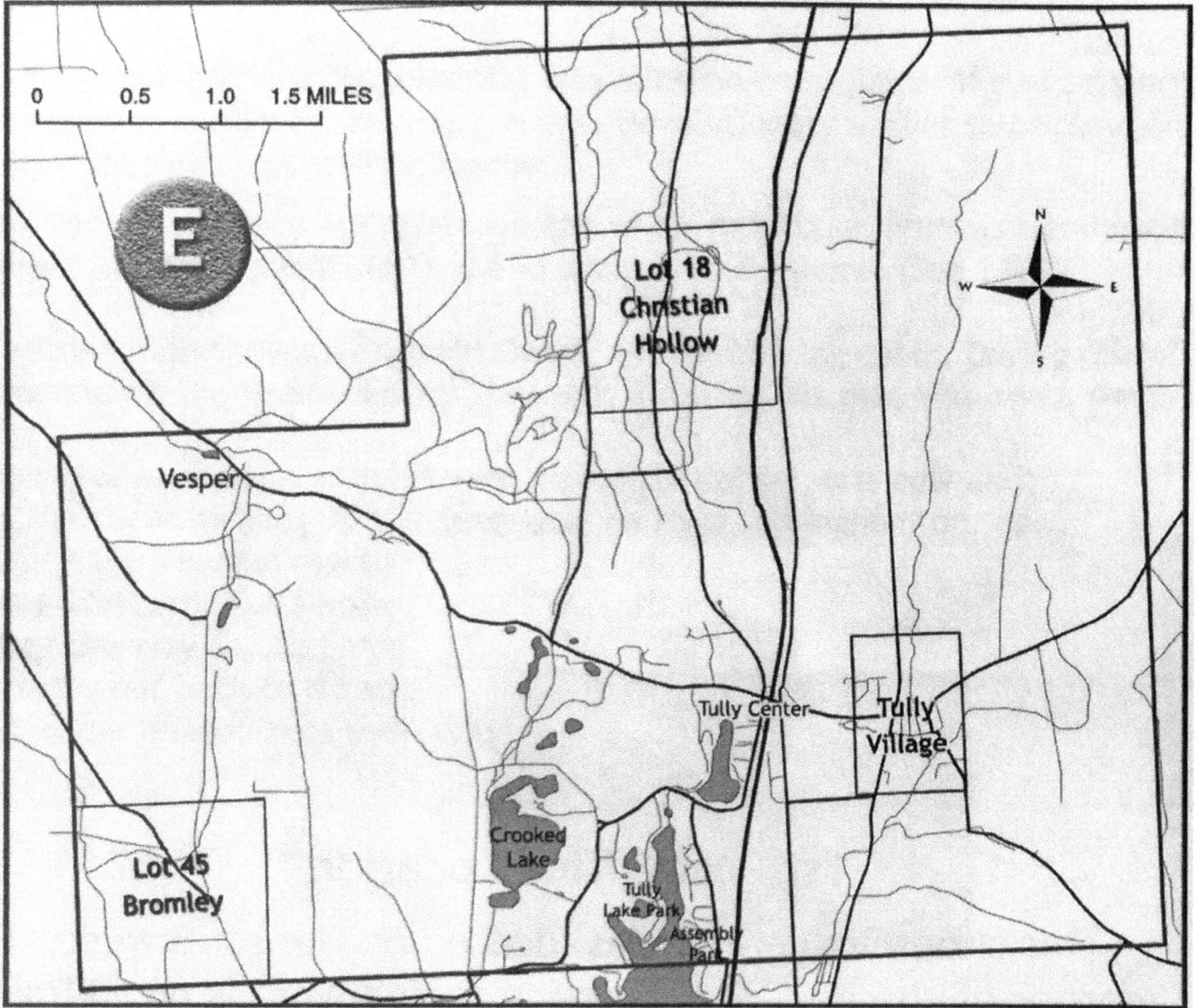

Drawing showing the location of several Town of Tully communities. Taken from the book, A Timeline History of the Town of Tully courtesy of the Town of Tully Area Historical Society.

1st Post Office Location

This shopping center was located on the southwest corner of the main intersection facing what is now Elm St. The old post office (perhaps the first) was on the left side of the building facing State St. You can see the post office sign in the painting above. Also see #1 on Map K

Taken from the book, A Timeline History of the Town of Tully courtesy of the Town of Tully Area Historical Society.

This photo was copied from the TAHS collection

3rd Post Office Location

This shows the first floor of the VanBergen Opera House. The Post Office is on the left. Also see #3 on Map K

Taken from the book, A Timeline History of the Town of Tully courtesy of the Town of Tully Area Historical Society.

A 1961 photo of the new shopping center on Elm Street consisting of the Victory Market, Wortley Drugstore, Hayes Insurance Office and the Tully Post Office. Taken from the book, A Timeline History of the Town of Tully courtesy of the Town of Tully Area Historical Society.

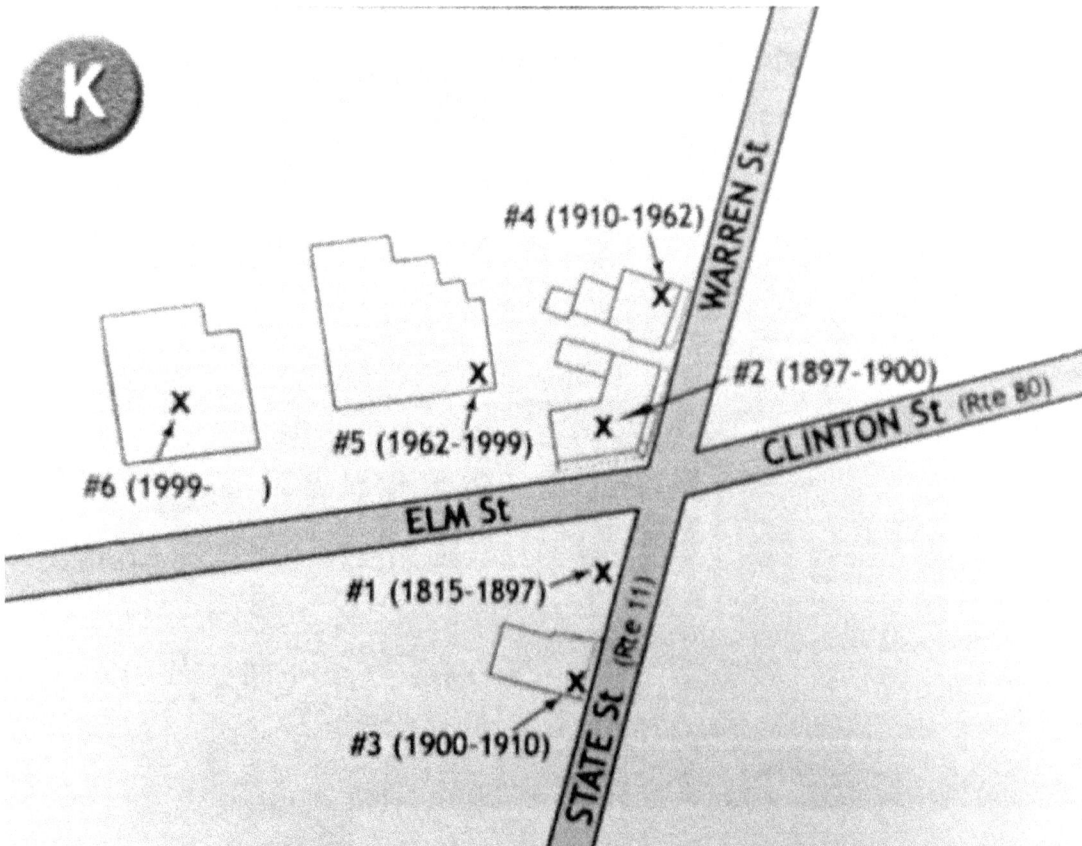

Drawing showing the locations of the Tully Post Offices. Taken from the book, A Timeline History of the Town of Tully courtesy of the Town of Tully Area Historical Society

The Tully Post Office is at 24 Elm Street, Tully, NY 13159-9998. It is leased by the US Postal Service, was constructed in 1999, has 4,165 Square feet and is located on a lot of a little over an acre.

CHAPTER 25

Post Offices in the Town of Van Buren

The Town of Van Buren was formed on March 26, 1829 and was named for Martin Van Buren who was Governor of New York at the time. It was derived from a portion of the Town of Camillus, which earlier had been formed from a portion of the Town of Marcellus, one of the original towns when Onondaga County came into being in 1794.

Page 490 of the *1860 Gazetteer of New York State*, by J.H. French provides some interesting statistics of two hamlets in Van Buren as follows:

Canal had a church and 188 inhabitants, Van Buren Center had a church and 16 dwellings.

Canal

Established: January 15, 1830 (from **Ionia**)
First Postmaster: Oliver Nichols
Name changed to **Memphis** on December 10, 1860

Canton, a growing community on the Erie Canal in the 1820s and now known as Memphis, wanted a post office but couldn't use the name Canton because there was an existing post office with that name in Northern NY. Canton was growing and had become more developed than its nearby neighbor Ionia, resulting in the closing of the Ionia Post Office. The post office at Canton was named Canal on January 15, 1830 when its post office was established.[1] Later its name was changed to Memphis which is still a post office today but at a location about a mile north but actually within a half-mile of where the old Ionia Post Office had been located.

Ionia

Established: February 22, 1820
First Postmaster: Charles H. Toll
Discontinued: January 15, 1830
Service provided by **Canal**

On March 29, 1811 the State Legislature ordered that a road be laid out from the bridge crossing Sodus Bay in the most direct route to the new bridge over the Seneca River on Lysander lot number 2 at Adam's Ferry, and from there on the most direct route to Gideon Brockway's house in the town and county of Onondaga. The actual survey wasn't done until 1813 but when the road was opened it brought an increased flow of traffic through both Ionia and Warners.[2] This brought more settlers and since Ionia, previously called Barnes Corners, was now on a major road a post office was established there in 1820.

Because of this early date, the post office at Ionia was in the Town of Camillus before the Town of Van Buren was formed. There was also a post office, at that time, in a hamlet of Earllville, (now Warners) for a little over two months before the formation of the Town of Van Buren. After the Town of Van Buren was formed the post office name was changed to Van Buren. Charles Turner became the new postmaster replacing John Patch the postmaster previous to the name change.[3]

The local residents requested that the post office be named Barnes Corners. The Post Office Department refused their request because there was already a post office with that name in Lewis County. The residents were slow in coming up with a name so the Post Office Department came up with the classic, 'Ionia'.[4]

---

1   Sisco, Louis Dow 1895, *Early History of the Town of Van Buren* p.20

2   Beauchamp, William M. 1908, *Past and Present of Onondaga County* p. 440
3   Kay, John L. & Smith, Chester M. Jr 1982, *New York Postal History* p.216
4   Christopher, Anthony, *Post Office Named Local Hamlets*, April 22, 1971

Ionia was not destined to be a thriving community for very long as the Erie Canal, which was being constructed at that time, passed less than a mile south through a small hamlet being laid out along the canal called Canton. The Erie Canal caused Canton to prosper and Ionia to diminish in importance, especially since the road to Sodus Bay was no longer used as a post road.

Memphis 13112

Established: December 10, 1860
First Postmaster: Wilson Bates
Serves a population of about 2,000 today with two rural routes and 50 postal boxes.

A new Memphis Post Office was constructed at the intersection of New York Route 31and old Route 31 in the late 1900's less than a half mile from where the old Ionia Post Office was located.

Van Buren

(previously had been **Earllville**)

Established: April 17, 1829
First Postmaster: Charles Turner
Discontinued: November 19, 1866
Re-established: December 18, 1867
Name changed to **Vanburen** December to April 30, 1901
Discontinued: April 30, 1901
Service from **Baldwinsville**

The Van Buren Post Office was located in Lot 22 of the town at approximately the intersection of the present Van Buren and Peck Roads in an area known as Hardscrabble. Van Buren Road was located on the road laid out in 1807 which extended from Onondaga Hill to Oswego that also passed through what is now Baldwinsville. The Postal System introduced Rural Free Delivery in the area around 1901, which resulted in the closing of the Vanburen Post Office with delivery service out of Baldwinsville. The Postal System was attempting to have post offices names be only one word is why its name was Vanburen for a few months before the post office closed.

Van Buren Centre

Established: December 27, 1837
First Postmaster: Jonathan Skinner
Name changed to **Warner's** January 13, 1870

Van Buren Centre was the name given to the post office at Warner's when it was established in 1837.[5] There were a number of members of the Warner family who were early settlers in the community which was the reason for the name Warners. The center of the community was originally near what is now the northern edge of Warners where there was a tavern and a schoolhouse erected around 1813. The community thrived with church, stores, physician and blacksmith, creating a need for a post office in 1837. The Van Buren Centre Post Office was only about two miles from the Van Buren Post Office, sometimes referred to as Hardscrabble. Postmasters of the two post offices had a difficult time with mail for Van Buren going to Van Buren Centre and vice-versa so the name of the Van Buren Centre Post Office was finally changed to Warner's in 1870.[6]

Warner's 13164

Established: January 13, 1870
First Postmaster: Stephen W. Betts
Spelling changed to Warner February 24, 1894
Spelling changed to Warners May 1, 1925
Serves a population of about 2,300 today with two rural routes and 100 postal boxes.

Warners prospered during the 1800s because of the Erie Canal passing about a mile to the South, a railroad passing through the community in 1851, a large brickyard and a cement works. The re-routing of the Erie Canal in the early 1900s, the closing of the railroad station and the closing of the brickyard and cement works all gradually diminished the village's prosperity. Today, the New York State Thruway passes through the village with its Warners rest stop giving only a token boost to the community.

The present Warner's Post Office is located just south of the Van Buren town line in the Town of Camillus, but during its years as Van Buren Centre and most of its

5   Scisco, Louis Dow, *Early History of the Town of Van Buren*, p. 22
6   Scisco, Louis Dow 1895, *Early History of the Town of Van Buren* p 22

years as Warners it has been located further north in the Town of Van Buren.

In the 1930s the Warners Post Office was in the home of Anna M. Isbell on the north side of Warners Rd. (Route 173) just past the cemetery. During the early 1950s, when Ella P. Olmstead was postmaster, it was also on Warners Road but across from its previous location. When Beatrice V. Conway was postmaster, the post office was in the first house on the east side of

Newport Road, still in the Town of Van Buren. It was in approximately the late 1950s that the present post office was constructed and it was the first time that the post office was in the Town of Camillus.

NOTE: *The courtesy of Marilyn Breakey, Town of Van Buren Historian, in sharing information concerning the post offices in Van Buren is appreciated.*

The Warners Post Office is at 6454 Newport Road, Warners, NY 13164-9998. It is leased by the US Postal Service, was constructed in 1962, has 1,219 square feet and is on a 3,946 square foot lot.

The Memphis Post Office is at 1749 State Route 173 Memphis, NY 13112-9998. It is leased by the US Postal Service, was constructed in 1989, has 1,602 square feet and is on a lot of more than an acre.

Postmasters

Postmasters in the Town of Camillus

AMBOY

POSTMASTER	TITLE	DATE APPOINTED
Delavan L. Hay	Postmaster	Feb. 24, 1886
A. Charles Armstrong	Postmaster	Dec. 23, 1889

BELLE ISLE

POSTMASTER	TITLE	DATE APPOINTED
Truman Skinner	Postmaster	Feb. 28, 1827
Alanson Ellis	Postmaster	Jan. 1, 1829
George Kimberly	Postmaster	Sept. 29, 1830
Marvin Armstrong	Postmaster	July 3, 1841
George Kimberly	Postmaster	Nov. 30, 1844
Ephraim Shead	Postmaster	June 8, 1849
William G. Armstrong	Postmaster	July 22, 1851
Henry G. White	Postmaster	Apr. 27, 1853
Oliver t. Goodfellow	Postmaster	June 5, 1857
Thomas Machan	Postmaster	Apr. 10, 1861
Sarah A. Zimmerman	Postmaster	May 14, 1897

CAMILLUS 13031

POSTMASTER	TITLE	DATE APPOINTED
Truman Adams	Postmaster	Apr. 9, 1810
David Munro	Postmaster	Feb. 1, 1816
James R. Lawrence	Postmaster	Aug. 28, 1825
Grove Lawrence	Postmaster	Aug. 25, 1829
Robert B. Dickey	Postmaster	June 16, 1838
Gaylord N. Sherwood	Postmaster	July 10, 1841
Samuel B. Rowe	Postmaster	Sept. 2, 1843
Gaylord B. Sherwood	Postmaster	Feb. 20, 1844
Henry C. Kimberly	Postmaster	Jan. 10, 1845
Samuel B. Rowe	Postmaster	Nov. 10, 1848
Gaylord N. Sherwood	Postmaster	May 11, 1849
Oliver Kimberly	Postmaster	Apr. 27, 1853

POSTMASTER	TITLE	DATE APPOINTED
Albert Harmon	Postmaster	Apr. 10, 1861
Benjamin Brown	Postmaster	Oct. 20, 1873
Fannie L. Carey	Postmaster	Jan. 5, 1885
Sidney H. Cook Jr.	Postmaster	Sept. 4, 1885
Benjamin Brown	Postmaster	Mar. 26, 1889
Sidney H. Cook	Postmaster	Mar. 2, 1894
Austin E. Daniels	Postmaster	Feb. 17, 1898
Information not available for postmasters of this time period		
Frank W. Palange	Acting PM	Nov. 30, 1960
Frank W. Palange	Postmaster	July 16, 1962
Vincent Pedele	Officer-In-Charge	June 9, 1978
Paul W. Pavius	Officer-In-Charge	Oct. 6, 1978
P. Campagna	Postmaster	Feb. 10, 1979
Mary G. Korzekwa	Officer-In-Charge	Feb. 3, 1984
G. Korzekwa	Officer-In-Charge	Feb. 4, 1984
Edward F. Phelan	Postmaster	Mar. 3, 1984
D. Lippa	Officer-In-Charge	Jan. 1, 1985
Mary Ellen Davis	Postmaster	Jan. 19, 1985
Thomas W. Shaffner	Officer-In-Charge	Sept. 15, 1992
Kevin I. Cunningham	Officer-In-Charge	Nov. 13, 1992
John J. Phelan	Postmaster	Jan. 23, 1993
Joseph W. Picciano	Officer-In-Charge	Apr. 1, 1996
William T. Vanderhyde	Officer-In-Charge	Oct. 18, 1996
Kim M. Hanscel	Officer-In-Charge	Feb. 11, 1997
Joseph W. Picciano	Postmaster	Mar. 15, 1997
Steven A. King	Officer-In-Charge	Aug. 20, 2002
Gail A. Weeks	Postmaster	Apr. 5, 2003
Suzanne M. McCann	Officer-In-Charge	Dec. 6, 2005
Maureen A. Hohl	Officer-In-Charge	Mar. 6, 2006
Anthony F. Zarachowicz	Officer-In-Charge	June 6, 2006

POSTMASTER	TITLE	DATE APPOINTED
Dawn Waldron	Postmaster	Aug. 19, 2006
Cynthia M. Donnelly	Officer-In-Charge	Jan. 14, 2009
Kelly J. Landers	Officer-In-Charge	Feb. 23, 2009
Brian K. Ratliff	Officer-In-Charge	Dec. 15, 2009
Stephen M. McAllister	Officer-In-Charge	May 17, 2010
John Czajkowski	Officer-In-Charge	Sept. 3, 2010
Kathleen Cusyk	Officer-In-Charge	Feb. 7, 2011
Barbara J. Almonte	Postmaster	June 30, 2012

FAIR MOUNT (previously TYLER)

POSTMASTER	TITLE	DATE APPOINTED
Wheeler Truesdell	Postmaster	Dec. 23, 1845
Henry C. Leavenworth	Postmaster	Apr. 11, 1851
Atwood Griffin	Postmaster	Feb. 2, 1855
Wheeler Truesdell	Postmaster	Mar. 4, 1859
Thomas Rhodes	Postmaster	Mar. 8, 1864
George Jerome	Postmaster	Apr. 24, 1865
Henry Jerome	Postmaster	Jan. 23, 1866
Patrick J Kelly	Postmaster	Sept. 4, 1895
Emily Jerome	Postmaster	May 25, 1896

LAKELAND

POSTMASTER	TITLE	DATE APPOINTED
John T. Clapp	Postmaster	Feb. 16, 1887
Herbert C. Fancher	Postmaster	Mar. 16, 1889
Stephan H. North	Postmaster	June 11, 1890
William A. Papworth	Postmaster	June 16, 1891
Herbert C. Fancher	Postmaster	Dec. 13, 1895

TYLER

POSTMASTER	TITLE	DATE APPOINTED
Wheeler Truesdell	Postmaster	Feb. 21, 1843

WELLINGTON

POSTMASTER	TITLE	DATE APPOINTED
Harvey Roberts	Postmaster	Mar. 5, 1828
William M. Canfield	Postmaster	Feb. 21, 1829
Nathan North	Postmaster	Apr. 10, 1837
Benjamin F. Sias	Postmaster	Dec. 8, 1837
David S. Bennett	Postmaster	Sept. 11, 1838
Joel B. Bennett	Postmaster	Apr. 6, 1839
Alexander J. Dallas	Postmaster	Nov. 19, 1845
Loron Tyler	Postmaster	Apr. 8, 1847
Lewis B. Bennett	Postmaster	Feb. 14, 1851

POSTMASTER	TITLE	DATE APPOINTED
Postmasters in the Town of Cicero		

BREWERTON 13029

POSTMASTER	TITLE	DATE APPOINTED
Wells Crumb	Postmaster	Jan. 23, 1828
Robert Boyd	Postmaster	Nov. 5, 1830
George Ramsey Jr.	Postmaster	Jan. 24, 1831 ?
William Bailey	Postmaster	Aug. 1, 1835
John Leach Jr.	Postmaster	June 26, 1845
George Walkup	Postmaster	Apr. 21, 1848
Asa U. Emmons	Postmaster	July 17, 1849
John L. Stevens	Postmaster	July 7, 1853
Orsamus Johnson	Postmaster	Apr. 10, 1861
William H. Carter	Postmaster	Feb. 15, 1869
Edward N. Emmons	Postmaster	Mar. 16. 1871
William W. Dority	Postmaster	Jan. 25, 1886
Modostus Holbrook	Postmaster	Apr. 12, 1889
Elizabeth C. Holbrook	Postmaster	Dec. 6, 1889
James W. Larkin	Postmaster	June 3, 1903
J. Floyd Larkin	Postmaster	Dec. 21, 1914
George Keating	Postmaster	July 29, 1915
Leah Keating	Postmaster	Apr. 5, 1920
Trulie Merritt	Acting PM	Apr. 26, 1921
Trulie Merritt	Postmaster	Aug. 24, 1921
Etta Merritt	Acting PM	Nov. 9, 1922
Etta Merritt	Postmaster	Jan. 31, 1923
Marion Kiehl	Acting PM	Aug. 28, 1933
Nina McKinney	Acting PM	May 31, 1937
Nina McKinney	Postmaster	Aug. 25, 1937
Marion L. Pontello	Acting PM	Feb. 16, 1968
Marion L. Pontello	Postmaster	Mar. 20, 1971
Henry A. Polech	Officer-in-Charge	June 4, 1979
Shirley A. Ames	Postmaster	Nov. 17, 1979
Richard J. Isyk	Officer-in-Charge	June 29, 1990
Keneth H. Myers	Officer-in-Charge	Aug. 30, 1990
Richard E. Fry	Officer-in-Charge	Feb. 1, 1991
Mary S. Frederick	Officer-in-Charge	May 3, 1991
Nancy A. Brown	Postmaster	Nov. 2, 1991
Jean L. Cisar	Officer-in-Charge	July 21, 2005
Ellen M. La Pine	Postmaster	Mar. 4, 2006
Rhonda Johnston	Officer-in-Charge	Aug. 24, 2011

Acting PM = Acting Postmaster

POSTMASTER	TITLE	DATE APPOINTED
leslie Hearne	Officer-in-Charge	Feb. 2, 2012
Rhonda Johnston	Officer-in-Charge	Mar. 9, 2012
Kathleen A. Cusyk	Postmaster	June 30, 2012
Rhonda Johnston	Officer-in-Charge	Aug. 15, 2012
Heidi L. Freeman	Postmaster	Oct. 6, 2012

CICERO 13039

POSTMASTER	TITLE	DATE APPOINTED
Isaac Cody	Postmaster	Apr. 7, 1821
Ebenezer Crowell	Postmaster	june 18, 1830
Hezekiah Joslin	Postmaster	May 22, 1834
Judson Gage	Postmaster	Nov. 5, 1841
Samuel T. Northrop	Postmaster	June 10, 1845
Zebulon Weaver	Postmaster	July 19, 1848
Judson Gage	Postmaster	May 11, 1849
Julius A. Dunham	Postmaster	Feb. 14, 1854
Zebulon Weaver	Postmaster	Feb. 9, 1857
Julius A. Dunham	Postmaster	July 22, 1857
Josiah H. Young	Postmaster	Apr. 10, 1861
Irving Coonley	Postmaster	Nov. 17, 1869
Robert Lower	Postmaster	Sept. 4, 1885
John H. Flosheim	Postmaster	Apr. 1, 1889
Melville Jackson	Postmaster	Oct. 9, 1893
Arthur Sterns	Postmaster	Mar. 4, 1898
Edwin Shepard	Postmaster	? (Greatest # of years)
Cadd Plant	Postmaster	? (11 Years)
Dorothy Mooney	Postmaster	? (15 Years)
Harold Eggleston	Postmaster	?
Blake Winter	Postmaster	?
Dorothy F. Crowell	Officer-in-Charge	Apr. 4, 1969
Dorothy F. Crowell	Postmaster	July 17, 1971
??	Officer-in-Charge	??
Rondal R. Holland	Postmaster	Aug. 17, 1985
Richard J. Isyk	Officer-in-Charge	June 12, 1987
Paul N. Schwenn	Officer-in-Charge	Dec. 4, 1987
William G. Donaghey	Officer-in-Charge	Jan. 26, 1988
Walter A. Brandt	Officer-in-Charge	Apr. 22, 1988
David J. Giantomasi	Officer-in-Charge	Dec. 9, 1988
Charles P. Hope	Officer-in-Charge	Mar. 24, 1989
John R. Andrianos	Officer-in-Charge	June 23, 1989

POSTMASTER	TITLE	DATE APPOINTED
Donald W. LaMontagne	Officer-in-Charge	Aug. 25, 1989
Gail L. Duke	Officer-in-Charge	Dec. 15, 1989
Eileen T. Hughes	Officer-in-Charge	July 20, 1990
Evelyn J. Savage	Officer-in-Charge	Sept. 28, 1990

Discontinued on December 26, 1990; Mail to Clay (Postal Bulletin 21788)

CICERO CENTRE

POSTMASTER	TITLE	DATE APPOINTED
Silvester Ball	Postmaster	July 12, 1852
Irving Welch	Postmaster	Feb. 7, 1890
Orin J. Daniels	Postmaster	June 7, 1895
Clerence Phelps	Postmaster	June 8, 1900

EAST CICERO

POSTMASTER	TITLE	DATE APPOINTED
Ashley Rathbun	Postmaster	Apr. 18, 1832

Postmasters in the Town of Clay

BELGIUM

POSTMASTER	TITLE	DATE APPOINTED
Albert E. Teall	Postmaster	May 19, 1892
John E. Drohen	Postmaster	June 5, 1895
Alonzo A. Winchell	Postmaster	Dec. 10, 1895
Andrew Brush	Postmaster	Feb. 6, 1900

CIGARVILLE

POSTMASTER	TITLE	DATE APPOINTED
Jacob W. Coughtry	Postmaster	Dec. 29, 1871
William Cullings	Postmaster	Sept. 4, 1885
Jacob W. Coughtry	Postmaster	Apr. 1, 1889
Francis E. Sandler	Postmaster	Dec. 29, 1892
Arthur H. Cullings	Postmaster	May 29, 1894
Fremont E. Strever	Postmaster	Nov. 30, 1898

CLAY 13041

POSTMASTER	TITLE	DATE APPOINTED
Nathaniel Teal	Postmaster	Jan. 29, 1828
Wilburn Hale	Postmaster	July 2, 1836
James Little	Postmaster	Jan. 31, 1845
Philander Childs	Postmaster	June 6, 1849
William B. Wandell	Postmaster	Apr. 27, 1853
Hial Crandall	Postmaster	Oct. 17, 1856
John W. Kenyon	Postmaster	Aug. 16, 1858
Orris Barnes	Postmaster	Apr. 30, 1861
James Little	Postmaster	Feb. 2, 1875
Orasmus Powell	Postmaster	Mar. 6, 1877

POSTMASTER	TITLE	DATE APPOINTED
Mary E. Potter	Postmaster	Jan. 14, 1878
Willis P. Lee	Postmaster	Dec. 20, 1880
William N. Teall	Postmaster	Oct. 22, 1884
Harriet Walter	Postmaster	Dec. 22, 1885
Albert E. Teall	Postmaster	Nov. 25, 1890
Mary E. Weller	Postmaster	May 2, 1903
Mary E. Carpenter	Postmaster	Jan. 21, 1915
Grace Neumann	Postmaster	Oct. 29, 1924
Information not available for postmasters of this time period		
Margaret K. Schneider	Postmaster	July 28, 1955
Patsy E. Campagna	Officer-In-Charge	July 31, 1978
John V. Boland	Postmaster	Dec. 2, 1978
Judy C. Binkerhoff	Officer-In-Charge	Aug. 31, 1985
John R. Moore	Postmaster	Dec. 21, 1985
John Lynch	Officer-In-Charge	Sept. 24, 1996
Sandra Williams	Officer-In-Charge	Dec. 6, 1996
Thomas W. Shaffner	Officer-In-Charge	Feb. 14, 1997
Ellen M. Brown	Officer-In-Charge	July 16, 1997
Anne M. Marafino	Postmaster	Sept. 27, 1997
Ronald W. LaRose	Officer-In-Charge	Feb. 8, 2000
Daniel E. Mulroy	Officer-In-Charge	July 5, 2000
Kevin I. Cunningham	Postmaster	July 29, 2000
Ralph J. Guida	Officer-In-Charge	July 12, 2002
Paul W. Francher	Postmaster	Aug. 24, 2002
Michelle DeStefano	Officer-In-Charge	Aug. 27, 2008
Marjorie L. Beebe	Officer-In-Charge	Oct. 1, 2008
Michelle DeStefano	Officer-In-Charge	Dec. 4, 2008
Trevor E. Stoyer	Officer-In-Charge	Dec. 30, 2008
Cynthia L. Foley	Officer-In-Charge	Mar. 4, 2009
David A. Simon	Postmaster	Aug. 1, 2009
Cynthia L. Foley	Officer-In-Charge	June 21, 2010
Trevor E. Stoyer	Officer-In-Charge	Mar. 25, 2011
Michelle DeStefano	Postmaster	Oct. 20, 2012
Barbara Stala	Officer-In-Charge	Jan. 4, 2016

EUCLID

POSTMASTER	TITLE	DATE APPOINTED
Andrew Johnson	Postmaster	Apr. 14, 1828
Nathan Soule	Postmaster	Aug. 6, 1833
William Coon	Postmaster	July 17, 1849
Allen V. Snyder	Postmaster	Sept. 28, 1853

POSTMASTER	TITLE	DATE APPOINTED
David I. Moyer	Postmaster	Nov. 1, 1856
Cyrus C. Warner	Postmaster	Aug. 7, 1861
Richard Platt	Postmaster	May 7, 1867
Enos Eastwood	Postmaster	July 30, 1872
John J. Barrus	Postmaster	Dec. 9, 1872
Richard Platt	Postmaster	Mar. 7, 1876
Orlando A. Rice	Postmaster	Sept. 4, 1885
James Hamlin	Postmaster	Mar. 27, 1889
Chauncey M. Soule	Postmaster	Nov. 26, 1890
Andrew J. McArthur	Postmaster	Aug. 16, 1895
Chauncey M. Soule	Postmaster	Feb. 20, 1899

LATIMER

POSTMASTER	TITLE	DATE APPOINTED
Royal J. Houghton	Postmaster	Mar. 21, 1889
Frederick H. Barnum	Postmaster	Feb. 25, 1891

NORTH SYRACUSE 13212

POSTMASTER	TITLE	DATE APPOINTED
William H. Collins	Postmaster	Aug. 5, 1887
Gage R. Crampton	Postmaster	Apr. 13, 1889
Eva McChesney	Postmaster	Dec. 13, 1893
Gage R. Crampton	Postmaster	Feb. 8, 1898

PLANK ROAD

POSTMASTER	TITLE	DATE APPOINTED
James Wallen	Postmaster	Mar. 17, 1846
Joseph Palmer	Postmaster	Apr. 4, 1849
George Woodward	Postmaster	Mar. 23, 1855
Jacob Kincaid	Postmaster	Jan. 19, 1857
Charles W. Clement	Postmaster	Jan. 21, 1858
Levi B. Skinner	Postmaster	Jan. 3, 1859
Jacob Kincaid	Postmaster	Apr. 10, 1861
Ralph Hirsh	Postmaster	Dec. 3, 1863
Henry Hoatland	Postmaster	May 7, 1864
Ralph Hirsh	Postmaster	May 21, 1864
Granville Baum	Postmaster	July 8, 1867
Horace Lawrence	Postmaster	Jan. 20, 1873
John Flagler	Postmaster	Jan. 11, 1881
William H. Collins	Postmaster	Sept. 4, 1885

THREE RIVER POINT

POSTMASTER	TITLE	DATE APPOINTED
Joseph W. Williams	Postmaster	Apr. 23, 1852
Horace P. Eno	Postmaster	Apr. 27, 1853
Frederick H. Barnum	Postmaster	Mar. 3, 1892

Acting PM = Acting Postmaster

POSTMASTER	TITLE	DATE APPOINTED
Susan Porter	Postmaster	July 23, 1896

THREE RIVERS

POSTMASTER	TITLE	DATE APPOINTED
Frederick H. Barnum	Postmaster	May 11, 1899
Emma Miller	Postmaster	Feb. 6, 1903

WOODARD

POSTMASTER	TITLE	DATE APPOINTED
Allen B Kinne	Postmaster	Dec. 29, 1871
Rudd Wetsel	Postmaster	Dec. 22, 1885
Ruel Wetsel	Postmaster	Dec. 31, 1885
Myron W. Clark	Postmaster	Mar. 2, 1887
Allen B Kinne	Postmaster	June 3, 1889
Myron W. Clark	Postmaster	June 7, 1895
Allen B Kinne	Postmaster	Feb. 20, 1899

YOUNG

POSTMASTER	TITLE	DATE APPOINTED
John G. Young	Postmaster	Dec. 29, 1871
Peter J. Young	Postmaster	Dec. 22, 1885

Postmasters in the Town of Dewitt

COLLAMER

POSTMASTER	TITLE	DATE APPOINTED
Henry E. Pierce	Postmaster	Dec. 17, 1849
James Terwilliger	Postmaster	Nov. 15, 1850
Conrad Terwilliger	Postmaster	Dec. 15, 1851
James Stevenson	Postmaster	Oct. 19, 1854
William J. Hemens	Postmaster	Sept. 18, 1857
Danial Young	Postmaster	June 9, 1858
William C. Stevenson	Postmaster	Apr. 10, 1861
John I. Furbeck	Postmaster	May 12, 1862
James E. Stewart	Postmaster	Apr. 25, 1884
Edwin Schuyler	Postmaster	Jan. 3, 1887
James E. Stewart	Postmaster	Apr. 13, 1889
Harrison Wands	Postmaster	June 5, 1895
Nellie J. Stewart	Postmaster	July 6, 1899

DEWITT

POSTMASTER	TITLE	DATE APPOINTED
George S. loomis	Postmaster	Apr. 9, 1835
Henry C. Goodell	Postmaster	Apr. 7, 1842
James H. King	Postmaster	Nov. 30, 1844
Henry C. Goodell	Postmaster	Apr. 28, 1849
James L. Willard	Postmaster	July 6, 1853
William Avery	Postmaster	Jan. 26, 1857

POSTMASTER	TITLE	DATE APPOINTED
Henry C. Goodell	Postmaster	Apr. 10, 1861
Edmund D. Cobb	Postmaster	Dec. 8, 1871
Philo Dutcher	Postmaster	Mar. 21, 1881
Angeline B. Avery	Postmaster	July 5, 1882
Dillaye Robert Snow	Postmaster	Dec. 22, 1885
Angeline B. Avery	Postmaster	Oct. 14, 1886

Information for postmasters after this time period not available

DEWITT CENTER

POSTMASTER	TITLE	DATE APPOINTED
Stephen Headson	Postmaster	Feb. 7, 1872
Lester C. Headson	Postmaster	Nov. 14, 1891
William Cowan	Postmaster	Mar. 9, 1898

EAST SYRACUSE

POSTMASTER	TITLE	DATE APPOINTED
Alvah Burnham	Postmaster	May 15, 1876
George W. Weaver	Postmaster	Dec. 22, 1885
Smith Rice	Postmaster	Dec. 7, 1889
Joseph H. Damon	Postmaster	Feb. 28, 1894
John L. Kyne	Postmaster	June 22, 1898
Michael J. Spillane	Postmaster	Feb. 22, 1915
Raymond L. Hodge	Acting PM	Nov. 15, 1923
Raymond L. Hodge	Postmaster	Jan. 8, 1924
Michael J. Spillane	Acting PM	May 21, 1934
Michael J. Spillane	Postmaster	Jan. 21, 1935
David B. McLaughlin	Acting PM	Dec. 15, 1940
David B. McLaughlin	Postmaster	Oct. 21, 1941
Maurice A. Reilihan	Acting PM	Apr. 24, 1964
Edward B. Bierman Jr.	Acting PM	Feb. 24, 1967
Edward B. Bierman Jr.	Postmaster	Oct. 5, 1967
Kenneth E. Wilbur	Officer-In-Charge	Mar. 23, 1973
Kenneth E. Wilbur	Postmaster	June 30, 1973
Edward F. Phelan Jr.	Officer-In-Charge	Dec. 1, 1989
John M. Pellenz	Officer-In-Charge	Mar. 9, 1990
David A. Simon	Postmaster	June 2, 1990
Janice A. Bieloski	Officer-In-Charge	Mar. 6, 1992
Janice A. Bieloski	Postmaster	Mar. 6, 1993
John Lynch	Postmaster	June 17, 2000
Kenneth Hoalcraft	Officer-In-Charge	Dec. 6, 2012
Florence Sitnik	Officer-In-Charge	June 13, 2013
John S. Armstrong	Postmaster	Sept. 7, 2013

Acting PM = Acting Postmaster

POSTMASTER	TITLE	DATE APPOINTED
EASTWOOD		
Byron Midler	Postmaster	Apr. 14, 1890
Abbie J. Shepardson	Postmaster	June 19, 1893
Alexander D. Chatelle	Postmaster	July 23, 1896
John S. Gourley	Postmaster	Oct. 5, 1899
JAMESVILLE 13078		
Thomas Rose	Postmaster	Sept. 2, 1811
Moses DeWitt Rose	Postmaster	Nov. 29, 1814
Isaac Croker	Postmaster	Mar. 31, 1817
Luther Badger	Postmaster	Apr. 30, 1818
Isaac W. Brewster	Postmaster	Dec. 12, 1825
George M. Richardson	Postmaster	July 10, 1841
Isaac W. Brewster	Postmaster	Sept. 17, 1844
Samuel Hill	Postmaster	May 17, 1849
Lemuel Hawley	Postmaster	Apr. 27, 1853
Samuel Hill	Postmaster	Apr. 10, 1861
Isaac K. Reed	Postmaster	Feb. 19, 1878
Dennis Quinlan	Postmaster	Dec. 22, 1885
Abram A. Wright	Postmaster	June 3, 1889
Dennis Quinlan	Postmaster	Oct. 18, 1893
Dwight B. Hotaling	Postmaster	Feb. 6, 1899
John D. Quinlan	Postmaster	Feb. 1, 1904
Harry P. Cross	Postmaster	Dec. 22, 1914
Archie Goodfellow	Postmaster	June 1, 1916
Elizabeth G. Kenyon	Postmaster	Nov. 21, 1918
Frances Dwyer	Acting PM	Sept. 4, 1920
Catherine Oley	Acting PM	Jan. 18, 1921
Katheryn M. Oley	Postmaster	July 29, 1921
James T. McConnell	Acting PM	Feb. 5, 1934
James T. McConnell	Postmaster	June 18, 1934
Frances D. McClenon	Acting PM	Apr. 15, 1943
Frances D. McClenon	Postmaster	Jan. 29, 1944
William J. Hopkins	Acting PM	Feb. 28, 1961
William J. Hopkins	Postmaster	July 26, 1963
Kevin I Cunningham	Officer-In-Charge	Dec. 18, 1987
William C. Markey	Postmaster	July 2, 1988
Ronald E. Barnhill	Officer-In-Charge	Oct. 23, 1995
Theresa B. Furlong	Officer-In-Charge	Feb. 9, 1996

POSTMASTER	TITLE	DATE APPOINTED
Anne M. Marafino	Postmaster	Apr. 27, 1996
Michael J. Prikazsky	Officer-In-Charge	Oct. 3, 1997
John H. Tambroni	Postmaster	Nov. 22, 1997
Michelle M. DeStefano	Officer-In-Charge	Nov. 23, 1999
Mary F. Foster	Officer-In-Charge	Jan. 7, 2000
John J. Furlong	Officer-In-Charge	June 2, 2000
Michael J. Prikazsky	Postmaster	Feb. 24, 2001
Renee Denny	Officer-In-Charge	July 30, 2012
Torry C. Lesh	Postmaster	Oct. 6, 2012
Michelle Cassavaugh	Officer-In-Charge	Sept. 12, 2014
Melinda Martin Robb	Officer-In-Charge	Nov. 13, 2014
Mary A. Simmons	Postmaster	Dec. 27, 2014
Joy Hotaling	Officer-In-Charge	May 20, 2015
MESSINA SPRINGS		
Miles Benham	Postmaster	Feb. 18, 1850
Henry P. Bogardus	Postmaster	Nov. 11, 1850
Rufus R. Kinne	Postmaster	July 22, 1853
ORVILLE		
Isaac Osgood	Postmaster	Nov. 11, 1815
William Barker	Postmaster	Oct. 10, 1826
James C. Vanslyke	Postmaster	Sept. 8, 1832
George S. Loomis	Postmaster	Mar. 28, 1834

Postmasters in the Town of Elbridge

POSTMASTER	TITLE	DATE APPOINTED
ELBRIDGE		
Truman Adams	Postmaster	Oct. 1, 1815
Gideon Wilcoxson	Postmaster	Jan. 29, 1816
Hiram F. Mather	Postmaster	Jan. 14, 1825
Elijah Kendrick	Postmaster	Mar. 4, 1830
Alonzo Wood	Postmaster	Jan. 28, 1837
Allen Monroe	Postmaster	Apr. 22, 1842 ?
Alonzo Wood	Postmaster	Sept. 14, 1844
Charles G. McGowan	Postmaster	Sept. 21, 1848
John D. Rhodes	Postmaster	June 8, 1849
Alonzo Wood	Postmaster	Apr. 29, 1853
Charles G. McGowan	Postmaster	Dec. 9. 1857
William G. Stevens	Postmaster	Oct. 16, 1861
Walter P VanVechten	Postmaster	Aug. 14, 1865

Acting PM = Acting Postmaster

POSTMASTER	TITLE	DATE APPOINTED
Alfred E. Stacey	Postmaster	Feb. 5, 1877
David M. Hill	Postmaster	May 5, 1885
Henry L. Hale	Postmaster	Mar. 26, 1889
Alonzo B. Wood	Postmaster	Sept. 6, 1893
Clare B. Cook	Postmaster	Sept. 15, 1897
Information not available for postmasters of this time period		
Russell L. DeWaters	Acting PM	Oct. 25, 1968
Russell L. DeWaters	Postmaster	Apr. 3, 1971
Charles F. Tanner	Officer-in-Charge	Feb. 1, 1989
James M. Burnett	Postmaster	Apr. 22, 1989
Kathleen Wingood	Officer-in-Charge	July 28, 2012
Holly M. Sharpe	Postmaster	Oct. 6, 2012

HALF WAY

POSTMASTER	TITLE	DATE APPOINTED
William A. Martin	Postmaster	June 23, 1868
Henry E. Van Vleit	Postmaster	Dec. 10, 1868
Gilbert S. Wright	Postmaster	Oct. 16, 1873
Alvin Campbell	Postmaster	Apr. 4, 1876
Alden A. Campbell	Postmaster	Apr. 18, 1876
Edward L. Ranney	Postmaster	Jan. 3, 1883
Mary J. Oliver	Postmaster	Sept. 27, 1888
Kyran Murphy	Postmaster	Sept. 27, 1893
Mary J. Oliver	Postmaster	Sept. 14, 1897

HART LOT

POSTMASTER	TITLE	DATE APPOINTED
Elisha P. Cornell	Postmaster	Jan. 15, 1850
Sylvester B. Noble	Postmaster	Sept. 16, 1850
Chauncey Cornell	Postmaster	May 1, 1851
Elisha P. Cornell	Postmaster	June 26, 1852
Julius Earll	Postmaster	Aug. 7, 1855
Almon D. Barr	Postmaster	May 18, 1865
Albert L. Chatfield	Postmaster	May 28, 1868
William G. Cottle	Postmaster	July 11, 1878
Patrick C. Carrigan	Postmaster	Sept. 19, 1888
William G. Cottle	Postmaster	June 17, 1889
Dennis J. Flynn	Postmaster	Oct. 9, 1893
John P. Cottle	Postmaster	July 3, 1897

JACK'S REEF

POSTMASTER	TITLE	DATE APPOINTED
Zera Shepard	Postmaster	Jan. 21, 1832
Stephen Ostrander	Postmaster	Apr. 10, 1837

POSTMASTER	TITLE	DATE APPOINTED
Vespasian Barns	Postmaster	Jan. 5, 1839
Calvin P. Richardson	Postmaster	Apr. 22, 1842
John Smith	Postmaster	July 29, 1845
Harvey Hall	Postmaster	June 2, 1849
Jackson Walker	Postmaster	May 30, 1850
Cornelius M. Emerick	Postmaster	Oct. 9, 1852
Daniel D. Suits	Postmaster	July 31, 1855
William Wilson Jr.	Postmaster	Apr. 25, 1857
Eli Tator	Postmaster	Mar. 24, 1859
Calvin McIntyre	Postmaster	Jan. 24, 1861
Daniel D. Suits	Postmaster	Apr. 10 1861
Eli Tator	Postmaster	Mar. 4, 1867
William W. Suits	Postmaster	June 5, 1872
William K. Pickard	Postmaster	Jan. 5, 1874
Harrison Evans	Postmaster	Mar. 26, 1877
William K. Pickard	Postmaster	June 9, 1884
Joseph M. Butler	Postmaster	Sept. 4, 1885
Thomas A. Cavenor	Postmaster	May 11, 1886
Francis E. Pickard	Postmaster	Jan. 28, 1889
Hiram Pickard	Postmaster	Nov. 21, 1893
Leslie R. Pickard	Postmaster	Mar. 6, 1897
Harrison Evans	Postmaster	Sept. 18, 1900

JORDAN 13080

POSTMASTER	TITLE	DATE APPOINTED
Seneca Hale	Postmaster	Mar. 23, 1824
Frederick Benson	Postmaster	Aug. 25, 1829
Lyman H. Mason	Postmaster	May 2, 1836
William T. Graves	Postmaster	Sept. 2, 1843
William Porter Jr.	Postmaster	Oct. 16, 1848
Justus Hough	Postmaster	June 6, 1949
James Rodgers	Postmaster	Feb. 24, 1853
Norman P. Eddy	Postmaster	Apr. 27, 1853
William T. Graves	Postmaster	Oct. 31, 1854
James Rodgers	Postmaster	Apr. 14, 1857
William C. Rodgers	Postmaster	Apr. 10, 1861
Ephraim Shead	Postmaster	Dec. 4, 1862
William C. Rodgers	Postmaster	May 29, 1863
Calvin F. Daggett	Postmaster	Dec. 7, 1870
William C. Rodgers	Postmaster	Apr. 3, 1871
Charles M. Warner	Postmaster	May 19, 1876

POSTMASTER	TITLE	DATE APPOINTED
Charles C. Cole	Postmaster	Apr. 3, 1883
William H. O'Donnell	Postmaster	Dec. 25, 1885
Fred C. Allen	Postmaster	June 24, 1889
Stephen L. Rockwell	Postmaster	Aug. 29, 1894
J. Dales Tullar	Postmaster	Dec. 15, 1898
James E. Peck	Postmaster	Feb. 4. 1903
Adelbert E. Brace	Postmaster	Feb. 6, 1911
Eugene E. Mann	Postmaster	Mar. 1, 1915
Joseph R. Cowell	Acting PM	Sept. 21, 1923
Joseph R. Cowell	Postmaster	Jan. 8, 1924
Allen M. Nesbitt	Acting PM	Feb. 17, 1936
Allen M. Nesbitt	Postmaster	June 20, 1936
Daniel P. Doran	Acting PM	May 15, 1944
Daniel P. Doran	Postmaster	Mar. 2, 1945
Barry Bassett	Officer-In-Charge	Oct. 10, 1980
Mary G. Koezekwa	Postmaster	Jan. 10, 1981
Richard E. Cushman	Officer-In-Charge	Sept. 17, 1982
John H. Tambroni	Postmaster	Nov. 27, 1982
Philip J. Kendal	Officer-In-Charge	Aug. 15, 1986
Nancy A. Brown	Postmaster	Jan. 31, 1987
James M. O'Shea	Officer-In-Charge	May 31, 1991
Barbara J. Beeles	Postmaster	Feb. 22, 1992
Bruce M. Emero	Officer-In-Charge	Mar. 2, 1998
Barbara L Weyand-Rogers	Officer-In-Charge	May 29, 1998
Barbara L. (Weyand-Rogers) Lukowski	Postmaster	Nov. 21, 1998
Michael T. Cantrell	Officer-In-Charge	Dec. 7, 2007
Holly M. Sharpe	Officer-In-Charge	Mar. 18, 2008
Melissa C. Peterson	Officer-In-Charge	Aug. 20, 2008
Mary A. Simmons	Officer-In-Charge	Sept. 29, 2008
Amy Charboneau	Officer-In-Charge	Dec. 23, 2008
Athanasios Tamoutselis	Postmaster	Aug. 1, 2009

WINDFALL

David Preston	Postmaster	Jan. 14, 1840

POSTMASTER	TITLE	DATE APPOINTED
Postmasters in the Town of Fabius		

APULIA

Stephen Miles	Postmaster	Dec. 27, 1825
Elijah H. St. John	Postmaster	July 15, 1828
John I. Doran	Postmaster	Feb. 8, 1833
Issac J. Higby	Postmaster	Nov. 6, 1833
Elijah H. St. John	Postmaster	Apr. 22, 1842
Justus Chollar	Postmaster	Jan. 20, 1845
Edwin Miles	Postmaster	June 15, 1849
John T. Colby	Postmaster	Mar. 5, 1858
Miles B. Hackett	Postmaster	Apr. 10, 1861
Judson F. Peck	Postmaster	July 10, 1873
Charles H. Hapgood	Postmaster	Feb. 21, 1876
Henry Rouse	Postmaster	Mar. 24, 1887
William H. Tibbitt	Postmaster	Dec. 28, 1887
Charles H. Hapgood	Postmaster	June 15, 1889
WilliamH. Tibbitt	Postmaster	Dec. 12, 1895
Reuben H. Gallinger	Postmaster	June 13, 1900
Carlton W. Ellis	Postmaster	Jan. 17, 1911
John R. Wood	Postmaster	Feb. 19, 1915
Emeline R. Wood	Postmaster	Apr. 29, 1916
Mary Wood Cory	Postmaster	Sept. 19, 1917
Lois N. Grant	Postmaster	Jan. 20, 1920
Irving C. Grant	Postmaster	Aug. 5, 1922
Lewis E. Klock	Postmaster	Dec. 4, 1923
Fannie B. Cummings	Postmaster	Feb. 24, 1926

APULIA STATION 13020

Frank June	Postmaster	June 16, 1898
Charles R. Briggs	Postmaster	Dec. 20, 1904
Walter E. Briggs	Acting PM	Nov. 2, 1925
Walter E. Briggs	Postmaster	Feb. 24, 1926
Robert V. Gorman	Acting PM	Nov. 30, 1962
Robert V. Gorman	Postmaster	July 26, 1965
Wilbur C. Rothery	Officer-In-Charge	Nov. 20, 1970
Wilbur C. Rothery	Postmaster	July 17, 1971
Barbara K. Wheeler	Officer-In-Charge	Oct. 13, 1972
Barbara K. Wheeler	Postmaster	Mar. 17, 1973

Acting PM = Acting Postmaster

POSTMASTER	TITLE	DATE APPOINTED
Robert E. DeJohn	Officer-In-Charge	June 22, 1989
Nicholas J. DeFurio	Officer-In-Charge	Mar. 23, 1990
Jean K. Paige	Officer-In-Charge	Apr. 13, 1990
Julia C. Conway	Postmaster	June 30, 1990
Peter Thomas Ames	Officer-In-Charge	Sept. 28, 2000
Frances R. Green	Officer-In-Charge	Nov. 20, 2000
Vicki A. Breyerton	Postmaster	Feb. 10, 2001
Stephen M. Florence	Officer-In-Charge	Aug. 17, 2005
Nancy L. Kirby	Postmaster	Nov. 12, 2005
Sharon D. Jones	Officer-In-Charge	Apr. 25, 2007
Brian K. Ratliff	Officer-In-Charge	Oct. 1, 2007
Davidd A. Read	Postmaster	Feb. 16, 2008
Sharon Dexter	Officer-In-Charge	July 30, 2012

FABIUS 13063

POSTMASTER	TITLE	DATE APPOINTED
Isaac Powers	Postmaster	May 7, 1821
George Pettit	Postmaster	Feb. 14, 1822
Thaddeus Archer	Postmaster	Feb. 3, 1841
Orvin E. Castle	Postmaster	July 15, 1841
Enoch Ely	Postmaster	Nov. 30, 1844
Elisha H. Sprague	Postmaster	June 8, 1849
Sherman H. Corbin	Postmaster	Apr. 27, 1853
Orel Pope	Postmaster	Apr. 7, 1861
Sherman H. Corbin	Postmaster	Oct. 1, 1866
Orel Pope	Postmaster	Nov. 27, 1867
James O. Hulbert	Postmaster	Mar. 18, 1873
Charles H. Wheaton	Postmaster	Mar. 19, 1883
William R Bush	Postmaster	Dec. 22, 1885
Charles H. Wheaton	Postmaster	Apr. 15, 1889
William R. Bush	Postmaster	Oct. 19, 1893
Clarence D. Kennedy	Postmaster	Feb. 3, 1898

Information for postmasters after this time period not available

Roger John Ryan	Postmaster	Feb. 19, 1946
Clyde J. Davis	Officer-In-Charge	June 30, 1972
Clyde J. Davis	Postmaster	Dec. 9, 1972
Jane M. Dwyer	Officer-In-Charge	June 25, 1982
Sally A. Seamans	Postmaster	July 24, 1982
James E. Lyons	Officer-In-Charge	Nov. 3, 1995
Carol A. Robinson	Postmaster	Mar. 2, 1996

POSTMASTER	TITLE	DATE APPOINTED
Suzanne L. Vinch	Officer-In-Charge	Dec. 9, 1996
Carey E. Sevier	Postmaster	Mar. 29, 1997
Jennifer A. umsey	Officer-In-Charge	Nov. 9, 2000
Roger John Ryan	Postmaster	Apr. 21, 2001
Donna L. Plummer	Officer-In-Charge	July 24, 2012
Julie Wheatley	Officer-In-Charge	Nov. 26, 2012
Donna L. Plummer	Postmaster	May 4, 2013
Julie Wheatley	Officer-In-Charge	July 22, 2014

SUMMIT STATION

John J. Blaney	Postmaster	Aug. 17, 1861
Charles S. Bovee	Postmaster	Feb. 2, 1894

Postmasters in the Town of Geddes

GEDDES

Elijah W. Curtis	Postmaster	Nov. 25, 1828
Joel Dickinson	Postmaster	July 3, 1841
Ferris Hubell	Postmaster	Dec. 1, 1842
Simeon Spaulding	Postmaster	June 8, 1849
Thomas Sammons	Postmaster	Apr. 30, 1853
Simeon Spaulding	Postmaster	July 26, 1856
Ferris Hubell	Postmaster	Apr. 10, 1861
Simeon Spaulding	Postmaster	Sept. 24, 1866
Hubbard Manzer	Postmaster	Mar. 26, 1867
Cornelius J. Ryan	Postmaster	Dec. 22, 1885

SOLVAY

Samuel S. DeWitt	Postmaster	Mar. 4, 1889
James W. Joslin	Postmaster	Dec. 28, 1889
James H. Rose	Postmaster	Dec. 23, 1890
Emmett R. Davidson	Postmaster	Jan. 23, 1896
Abraham Van Heusen	Postmaster	Feb. 17, 1898

STYLES STATION

Jacob D. Jewell	Postmaster	Sept. 11, 1871
Freeman D. Blanding	Postmaster	Apr. 29, 1874
Amos D. Hoffman	Postmaster	Dec. 22, 1885
Thomas B. Grace	Postmaster	Apr. 24, 1890
Jean C. Powers	Postmaster	Sept. 22, 1896

POSTMASTER	TITLE	DATE APPOINTED
Postmasters in the Town of LaFayette		

CARDIFF

POSTMASTER	TITLE	DATE APPOINTED
John Spencer	Postmaster	Jan. 15, 1830
Henry T. O'Farrell	Postmaster	Aug. 22, 1848
Isaac Garfield	Postmaster	May 11, 1849
Timothy Cuddiback	Postmaster	Apr. 27, 1853
Volney C. Haughton	Postmaster	Aug. 7, 1861
Robert S. Park	Postmaster	Nov. 6, 1865
Sabra E. Park	Postmaster	Jan. 16, 1882

CHRISTIAN HOLLOW

POSTMASTER	TITLE	DATE APPOINTED
Salmon S. Merriman	Postmaster	Feb. 5, 1828

COLLINGWOOD

POSTMASTER	TITLE	DATE APPOINTED
Luther Cole	Postmaster	Apr. 22, 1865
Avery R. Palmer	Postmaster	Dec. 10, 1868
Jerah D. Palmer	Postmaster	Dec. 17, 1875

LAFAYETTE

POSTMASTER	TITLE	DATE APPOINTED
Johnson Hall	Postmaster	May 6, 1825
Samuel S. Baldwin	Postmaster	Dec. 4, 1838
Chauncey Williams	Postmaster	June 16, 1841
Harvey G. Andrews	Postmaster	Nov. 30, 1844
Ira Green	Postmaster	May 24, 1845
Philander Trowbridge	Postmaster	Oct. 21, 1847
James B. Gilbert	Postmaster	Dec. 7, 1848
Chester Baker	Postmaster	June 16, 1849
Milton S. Price	Postmaster	Apr. 17, 1852
Reuben M. Handy	Postmaster	Apr. 27, 1853
Harvey G. Andrews	Postmaster	Apr. 10, 1861
Charles G. Robinson	Postmaster	July 1, 1862
Chester Baker	Postmaster	May 29, 1866
Asahel R. Palmer	Postmaster	July 29, 1885
John Carey	Postmaster	Apr. 1, 1889
James Crowe Jr.	Postmaster	June 28, 1893
James J. Conan	Postmaster	Feb. 4, 1898
Information for postmasters after this time period not available		
Iva B. Locke	Acting PM	May 29, 1933
Iva B. Locke	Postmaster	Aug. 29, 1933
Vernon E. Field	Acting PM	Oct. 31, 1959
George L. Longyear	Acting PM	Apr. 14, 1961

POSTMASTER	TITLE	DATE APPOINTED
George L. Longyear	Postmaster	Apr. 25, 1963
Rachel M. Field	Officer-In-Charge	Oct. 31, 1969
Glenn J. Miller	Officer-In-Charge	Jan. 30, 1970
Glenn J. Miller	Postmaster	Feb. 20, 1971
Eddie R. Thompson	Officer-In-Charge	July 25, 1980
Marilyn J. DeWolfe	Postmaster	Sept. 6, 1980
John H. Tambroni	Officer-In-Charge	Sept. 25, 1992
Susan M. Pollock	Postmaster	Jan. 23, 1993
Nancy L. Kirby	Officer-In-Charge	Mar. 24, 2000
Cynthia L. Foley	Postmaster	June 17, 2000
Sylvia Conte	Officer-In-Charge	Mar. 12, 2004
Teresa M. Hoxie	Officer-In-Charge	July 1, 2004
Steven A. King	Postmaster	Jan. 22, 2005
Nancy L. Kirby	Officer-In-Charge	Dec. 2, 2005
Cynthia M. Donnelly	Officer-In-Charge	Mar. 27, 2006
Marjorie L Beebe	Postmaster	June 10, 2006
Nancy L. Kirby	Officer-In-Charge	July 13, 2011
Nancy L. Kirby	Postmaster	June 30, 2012

LINN

POSTMASTER	TITLE	DATE APPOINTED
Reuben Bryan Jr.	Postmaster	Sept. 27, 1852
Lurher Cole	Postmaster	Feb. 23, 1865

POMPEY WEST HILL

POSTMASTER	TITLE	DATE APPOINTED
Asahel Smith	Postmaster	Nov. 1, 1816
John Hall	Postmaster	June 16, 1820

Postmasters in the Town of Lysander

BALDWINSVILLE

POSTMASTER	TITLE	DATE APPOINTED
Jonas C. Baldwin	Postmaster	Jan. 8, 1815
Stephen W. Baldwin	Postmaster	Feb. 22, 1821
Otis Bigelow	Postmaster	Dec. 5, 1829
E. Austin Baldwin	Postmaster	July 20, 1841
Daniel T. Jones	Postmaster	Nov. 20, 1844
Lucien B. Hall	Postmaster	June 6, 1849
Edward B. Wigent	Postmaster	Apr. 9, 1853
Irvine Williams	Postmaster	Apr. 10, 1861
David S. Wilkins	Postmaster	Feb. 15, 1864
William W. Perkins	Postmaster	Apr. 5, 1869
William H. Tappan	Postmaster	Jan. 27, 1886

POSTMASTER	TITLE	DATE APPOINTED
Lucien E. Smith	Postmaster	Dec. 21, 1889
Stephen J. Lonergan	Postmaster	Jan. 24, 1894
Martin Harrington	Postmaster	Mar. 9, 1898
Mathew G. Frawley	Postmaster	Mar. 14, 1902
Willard H. Tappan	Postmaster	Oct. 13, 1914
Arthur L. Howard	Acting PM	Oct. 16, 1923
Arthur L. Howard	Postmaster	Jan. 8, 1924
William H. O'Brien Jr.	Acting PM	Mar. 18, 1936
William H. O'Brien Jr.	Postmaster	June 16, 1936
Margaret L. O'Brien	Acting PM	Mar. 31, 1948
James R. Walker	Acting PM	Apr. 30, 1953
James R. Walker	Postmaster	July 28, 1954
Charles C. Vredenburg	Officer-In-Charge	Feb. 28, 1970
Charles C. Vredenburg	Postmaster	Mar. 30, 1971
Robert B. Chamberlain	Officer-In-Charge	Dec. 28, 1972
Robert B. Chamberlain	Postmaster	Apr. 7, 1973
Henry A. Fleming	Officer-In-Charge	Nov. 12, 1982
William T. Moore	Postmaster	Feb. 19, 1983
Ray Venuti	Officer-In-Charge	Mar. 2, 1985
Raymond F. Killiam	Postmaster	June 22, 1985
John M. Pellenz	Officer-In-Charge	Aug. 14, 1987
John N. Puopolo	Officer-In-Charge	Feb. 12, 1988
Charlotte A. Tarwacki	Officer-In-Charge	Apr. 15, 1988
Mary Gale Korzekwa	Postmaster	Dec. 31, 1988
Neil R. Landers	Officer-In-Charge	Dec. 29, 1999
Cheryl M. Matt	Postmaster	Mar. 25, 2000
Gail A. Weeks	Officer-In-Charge	Oct. 23, 2002
Ronald W. La Rose	Officer-In-Charge	Dec. 3, 2002
Charles H. France	Officer-In-Charge	Mar. 21, 2003
Charles H. France	Postmaster	May 31, 2003
Michelle DeStefano	Officer-In-Charge	Dec. 30, 2008
Mark Johnson	Officer-In-Charge	May 5, 2009
Maureen A. Hohl	Officer-In-Charge	June 16, 2009
Maureen A. Hohl	Postmaster	Aug. 29, 2009
Brian Czarnecki	Officer-In-Charge	Dec. 7, 2010
Cynthia L. Foley	Officer-In-Charge	Mar. 29, 2011
Cynthia L. Foley	Postmaster	Aug. 27, 2011

DUNHAMVILLE

POSTMASTER	TITLE	DATE APPOINTED
Noah Payn Jr.	Postmaster	Apr. 15, 1832

POSTMASTER	TITLE	DATE APPOINTED
LAMSON		
John H. Lamson	Postmaster	Aug. 25, 1849
James H. Lamson	Postmaster	June 25, 1850
Merrick S.. Thompson	Postmaster	Oct. 22, 1852
Charles W. thompson	Postmaster	Mar. 25, 1886
John Butler	Postmaster	July 25, 1894
Lewis E. Scriber	Postmaster	Jan. 10, 1899
LITTLE UTICA		
Albert Harrington	Postmaster	Sept. 16, 1863
Lansing W. Connell	Postmaster	Mar. 17, 1864
Loran Dunham	Postmaster	Nov. 14, 1864
Fred H. Morgan	Postmaster	Dec. 24, 1883
John C. Fancher	Postmaster	May 11, 1885
Fred H. Morgan	Postmaster	Dec. 7, 1889
William E. Parke	Postmaster	Feb. 2, 1894
Charles A. Losey	Postmaster	Feb. 8, 1898
LYSANDER		
Chauncey Betts	Postmaster	Feb. 8, 1821
Cornelius C. Hubbard	Postmaster	Dec. 20, 1834
Willard P. Bump	Postmaster	Jan. 5, 1839
George A. Allen	Postmaster	Dec. 23, 1839
Chauncey Betts	Postmaster	May 17, 1841
George A. Allen	Postmaster	Dec. 19, 1844
Chauncey Betts	Postmaster	June 19, 1849
Henry W. Andrews	Postmaster	Sept. 25, 1851
Barclay Wooster	Postmaster	Apr. 27, 1853
William Culver	Postmaster	July 16, 1861
Richard L. Smith	Postmaster	Sept. 28, 1863
Sarah C. Winchel	Postmaster	Mar. 9, 1876
William C. Winchel	Postmaster	Dec. 22, 1885
George S. Hayden	Postmaster	June 11, 1889
James E. Decker	Postmaster	Dec. 13, 1893
George S. Hayden	Postmaster	Feb. 3, 1898
Milan McCarty	Postmaster	Jan. 13, 1900
Willis M. Gillett	Postmaster	June 16, 1906
Dettie M. Gillett	Postmaster	Dec. 22, 1914
Lewis D. Merrifield	Acting PM	Feb. 17, 1928
Frederick M. Blake Jr.	Acting PM	Mar. 9, 1928

POSTMASTER	TITLE	DATE APPOINTED
Frederick M. Blake Jr.	Postmaster	July 11, 1928
Francis Grove Rice	Acting PM	Mar. 23, 1937
Francis Grove Rice	Postmaster	Aug. 10, 1937
Mary E. Baker	Acting PM	July 26, 1938
Mary E. Baker (Welch)	Postmaster	Aug. 15, 1938
Rose I. Litterbrant	Officer-In-Charge	May 27, 1971
Rose I. Litterbrant	Postmaster	May 27, 1972
June M. Wilson	Postmaster	Sept. 23, 1978
Mary E. Mosher	Officer-In-Charge	Nov. 20, 1992

PAYNVILLE

POSTMASTER	TITLE	DATE APPOINTED
Noah Payn Jr.	Postmaster	July 23, 1834
Nelson C. Dunham	Postmaster	Sept. 1, 1836

PLAINVILLE

POSTMASTER	TITLE	DATE APPOINTED
William Wilson	Postmaster	Feb. 20, 1826
Sylvester Stoddard	Postmaster	Apr. 9, 1827
Simon Town	Postmaster	Mar. 31, 1830
John Buck	Postmaster	Mar. 3, 1831
Benjamin B. Schenck	Postmaster	Aug. 22, 1849
Lyman Norton	Postmaster	Apr. 27, 1853
Benjamin B. Schenck	Postmaster	Oct. 13, 1863
Thomas McCall	Postmaster	Apr. 27, 1883
Jabez H. Norton	Postmaster	Apr. 6, 1888
Charles W. Sizeland	Postmaster	July 24, 1889
Major E. Rowell	Postmaster	June 16, 1893
Ulysess G. Dunham	Postmaster	Nov. 11, 1897

Information for postmasters after this time period not available

Earl H. Woodraff	Postmaster	Est. 1930-1950
Roy Roberts	Postmaster	Est. 1950-1955
Edythe P. Forsythe	Postmaster	Mar. 4, 1955
Virginia A. Billings	Officer-In-Charge	May 21, 1976
Virginia A. Billings	Postmaster	July 2, 1977
Shirles E. Stock	Officer-In-Charge	Nov. 20, 1992
Carey E. Sevier	Postmaster	June 26, 1993
Thomas J. O'Neil	Officer-In-Charge	Nov. 25, 1996
Gerald E. Santimaw	Officer-In-Charge	Feb. 18, 1997
Grover C. Horn	Officer-In-Charge	Feb. 29, 1998
Carole A. Conlan	Postmaster	July 4, 1998
Robin M. Bridenbaker	Officer-In-Charge	July 14, 2012

POSTMASTER	TITLE	DATE APPOINTED
POLKVILLE		
Hugh McKiernan	Postmaster	Aug. 18, 1845
Hugh McKiernan	Postmaster	Sept. 28, 1853
Ebenezer Allen	Postmaster	Apr. 11, 1856
Henry Cram	Postmaster	Mar. 28, 1860
Alanson Fancher	Postmaster	Feb. 12, 1861

Postmasters in the Town of Manlius

ELKHORN

POSTMASTER	TITLE	DATE APPOINTED
Cortland A. Snook	Postmaster	Apr. 26, 1890
David T. Bennett	Postmaster	Dec. 28, 1892

FAYETTEVILLE 13066

POSTMASTER	TITLE	DATE APPOINTED
John W. Hyde	Postmaster	Apr. 10, 1818
Aaron C. Hoar	Postmaster	June 4, 1821
Henry Edwards	Postmaster	Apr. 29, 1823
Curtiss J. Hurd	Postmaster	June 16, 1841
Hicks Worden	Postmaster	Apr. 29, 1844
James Mead	Postmaster	June 1, 1849
Andrew T. Gilmor	Postmaster	Apr. 27, 1853
Henry Ecker	Postmaster	Apr. 10, 1861
Franklin M. Severance	Postmaster	Mar. 3, 1878
William Austin	Postmaster	Apr. 23, 1880
Howard H. Edwards	Postmaster	May 10, 1888
John A. Ecker	Postmaster	June 20, 1892
Frank Boynton	Postmaster	June 6, 1896
Arthur C. Agan	Postmaster	June 29, 1900
Delbert M. O'Brien	Postmaster	July 21, 1917
Harry J. Goodfellow	Postmaster	Mar. 7, 1922
Frederick A. Lowe	Postmaster	Dec. 18, 1930
Milton L. Rogers	Acting PM	Dec. 31, 1934
Milton L. Rogers	Postmaster	June 28, 1935
Charles A. O'Brien	Acting PM	June 1, 1936
Charles A. O'Brien	Postmaster	Feb. 4, 1937
Robert K. Norton	Acting PM	July 26, 1963
Robert K. Norton	Postmaster	July 26, 1965
Alfred P. Zappala	Officer-In-Charge	Oct. 2, 1987
John M. Pellenz Jr.	Postmaster	Feb. 13, 1988
Charles H. Houghton	Postmaster	Jan. 23, 1993

Acting PM = Acting Postmaster

POSTMASTER	TITLE	DATE APPOINTED
Ronald W. Larose	Officer-In-Charge	May 1, 2007
Ronald W. Larose	Postmaster	Oct. 13, 2007
Michelle M. Destefano	Officer-In-Charge	Sept. 30, 2008
Eva M. Gigon	Officer-In-Charge	Dec. 4, 2008
Eva M. Gigon	Postmaster	Aug. 29, 2009
Mark Johnson	Officer-In-Charge	Mar. 8, 2013
Daniel E. Mulroy	Postmaster	Sept. 7, 2013
James Jones	Officer-In-Charge	Nov. 13, 2014
Janette L. Roskoff	Postmaster	Feb. 7, 2015

HARTSVILLE

POSTMASTER	TITLE	DATE APPOINTED
Henry H. Potter	Postmaster	Mar. 1, 1826
Origen Eaton Jr.	Postmaster	Oct. 28, 1826
Elisha Raymond	Postmaster	Aug. 14, 1832
Elisha Raymond Jr.	Postmaster	July 7, 1837
Pardon Thompson	Postmaster	Aug. 29, 1842
Silas T. Hinds	Postmaster	Mar. 12, 1846
Pardon Thompson	Postmaster	July 17, 1849

HURLGATE

POSTMASTER	TITLE	DATE APPOINTED
William C. Shute	Postmaster	June 2, 1855

KIRKVILLE 13082

POSTMASTER	TITLE	DATE APPOINTED
Robert Cunningham	Postmaster	May 12, 1824
Eddward Kirkland	Postmaster	Dec. 5, 1829
Clark Hebbard	Postmaster	June 17, 1833
Alonzo L. Scranton	Postmaster	July 7, 1841
Obadiah Hubbs	Postmaster	Mar. 24, 1842
Anson W. Sackett	Postmaster	Oct. 7, 1851
Obadiah Hubbs	Postmaster	July 6, 1852
Joseph Hoag	Postmaster	Sept. 3, 1853
Lawrence Delany	Postmaster	Aug. 7, 1861
William J. Overhiser	Postmaster	Oct. 13, 1863
Nathan S. Moses	Postmaster	Mar. 24, 1865
Asa Ballon	Postmaster	Sept. 7, 1865
Joseph Hoag	Postmaster	May 15, 1867
James A. Brown	Postmaster	Dec. 3, 1884
Charles Hoag	Postmaster	Sept. 4, 1885
James A. Brown	Postmaster	Apr. 4, 1889
Charles Hoag	Postmaster	Oct. 13, 1893
Herbert H. Brown	Postmaster	June 21, 1898

POSTMASTER	TITLE	DATE APPOINTED
William C. Moore	Postmaster	Dec. 29, 1900
Alice B. Moore	Postmaster	Feb. 26, 1915
Mary E. Mather	Postmaster	July 14, 1921
Elmer O. Plopper	Acting PM	Oct. 16, 1922
Elmer O. Plopper	Postmaster	Jan. 23, 1923
Katharine M. Carhart	Acting PM	Jan. 25, 1944
Katharine M. Carhart	Postmaster	July 17, 1947
Marjorie C. Petrie	Acting PM	Feb. 29, 1968
Daisy A. Myers	Officer-In-Charge	Sept. 19, 1969
Daisy A. Myers	Postmaster	June 26, 1971
Charles H. Houghton	Officer-In-Charge	Sept. 16, 1983
Carolyn T. McCarthy	Postmaster	Nov. 26, 1983
Janet L. Mattox	Officer-In-Charge	Sept. 25, 1992
Thomas W. Shaffner	Postmaster	Jan. 23, 1993
Rebecca Jenkins	Officer-In-Charge	July 30, 2012
John Lynch	Postmaster	Oct. 6, 2012
Rebecca Jenkins	Postmaster	Sept. 21, 2013

KIRKVILLE STATION

POSTMASTER	TITLE	DATE APPOINTED
Herbert H. Brown	Postmaster	Sept. 7, 1898

MANLIUS 13104

POSTMASTER	TITLE	DATE APPOINTED
Colonel Luther Bingham	Postmaster	Nov. 26, 1800
Robert Wilson	Postmaster	Apr. 1, 1803
Hezekiah L Granger	Postmaster	June 19, 1811
Nathan Williams	Postmaster	Apr. 19, 1819
Dearborn B. Beckford	Postmaster	Aug. 21, 1835
Joseph S. Rhoades	Postmaster	Aug. 6, 1841
John Grinnell	Postmaster	Feb. 7, 1845
Horace Nims	Postmaster	June 6, 1849
Hiram Smith	Postmaster	Apr. 27, 1853
Eben Duell	Postmaster	Apr. 10, 1861
Joseph Baker	Postmaster	July 20, 1868
William W. Candee	Postmaster	June 27, 1881
Ailliam W. Agar	Postmaster	Jan. 25, 1886
James A. O'Neill	Postmaster	June 3, 1889
Frank P. Emmons	Postmaster	Apr. 11, 1892
William F. Sponenburg	Postmaster	Jan. 7, 1897
George W. Armstrong	Postmaster	Feb. 4, 1901
John J. Costello	Postmaster	Aug. 27, 1913

POSTMASTER	TITLE	DATE APPOINTED
Leslie R. Bell	Postmaster	Apr. 11, 1922
Henry S. Whitney	Acting PM	July 24, 1922
Henry S. Whitney	Postmaster	Jan. 31, 1923
John L. McDermott	Acting PM	Feb. 25, 1935
John L. McDermott	Postmaster	Aug. 27, 1935
Emily B. Koons	Acting PM	July 9, 1939
Emily B. Koons	Postmaster	Mar. 21, 1940
Willis Clayton Farnham	Acting PM	July 31, 1954
Willis Clayton Farnham	Postmaster	July 19, 1956
Guy E. Hobbs Jr.	Acting PM	Aug. 24, 1962
Guy E. Hobbs Jr.	Postmaster	Apr. 25, 1963
Joseph A. Trovato	Officer-In-Charge	Dec. 31, 1987
Charles H. France	Postmaster	July 2, 1988
Michelle M. DeStefano	Officer-In-Charge	Mar. 20, 2003
Sharon M. Parmley	Officer-In-Charge	May 30, 2003
Cynthia L. Foley	Officer-In-Charge	Aug. 11, 2003
Michellle M. DeStefano	Postmaster	Oct. 18, 2003
Mark E. Lawrence	Officer-In-Charge	Aug. 26, 2008
David H. Moore	Postmaster	Mar. 27, 2010
Peter J. Egitton	Postmaster	Nov. 5, 2011

MANLIUS CENTRE

Alfred Palmer	Postmaster	Mar. 20, 1824
John Mabie	Postmaster	Mar. 1, 1831
Timothy H. Taylor	Postmaster	June 26, 1841
Jonas P. Haner	Postmaster	Aug. 29, 1842
Charles Huntley	Postmaster	June 2, 1845
John Mabie	Postmaster	July 8, 1846
Ralph Chapin	Postmaster	Aug. 18, 1853
Franklin W. Walrath	Postmaster	Jan. 3, 1859
Ralph Chapin	Postmaster	Jan. 4, 1865
Orrin W. Brown	Postmaster	Nov. 17, 1884

MANLIUS STATION

Peter J. Terpening	Postmaster	June 21, 1855
Joseph Mead	Postmaster	Sept. 3, 1857
Perry O. Weaver	Postmaster	June 5, 1868
James E. Weaver	Postmaster	Jan. 27, 1881
Oliver B. Mead	Postmaster	Sept. 4, 1885
Richard W. McKinley	Postmaster	June 18, 1889
Ephraim E. Woodward	Postmaster	July 10, 1893

POSTMASTER	TITLE	DATE APPOINTED
MINOA		
Ephraim E. Woodward	Postmaster	Aug. 16, 1895
Blanche Morrison	Postmaster	Mar. 2, 1898
Stanley E. Terwillger	Postmaster	June 23, 1904
Helen C. B. Rube	Postmaster	Dec. 22, 1914
Albert J. Helfer	Postmaster	Aug. 14, 1918
Clifford E. Brown	Postmaster	Dec. 11, 1926
Joseph A. Strodel	Acting PM	Dec. 31, 1934
Joseph A. Strodel	Postmaster	July 24, 1935
Walter A. Soule	Acting PM	Feb. 22, 1937
Walter A. Soule	Postmaster	Aug. 2, 1937
Mary Louise Soule	Acting PM	Jan. 28, 1944
Mary Louise Soule	Postmaster	Nov. 16, 1945
Wayne V. Tapper	Acting PM	May 15, 1959
Earl F. Huller	Acting PM	Apr. 14, 1961
Earl W. Fleegel	Officer-In-charge	Apr. 10, 1970
Robert W. Heaps	Officer-In-charge	Apr. 24, 1970
Robert W. Heaps	Postmaster	June 26, 1971
Richard C. Knopp	Officer-In-charge	Feb. 3, 1984
Alfred P. Zappala	Postmaster	Apr. 28, 1984
Torry C. Lesh	Officer-In-charge	Sept. 28, 2005
Barbara J. Almonte	Postmaster	Nov. 12, 2005
Leah T. Cushing	Officer-In-charge	July 14, 2012

MYCENAE

Jay G. Dewey	Postmaster	Apr. 4, 1889
Bessie Terry	Postmaster	Mar. 14, 1892
Seymour B. Moyer	Postmaster	Mar. 23, 1892

NORTH MANLIUS

Cyrus P. Camp	Postmaster	Dec. 31, 1851
David J. Dewey	Postmaster	Aug. 7, 1861

Postmasters in the Town of Marcellus

CLINTONVILLE

Manapeh Eaton	Postmaster	Jan. 8, 1818
James Meade Allen	Postmaster	May 13, 1820

ELLISTON

Furman B. North	Postmaster	Feb. 22, 1849
Isaac Mills	Postmaster	Mar. 2, 1852

POSTMASTER	TITLE	DATE APPOINTED
EMPIRE		
Norman B. Sheppard	Postmaster	May 20, 1898
Sidney Sheppard	Postmaster	June 24, 1898
MARCELLUS 13108		
Dr. Jesse Munger	Postmaster	Apr. 17, 1797
Elnathan Beech/Beach	Postmaster	Feb. 18, 1799
Samuel Bishop	Postmaster	Feb. 20, 1801
Guy Humphreys	Postmaster	Feb. 1, 1803
Ebenezer Rice	Postmaster	Apr. 1, 1808
Joseph Olmsted	Postmaster	Oct. 1, 1809
Erastus Humphreys	Postmaster	Oct. 14, 1811
Daniel Ball	Postmaster	Oct. 17, 1818
Sanford C. Parker	Postmaster	Dec. 21, 1831
George Kennedy	Postmaster	Nov. 1, 1836
Sanford Dalliba	Postmaster	July 3, 1841
Newton G. Case	Postmaster	Aug. 19, 1845
Elijah Rowley	Postmaster	July 3, 1849
Henry T. Kennedy	Postmaster	Apr. 27, 1853
Joseph S. Platt	Postmaster	Apr. 10, 1861
Thomas DeCondres	Postmaster	July 20, 1865
John M. Seymour	Postmaster	Feb. 11, 1885
Michael Sheehan	Postmaster	Jan. 25, 1886
John M. Seymour	Postmaster	Mar. 26, 1889
Maurice H. Donahue	Postmaster	Mar. 2, 1894
Frank J. Lawless	Postmaster	Mar. 21, 1898
Watson J. Matteson	Postmaster	Mar. 2, 1901
Edward V. Baker	Postmaster	Apr. 8, 1909
James Hogan	Postmaster	June 5, 1913
Marion L. Woodford	Postmaster	Dec. 22, 1921
Robert McHale	Acting PM	Feb. 28, 1934
Robert McHale	Postmaster	June 25, 1936
William T. Conley	Postmaster	Aug. 22, 1940
Jane Ann Conley	Acting PM	Jan. 1, 1949
John E. Conley	Postmaster	Sept. 14, 1951
Robert P. Siersma	Acting PM	June 30, 1955
Robert P. Siersma	Postmaster	Apr. 8, 1957
Andrew Vanags	Officer-In-Charge	
John R. Moore	Postmaster	Jan. 24, 1981

POSTMASTER	TITLE	DATE APPOINTED
James A. McCann	Officer-In-Charge	Feb. 2, 1985
Helga L. Castor	Postmaster	June 22, 1985
Joseph W. Picciano	Officer-In-Charge	Dec. 27, 1991
Samuel S. Martino Jr.	Postmaster	June 13, 1992
Theresa B. Furlong	Officer-In-Charge	Nov. 30, 2001
Dennis J. O'Donnell	Postmaster	July 13, 2002
MARCELLUS FALLS		
Salmon C. Norton	Postmaster	Sept. 24, 1840
George P. Herring	Postmaster	May 9, 1843
Joseph H. Steele	Postmaster	Aug. 5, 1850
Edwin Steele	Postmaster	Aug. 7, 1861
Addison M. Seymour	Postmaster	Dec. 17, 1885
David J. Lawless	Postmaster	Apr. 15, 1889
Addison M. Seymour	Postmaster	Oct. 7, 1893
Kate L. Seymour	Postmaster	July 23, 1896
Kate L. Bennett	Postmaster	Nov. 28, 1899
MARIETTA 13110		
Thaddeus Thompson	Postmaster	Mar. 8, 1832
Alanson Hicks	Postmaster	May 18, 1842
George B. Fish	Postmaster	Dec. 15, 1856
Alanson Hicks	Postmaster	Mar. 24, 1860
Salem T. Beebe	Postmaster	Aug. 25, 1861
John M. DeWitt	Postmaster	Apr. 6, 1863
James DeWitt	Postmaster	Oct. 27, 1863
Richard Salisbury	Postmaster	June 26, 1867
James DeWitt	Postmaster	June 9, 1873
John T. Hicks	Postmaster	Mar. 13, 1886
Frank A. Rathbun	Postmaster	July 2, 1891
Peter FitzPatrick	Postmaster	July 25, 1894
Frank S. Norton	Postmaster	Dec. 9, 1898
Arthur L. Sayles	Postmaster	Oct. 1, 1900
Olm J. Baker	Postmaster	Feb. 6, 1906
Lillie E. Baker	Postmaster	Dec. 22, 1914
Lawrence J. Kennedy	Acting PM	June 1, 1942
Eileen B. Kennedy	Postmaster	June 21, 1944
William V. Compson	Officer-In-Charge	July 12, 1974
Charles E. DeVoe Jr.	Postmaster	July 20, 1974
Joseph V. Coleman	Officer-In-Charge	Dec. 17, 1982

POSTMASTER	TITLE	DATE APPOINTED
Charles W. Woeller	Postmaster	Mar. 19, 1983
Laraine A. Rapple	Officer-In-Charge	Dec. 31, 2008
Laraine A. Rapple	Postmaster	Mar. 27, 2010

RHODES

John Adams	Postmaster	Feb. 23, 1828

ROSE HILL

Frank B. Mills	Postmaster	Oct. 24, 1890
William E. Mills	Postmaster	Oct. 6, 1892
William E. Mills	Postmaster	Jan. 23, 1900

SHAMROCK

Charles M. Goodspeed	Postmaster	Dec. 15, 1890

SOUTH MARCELLUS

Caleb N. Potter	Postmaster	Feb. 1, 1832
John Burns	Postmaster	Aug. 6, 1841
Hiram Slade	Postmaster	Aug. 22, 1842
Caleb N. Potter	Postmaster	May 15, 1844

THORN HILL

Obadiah Thorne	Postmaster	Aug. 24, 1853
Stephen Vanderburgh	Postmaster	Mar. 7, 1855
George F. Knapp	Postmaster	Dec. 9, 1857
Allen Brown	Postmaster	May 28, 1868
David S. Church	Postmaster	Apr. 28, 1884
Allen Brown	Postmaster	May 15, 1884
Charles H. Haas	Postmaster	May 4, 1886
Ann Hawton	Postmaster	Mar. 18, 1887
Ann Hawton	Postmaster	Dec. 23, 1890
Albert Easton	Postmaster	Feb. 2, 1894

Postmasters in the Town of Onondaga

CEDARVILLE

Lewis Amidon	Postmaster	June 29, 1871
Ezra F. Lounsbury	Postmaster	May 13, 1873
R. Angie Lounsbury	Postmaster	Aug. 27, 1886
Willis G. Hull	Postmaster	July 20, 1893

EAST ONONDAGA

George B. Clark	Postmaster	Jan. 22, 1883
Leonard H. Church	Postmaster	Dec. 22, 1885

POSTMASTER	TITLE	DATE APPOINTED
James C. Redding	Postmaster	Apr. 27, 1889
Edward C. Fay	Postmaster	Dec. 13, 1893
Emmet G. Fairchild	Postmaster	Feb. 3, 1898

ELMWOOD PARK

Walter W Norris	Postmaster	May 7, 1891
Frank L. Hall	Postmaster	Aug. 16, 1895
Ada P. Widdrington	Postmaster	July 28, 1897

HOWLET HILL

Wheeler Truesdell	Postmaster	May 18, 1829
Stephen S. Jewett	Postmaster	Aug. 12, 1831
B. H. Case	Postmaster	Feb. 1, 1833
Wheeler Truesdell	Postmaster	Jan. 2, 1836
John Case	Postmaster	July 11, 1837
Leonard Caten	Postmaster	June 6, 1849
Ralph D. Marvin	Postmaster	Feb. 21, 1855
John Q. Robinson	Postmaster	Dec. 24, 1860
Helen C. Robinson	Postmaster	June 22, 1865
Caroline C. Berry	Postmaster	Nov. 1, 1869
William O. Powell	Postmaster	Jan. 18, 1875
Helen C. Powell	Postmaster	Mar. 29, 1880
Albert Marshfield	Postmaster	Aug. 19, 1895

JOSHUA

Charles V. Webber	Postmaster	Oct. 29, 1896

NAVARINO

Alexander H. Cowles	Postmaster	Feb. 28, 1828
Oren Hull	Postmaster	Aug. 5, 1835
Andrew J. Cummings	Postmaster	Jan. 3, 1842
Almon B. Edmonds	Postmaster	Apr. 28, 1948
John T. Gillet	Postmaster	June 8, 1849
Martin L. Gardner	Postmaster	June 21, 1853
Theophilus Hall	Postmaster	Feb. 27, 1857
John P. Hull	Postmaster	Nov. 28, 1857
George Stocking	Postmaster	Apr. 22, 1859
Martin L. Gardner	Postmaster	Apr. 4, 1861
Byron C. Grennell	Postmaster	Sept. 4, 1885
Martin L. Gardner	Postmaster	Apr. 13, 1889
Lee A. Cummings	Postmaster	Oct. 9, 1893
Olin W. Crysler	Postmaster	Feb. 8, 1898

Acting PM = Acting Postmaster

NEDROW 13120

POSTMASTER	TITLE	DATE APPOINTED
Alfred E. Perry	Postmaster	Sept. 5, 1917
Clarence H. Ash	Postmaster	May 5, 1919
R. Walter Riehlman	Postmaster	June 16, 1921
Clarence H. Ash	Postmaster	Feb. 15, 1922
Oliver Kamm	Postmaster	May 18, 1922
Clarence H. Ash	Postmaster	Jan. 15, 1923

Information for postmasters after this time period not available

Vincent J. Behm	Postmaster	July 20, 1956
Doris K. Moore	Officer-In-Charge	Sept. 30, 1979
Orlando A. Houghtaling	Postmaster	Nov. 17, 1979
Fred J. Heins	Officer-In-Charge	June 6, 1980
James A. McCann	Postmaster	Sept. 6, 1980
Marilyn J. DeWolfe	Officer-In-Charge	Nov. 14, 1986
Thomas E. Heisey	Postmaster	Apr. 25, 1987
Donald A. Bausman Jr.	Officer-In-Charge	Sept. 28, 1992
Central A. Williams	Postmaster	Jan. 23, 1993
Jeanne L. Murphy	Officer-In-Charge	Mar. 28, 1996
Theresa B. Furlong	Postmaster	June 22, 1996

ONONDAGA

POSTMASTER	TITLE	DATE APPOINTED
Nehemiah H. Earll	Postmaster	Apr. 17, 1830
Reuben West	Postmaster	Jan. 6, 1831
Lewis M. Morton	Postmaster	Apr. 20, 1832
Hezekiah Strong	Postmaster	June 21, 1833
Danial Smith	Postmaster	Jan. 12, 1837
Nathan R. Tefft	Postmaster	Feb. 14, 1839
Charles D. Easton	Postmaster	Apr. 7, 1842
Henry P. Shove	Postmaster	Nov. 30, 1844
Charles D. Easton	Postmaster	June 5, 1849
Henry P. Shove	Postmaster	Apr. 27, 1853
William T. Mosely	Postmaster	Mar. 22, 1856
Stephen Yielding	Postmaster	Aug. 29, 1862
John W. Stackhouse	Postmaster	June 26, 1871
Edward S. Tefft	Postmaster	Nov. 22, 1880
John Raynor	Postmaster	Sept. 28, 1881
George Curtis	Postmaster	Sept. 4, 1885
Charles T. Raynor	Postmaster	June 17, 1889

ONONDAGA C. H.

POSTMASTER	TITLE	DATE APPOINTED
Nehemiah H. Earll	Postmaster	Feb. 9, 1816

ONONDAGA CASTLE

Albion Jackson	Postmaster	Sept. 22, 1849
John W. Decker	Postmaster	Mar. 4, 1859
Jerome J. Cook	Postmaster	Jan. 23, 1860
Lemuel G. Clark	Postmaster	Aug. 18, 1862
Joseph T. Card	Postmaster	Nov. 1, 1865
John G. Jackson	Postmaster	Jan. 23, 1866
George W. Card	Postmaster	June 26, 1867
Henry Conklin	Postmaster	Jan. 6, 1869
Henry Conklin	Postmaster	Nov. 9, 1875
Barney Kelly	Postmaster	Nov. 15, 1886
Samuel C. Worden	Postmaster	May 25, 1889
Henry Conklin	Postmaster	Oct. 3, 1892
Daniel A. Kelley	Postmaster	Dec. 10, 1896

ONONDAGA HOLLOW

Comfort Tyler	Postmaster	Apr. 1, 1795
George Hall	Postmaster	July 1, 1799
Jasper Hopper	Postmaster	Mar. 28, 1803
Lewis H. Redfield	Postmaster	June 20, 1820
Royal Stewart	Postmaster	May 27, 1829
Robert Hamilton	Postmaster	Dec. 20, 1833
Joseph W. Loomis	Postmaster	Dec. 27, 1838
John J. Hopper	Postmaster	June 17, 1839
Arthur Pattison	Postmaster	July 3, 1841
John J. Hopper	Postmaster	Aug. 19, 1845
Arthur Pattison	Postmaster	June 8, 1849

ONONDAGA VALLEY

Arthur Pattison	Postmaster	Sept. 18, 1849
Francis W. Hastings	Postmaster	Sept. 28, 1853
Richard R. Slocum	Postmaster	Feb. 14, 1855
Charles Rowe	Postmaster	Apr. 10, 1861
Lorenzo M. Withey	Postmaster	Apr. 8, 1864
Thomas T. Clark	Postmaster	Dec. 20, 1865
Frederick Kimber	Postmaster	Oct. 29, 1866
George B. Clark	Postmaster	Mar. 13, 1867

POSTMASTER	TITLE	DATE APPOINTED
Frank N. Dickinson	Postmaster	Jan. 29, 1875
Cornelius C. Marletto	Postmaster	Apr. 30, 1885
Benjamin F. Churchill	Postmaster	Apr. 4, 1889
William H. Card	Postmaster	Oct. 9, 1893
Henry A. Maynard	Postmaster	Apr. 26, 1895

ROCK CUT

POSTMASTER	TITLE	DATE APPOINTED
George A. Hoyt	Postmaster	Feb. 21, 1890

SOUTH ONONDAGA

POSTMASTER	TITLE	DATE APPOINTED
Samuel Kingsley	Postmaster	Feb. 15, 1828
Titus J. Fenn	Postmaster	July 6, 1841
Jesse Salmons	Postmaster	July 29, 1845
CheneyAmidon	Postmaster	June 6, 1849
Jesse Salmons	Postmaster	Apr. 27, 1853
Olmsted Quick	Postmaster	Dec. 12, 1854
Jesse Salmons	Postmaster	July 26, 1856
Eben L. North	Postmaster	Mar. 1, 1865
Merton L. Beach	Postmaster	Feb. 19, 1878
Victory Day	Postmaster	Dec. 8, 1881
George Anderson	Postmaster	Dec. 22, 1885
Daniel Pinckney	Postmaster	Apr. 12, 1889
John R. Lord	Postmaster	Apr. 2, 1894
Lois E. Lord	Postmaster	Jan. 26, 1897

SPLIT ROCK

POSTMASTER	TITLE	DATE APPOINTED
Stephen H. North	Postmaster	Apr. 3, 1890
Oren W. Fyler	Postmaster	June 11, 1890
Mary Connors	Postmaster	July 25, 1894
Burnett Reagan	Postmaster	Apr. 25, 1899

WEST ONONDAGA

POSTMASTER	TITLE	DATE APPOINTED
Myron Clift	Postmaster	Feb. 5, 1851
Denison Hull	Postmaster	Apr. 28, 1854
Alanson Woodford	Postmaster	Nov. 15, 1856

POSTMASTER	TITLE	DATE APPOINTED

Postmasters in the Town of Otisco

AMBER

POSTMASTER	TITLE	DATE APPOINTED
William V. R. Lansurgh	Postmaster	Apr. 21, 1817
David S. Van Rensselaer	Postmaster	Sept. 21, 1821
Lewis Gelding	Postmaster	Mar. 20, 1827
Albert Niles	Postmaster	Dec. 22, 1831
Alanson Adams	Postmaster	Oct. 2, 1849
Myron Hillyer	Postmaster	Dec. 26, 1849
Albert Niles	Postmaster	Feb. 28, 1855
Alfred J. Niles	Postmaster	Oct. 23, 1857
Anson L. Kinyon	Postmaster	Aug. 23, 1861
Zenas Barrows	Postmaster	Mar. 28, 1864
Alfred J. Barrows	Postmaster	May 7, 1864
Alfred J. Niles	Postmaster	Oct. 29, 1866
Franklin D. Griffin	Postmaster	Feb. 21, 1881
Alfred J. Niles	Postmaster	Dec. 22, 1885
Franklin D. Griffin	Postmaster	June 17, 1889
Byron C. Grennell	Postmaster	July 10, 1893
Henry S. Jones	Postmaster	July 6, 1899

CASE

POSTMASTER	TITLE	DATE APPOINTED
Edith L. Russell	Postmaster	Feb. 17, 1898

OTISCO

POSTMASTER	TITLE	DATE APPOINTED
Luther French	Postmaster	Jan. 21, 1815
Jesse Swan	Postmaster	Feb. 5, 1817
Chauncey Swan	Postmaster	Sept. 4, 1826
Oliver H. Kingsley	Postmaster	Feb. 20, 1833
Chauncey Swan	Postmaster	May 23, 1833
Oliver H. Kingsley	Postmaster	Jan. 23, 1834
Henry K. Graves	Postmaster	Oct. 30, 1835
Horatio Smith	Postmaster	Sept. 17, 1840
Ashbel Searl	Postmaster	June 6, 1849
Anson Whitcomb	Postmaster	July 15, 1853
Henry A. Shaw	Postmaster	Feb. 21, 1859
Darius D. Tuttle	Postmaster	Apr. 10, 1861
Anthony C. Stone	Postmaster	Feb. 1, 1866
James C. Gardner	Postmaster	Feb. 5, 1867
Frederick C. Child	Postmaster	July 15, 1869
James Henderson	Postmaster	May 2, 1871

POSTMASTER	TITLE	DATE APPOINTED
Michael Cummings	Postmaster	Dec. 22, 1885
Lester Judson	Postmaster	Mar. 27, 1889
Ellen E. Cain	Postmaster	Sept. 13, 1893
Ellen E. Long	Postmaster	Dec. 17, 1894
Emerson J. Burroughs	Postmaster	Apr. 19, 1911

OTISCO CENTRE

Oliver H. Kingsley	Postmaster	May 23, 1833

OTISCO VALLEY

Hannah Webster	Postmaster	May 20, 1868
Mary J. Frisbie	Postmaster	May 10, 1869
Edwin Rice	Postmaster	Apr. 3, 1886
George A. Patton	Postmaster	Jan. 3, 1887
James Ready	Postmaster	May 19, 1887
Henry B. Swetland	Postmaster	Apr. 1, 1889
James Ready	Postmaster	Dec. 13, 1893
James Murphy	Postmaster	Jan. 23, 1896
Milton A. Swetland	Postmaster	Feb. 5, 1898

ZEALAND

Carrie Rice	Postmaster	Sept. 28, 1892
Edward L. Williams	Postmaster	Feb. 17, 1898

Postmasters in the Town of Pompey

BERWYN (previously MARIONVILLE)

Daniel Woodford	Postmaster	Jan. 4, 1893
Raymond D. Swift	Postmaster	Feb. 13, 1894
Lucien L. Woodford	Postmaster	Feb. 17, 1898

DELPHI

Schuyler Van Renssalear	Postmaster	Apr. 14, 1814
Elisha Litchfield	Postmaster	Nov. 28, 1817
Sanders Vam Remssa;ear	Postmaster	June 25, 1821
Elisha Litchfield	Postmaster	May 5, 1826
Charles C. Slocum	Postmaster	Apr. 28, 1845
William A. Bates	Postmaster	June 1, 1849
Charles C. Slocum	Postmaster	Apr. 27, 1853
Egbert H. Hill	Postmaster	Feb. 7, 1854
Charles R. K. Hill	Postmaster	Jan. 25, 1856
William A. Bates	Postmaster	Apr. 10, 1861
Frederick W. Drury	Postmaster	Dec. 26, 1862

POSTMASTER	TITLE	DATE APPOINTED
Willam A. Bates	Postmaster	June 2, 1863
James S. Galloway	Postmaster	Apr. 6, 1870
James R. Fenner	Postmaster	Apr. 3, 1871
Job D. Potter	Postmaster	Sept. 4, 1885
James R. Fenner	Postmaster	Apr. 2, 1889
Thomas J. Piester	Postmaster	July 10, 1893
James R. Fenner	Postmaster	Nov. 11, 1889

DELPHI FALLS 13051

James R, Fenner	Postmaster	Apr. 21, 1902
Ernest L. Blowers	Postmaster	Apr. 7, 1909
George B. Tuttle	Postmaster	July 8, 1922
Howard J. Furlong	Postmaster	Sept. 30, 1922

Information for postmasters after this time period not available

Ethel L. Mueller	Acting PM	Aug. 31, 1968
Ethel L. Mueller	Postmaster	May 1, 1971
Carolyn L. Houck	Officer-In-Charge	Oct. 20, 1978
Carolyn L. Houck	Postmaster	Jan. 13, 1979
Karen L. Reynolds	Officer-In-Charge	Nov. 8, 1996
John C. Altman	Officer-In-Charge	Mar. 21, 1997
Barbara M. Vanderwerken	Officer-In-Charge	May 2, 1997
Delores Pontillo IIacqua	Officer-In-Charge	July 14, 1997
Nila R. Rodgers	Officer-In-Charge	Sept. 26, 1997

MARIONVILLE

Daniel Woodford	Postmaster	Apr. 18, 1878

ORAN

Philo Cleveland	Postmaster	May 23, 1816
Luther Scovil	Postmaster	Mar. 20, 1819
Cyrenus Bartholomew	Postmaster	June 12, 1822
Anson H. Taylor	Postmaster	May 15, 1828
Daniel Dennison	Postmaster	June 26, 1833
Lorenzo D. Loomis	Postmaster	Jan. 10, 1842
Josiah Brintnall	Postmaster	Apr. 28, 1845
David H. Lines	Postmaster	Oct. 23, 1846
Harvey Morse	Postmaster	Nov. 13, 1846
Lorenzo D. Loomis	Postmaster	Dec. 23, 1847
Julius Candee	Postmaster	June 9, 1849
James C. Midler	Postmaster	Apr. 19, 1886

POSTMASTER	TITLE	DATE APPOINTED
Clarence R. Wells	Postmaster	Apr. 12, 1889
John F. Lewis	Postmaster	Apr. 11, 1890
James C. Midler	Postmaster	May 10, 1894
Roger D. Boyd	Postmaster	June 21, 1898
Information for postmasters after this time period not available		
Ralph C. Cathers	Postmaster	Mar. 7, 1942
Mae P. Cathers	Acting PM	Feb. 25, 1943
Mae P. Cathers	Postmaster	Apr. 3, 1943
Anna M. Penoyer	Acting PM	Aug. 31, 1968
Veronica C. Vanderwerken	Postmaster	Nov. 13, 1971
Ronald W. Dunn	Officer-In-Charge	July 5, 1974
Jerry E. Goodfellow	Postmaster	Oct. 26, 1974
Unknown	Officer-In-Charge	
Joan K. Kosalek	Postmaster	Oct. 26, 1985
Julia C. Conway	Officer-In-Charge	June 19, 1987
Kathie M. L. Oot	Postmaster	Oct. 24, 1987
Michelle M. Berry	Officer-In-Charge	July 26, 1991
Delores L. Pontillo	Officer-In-Charge	Oct. 4, 1991
Patricia A. Wright	Officer-In-Charge	Nov. 8, 1991
Gail L. Harringron	Officer-In-Charge	Apr. 10, 1992
Nancy J. Campagna	Officer-In-Charge	June 12, 1992
Connie Crayton	Officer-In-Charge	Aug. 20, 1993
Bonnie S. Burnatowski	Officer-In-Charge	Dec. 17, 1993
Roslyn M. McConnell	Officer-In-Charge	Apr. 15, 1994
Peggy A. Lewis	Officer-In-Charge	July 5, 1994
Maureen A. Hohl	Officer-In-Charge	Nov. 4, 1994
Alaina E. Lapoint	Officer-In-Charge	Mar. 2, 1995
Mary Anne Kelly	Officer-In-Charge	June 12, 1995
Gerald P. Connelly	Officer-In-Charge	Sept. 18, 1995

POMPEY

POSTMASTER	TITLE	DATE APPOINTED
Daniel Woods	Postmaster	May 2, 1803
Luther Marsh	Postmaster	Feb. 14, 1816
Victory Birdseye	Postmaster	Apr. 25, 1817
Horace Wheaton	Postmaster	Dec. 20, 1838
William J. Curtis	Postmaster	Nov. 10, 1843
Calvin S. Ball	Postmaster	June 19, 1849
John J. Taylor	Postmaster	Apr. 28, 1853
Samuel P. Hayden	Postmaster	Apr. 10, 1861

POSTMASTER	TITLE	DATE APPOINTED
John J. Taylor	Postmaster	Sept. 24, 1866
Daniel E. Hayden	Postmaster	May 15, 1867
Lemuel S. Pomeroy	Postmaster	Apr. 6, 1870
Carmi Heyden	Postmaster	Mar. 18, 1873
John F. Petrie	Postmaster	Nov. 13, 1877
James V. Butts	Postmaster	June 4, 1884
William W. Van Brocklin	Postmaster	July 20, 1885
James V. Butts	Postmaster	Apr. 1, 1889
Wells M. Butler	Postmaster	July 25, 1894
Elijah L. Wheeler	Postmaster	Apr. 19, 1899
Information for postmasters after this time period not available		
Francis W. Cox	Acting PM	July 17, 1941
Francis W. Cox	Postmaster	Mar. 3, 1942
Charles R. Whitton	Acting PM	Sept. 21, 1956
David K. Pearson	Acting PM	Jan. 24, 1958
David K. Pearson	Postmaster	Sept. 2, 1958
Charles R. Whitton	Acting PM	Sept. 24, 1959
Charles R. Whitton	Postmaster	Feb. 15, 1960
Bettey R. Sullivan	Officer-In-Charge	June 30, 1972
Bettey R. Sullivan	Postmaster	Dec. 23, 1972
Donna L. Chubb	Officer-In-Charge	Mar. 22, 1991
Kathie M. L. Oot	Postmaster	July 27, 1991
M. Colleen DeVere	Officer-In-Charge	Dec. 2, 1999
Nancy J. Hammond	Officer-In-Charge	Mar. 3, 2000
Sylvia E. Conte	Postmaster	Mar. 25, 2000
Shannon Dexter	Officer-In-Charge	Sept. 26, 2014

POMPEY CENTRE

POSTMASTER	TITLE	DATE APPOINTED
Charles G. Merrell	Postmaster	Oct. 10, 1831
James Dunning	Postmaster	June 17, 1833
Harmon Marsh	Postmaster	Apr. 12, 1836
Levi S. Holbrook	Postmaster	Apr. 8, 1840
Daniel W. Holbrook	Postmaster	Dec. 23, 1845
Judson Candee	Postmaster	Sept. 28, 1846
Robert Moore	Postmaster	Apr. 6, 1870
Daniel W. Holbrook	Postmaster	Oct. 6, 1887
Frank N. Jennings	Postmaster	Apr. 16, 1890
Mary E. Jennings	Postmaster	May 19, 1892
Virgil J. Purington	Postmaster	Sept. 1, 1892

Acting PM = Acting Postmaster

POSTMASTER	TITLE	DATE APPOINTED
Spelling on name changed to POMPEY CENTER		
Daniel W. Holbrook	Postmaster	May 8, 1893
Frank J. Purington	Postmaster	Apr. 22, 1898
WATERVILLE		
Ansell Judd	Postmaster	Dec. 20, 1826
Elijah D. Goodwin	Postmaster	Sept. 17, 1831
Ira Curtis	Postmaster	Dec. 21, 1833
Joseph Baker	Postmaster	Dec. 15, 1845
William Ely	Postmaster	July 20, 1849
Ralph T. Reed	Postmaster	July 10, 1855
Edward M. Thompson	Postmaster	Feb. 15, 1869
Charles Brown	Postmaster	Dec. 18, 1871
Edward M. Thompson	Postmaster	Sept. 16, 1872
Charles D. Brown	Postmaster	Oct. 21, 1875
George Miles	Postmaster	Dec. 22, 1885
George T. Niles	Postmaster	Jan. 21, 1886
Thomas W. Jones	Postmaster	Mar. 26, 1889
Simon Clark	Postmaster	Apr. 29, 1890
Katie Blaich	Postmaster	Dec. 12, 1891
George T. Niles	Postmaster	Dec. 10, 1895

Postmasters in the Town of Salina

POSTMASTER	TITLE	DATE APPOINTED
LIVERPOOL 13088		
Henry Case	Postmaster	Sept. 9, 1811
Joseph Jaqueth	Postmaster	July 11, 1833
Henry Paddock	Postmaster	July 3, 1841
Caleb Hubbard	Postmaster	Sept. 2, 1843
Sampson Jaqueth	Postmaster	Mar. 31, 1846
John S. Forger	Postmaster	June 6, 1849
Arthur Macarthur	Postmaster	Apr. 27, 1853
Thomas B. Anderson	Postmaster	Nov. 24, 1856
Jason H. Learned	Postmaster	Apr. 10, 1861
Jasper T. Crawford	Postmaster	July 13, 1865
William H. Lynn	Postmaster	May 7, 1886
George Richberg	Postmaster	Apr. 4, 1889
Martin J. Dinehart	Postmaster	Feb. 3, 1894
George Smith	Postmaster	Feb. 3, 1898
Valentine Bahn	Postmaster	May 31, 1907
Francis H. Alvord	Postmaster	Mar. 28, 1916

POSTMASTER	TITLE	DATE APPOINTED
Harold E. Sargent	Postmaster	Jan. 5, 1922
Charles F. Brandt	Acting PM	May 1, 1928
Charles F. Brandt	Postmaster	Dec. 8, 1928
James J. Gaffney	Acting PM	Aug. 1, 1933
John P. Young	Postmaster	June 5, 1934
John J. Gaffney	Acting PM	June 3, 1939
John J. Gaffney	Postmaster	Apr. 2, 1940
Dominic F. Mazza	Acting PM	Dec. 26, 1964
Dominic F. Mazza	Postmaster	July 26, 1965
Thomas S. Loop	Officer-In-Charge	May 12, 1972
Edward B. Bierman Jr.	Postmaster	Mar. 17, 1973
Edward F. Phelan	Officer-In-Charge	Sept. 30, 1978
Anthony J. Spagnola	Postmaster	Mar. 24, 1979
Timothy J. Milicich	Officer-In-Charge	Mar. 18, 1983
Joseph F. Castro	Postmaster	Sept. 3, 1983
Adele M. Moore	Officer-In-Charge	Aug. 24, 1990
Joseph A. Trovato	Officer-In-Charge	Oct. 26, 1990
David E. Boardman	Officer-In-Charge	Feb. 1, 1991
Kenneth A. Andrews	Postmaster	June 1, 1991
Lindsey B. Hicks	Officer-In-Charge	Dec. 17, 1997
Lindsey B. Hicks	Postmaster	July 18, 1998

POSTMASTER	TITLE	DATE APPOINTED
SALINA		
Isaiah Bunce	Postmaster	July 1, 1807
Henry J. Baldwin	Postmaster	Apr. 1, 1810
Nehemiah H. Earll	Postmaster	Oct. 1, 1810
John P. Sherwood	Postmaster	July 1, 1813
Ashbell Kellogg	Postmaster	June 24, 1814
Daniel Gilbert	Postmaster	July 1, 1816
Jonathan Baldwin	Postmaster	Oct. 13, 1820
William Clark	Postmaster	Sept. 7, 1822
Erasmus Stone	Postmaster	Jan. 29, 1830
Andrew H. Newcomb	Postmaster	May 28, 1841
Isaac R. Quereau	Postmaster	Aug. 14, 1843
Isaac R. Quereau	Postmaster	Feb. 17, 1848
William B. Whitmore	Postmaster	July 3, 1849
William H. Hoyt	Postmaster	Jan. 8, 1851
Harry Gifford	Postmaster	July 26, 1853
John Eastwood	Postmaster	Apr. 10, 1861
Garrett Doyle	Postmaster	Oct. 1, 1866
Samuel J. Abbott	Postmaster	Mar. 27, 1867

Postmasters in the Town of Skaneateles

MANDANA

POSTMASTER	TITLE	DATE APPOINTED
Tunis Van Houghten	Postmaster	May 21, 1828
Josias Garlock	Postmaster	Apr. 12, 1836
Alexander H. Allen	Postmaster	Oct. 23, 1843
David T. Fowler	Postmaster	June 1, 1849
John S. Fowler	Postmaster	Nov. 19, 1849
Alexander H. Allen	Postmaster	July 8, 1852
Lewis Van Inwegen	Postmaster	Apr. 19, 1854
Daniel B. Northrup	Postmaster	Aug. 29, 1862
Harvey Folts	Postmaster	Dec. 26, 1862
Roswell S. Parish	Postmaster	Aug. 22, 1877
James E. Keefe	Postmaster	Apr. 15, 1898
Oscar Folts	Postmaster	Oct. 9, 1899

MOTTVILLE

POSTMASTER	TITLE	DATE APPOINTED
Ansel Frost	Postmaster	Mar. 1, 1832
Leonard Mason	Postmaster	Feb. 12, 1835
Benjamin Nye	Postmaster	Feb. 3, 1837
Howard Delano	Postmaster	July 15, 1841
Ezekiel B. Hoyt	Postmaster	Oct. 1, 1849
Deloss Earll	Postmaster	Sept. 23, 1851
Alanson Watson	Postmaster	Apr. 27, 1853
Henry Hunsiker	Postmaster	Apr. 2, 1856
Sidney L. Benedict	Postmaster	Apr. 10, 1861
Olive A. Eastwood	Postmaster	Mar. 21, 1871
Sidney L. Benedict	Postmaster	Aug. 15, 1876
Ellen Smith	Postmaster	Dec. 22, 1885
David Hall	Postmaster	Dec. 7, 1889
Ellen Smith	Postmaster	Oct. 17, 1891
Mary Evans	Postmaster	Dec. 28, 1897

Information for postmasters after this time period not available

Salvatore T. Catalano	Officer-In-Charge	Aug. 31, 1969
Charles E. DeVoe Jr.	Postmaster	May 1, 1971
William V. Compson	Officer-In-Charge	July 19, 1974
William V. Compson	Postmaster	Nov. 9, 1974
C. Robert Jordan	Officer-In-Charge	Feb. 20, 1981
Charles R. Jordan	Postmaster	May 30, 1981
Edward J. Maywald	Officer-In-Charge	My 3, 1988

SKANEATELES

POSTMASTER	TITLE	DATE APPOINTED
William J. Vredenburg	Postmaster	Oct. 1, 1804
John Ten Eyck	Postmaster	June 1, 1813
Charles J. Burnett	Postmaster	Mar. 28, 1817
Joel Thayer	Postmaster	July 1, 1843
John Snook Jr.	Postmaster	Apr. 11, 1849
Josias Garlock	Postmaster	Apr. 27, 1853
Horace Hazen	Postmaster	Apr. 10, 1861
Forrest G. Weeks	Postmaster	Apr. 16, 1869
John B. Marshall	Postmaster	Dec. 20, 1872
Edson D. Gillett	Postmaster	Feb. 11, 1885
J. Horatio Earll	Postmaster	Jan. 24, 1894
William J. Bright	Postmaster	Mar. 9, 1898
George B. Harwood	Postmaster	Apr. 22, 1902
Henry T. Tucker	Postmaster	June 10, 1910
William H. Hennessey	Postmaster	Oct. 13, 1914
William A. Hilton	Acting PM	Sept. 15, 1923
William A. Hilton	Postmaster	Jan. 8, 1924
Walter F. Herring	Acting PM	Feb. 17, 1936
Walter F. Herring	Postmaster	May 22, 1936
Paul H. Irving	Acting PM	June 30, 1951
Paul H. Irving	Postmaster	July 3, 1952
Paul W. Pavlus	Officer-In-Charge	June 29, 1973
Paul W. Pavlus	Postmaster	Dec. 8, 1973
Charles F. Tanner	Officer-In-Charge	Sept. 24, 1992
Charles F. Tanner	Postmaster	Jan. 23, 1993
Cynthia M. Donnelly	Officer-In-Charge	Feb. 26, 2009
Cynthia M. Donnelly	Postmaster	Aug. 29, 2009
Mark E. Lawrence	Postmaster	Apr. 5, 2014

SKANEATELES FALLS

POSTMASTER	TITLE	DATE APPOINTED
Eben Bean	Postmaster	Nov. 24, 1874
John W. Feeley	Postmaster	Oct. 27, 1875
Patrick S. Feeley	Postmaster	Jan. 24, 1879
Charles J. Keegan Jr.	Postmaster	Sept. 4, 1885
Patrick S. Feeley	Postmaster	June 17, 1889
James D. Feeley	Postmaster	Dec. 13, 1893
Albert E. Ketcham	Postmaster	Feb. 3, 1898
Samuel Bradshaw	Postmaster	Mar. 17, 1903

Acting PM = Acting Postmaster

POSTMASTER	TITLE	DATE APPOINTED
Anna H. Walsh	Postmaster	Apr. 10, 1915
Michael McGinn	Postmaster	Jan. 24, 1919
Thomas F. Powers	Postmaster	Apr. 30, 1921
Edward A. Cronauer	Acting PM	Apr. 17, 1922
Edward A. Cronauer	Postmaster	June 1, 1922
Nora E. Feeley	Acting PM	July 1, 1933
Nora E. Feeley	Postmaster	Jan. 31, 1934
Florence K. Bryant	Acting PM	June 30, 1948
Donald S. Jackson	Postmaster	Oct. 19, 1949
William V. Compson	Officer-In-Charge	Jan. 13, 1978
John H. Tambroni	Postmaster	Aug. 26, 1978
Freda M. Crary	Officer-In-Charge	Dec. 10, 1982
Mark E. Krohl	Postmaster	Apr. 2, 1983
Nancy A. Brown	Officer-In-Charge	Jan. 27, 1986
Lorna E. Moore	Postmaster	July 19, 1986

Postmasters in the Town of Spafford

BORODINO

Daniel Baxter	Postmaster	Jan. 22, 1821
John Baxter	Postmaster	Oct. 31, 1833
William Legg	Postmaster	Sept. 24, 1844
Eleazer E. Fulton	Postmaster	Apr. 11, 1849
David Becker	Postmaster	Apr. 27, 1853
Isaac Morrell	Postmaster	Apr. 10, 1861
Charles M. Rich	Postmaster	Nov. 17, 1865
William W. Legg	Postmaster	May 6, 1869
Edward J. Churchell	Postmaster	Dec. 22, 1885
William H. Boss	Postmaster	Nov. 19, 1888
Charles M. Rich	Postmaster	Mar. 29, 1889
James Sweet	Postmaster	July 10, 1893
Estella Rich	Postmaster	Nov. 10, 1897

EDGEWATER

William H. Harris	Postmaster	Dec. 21, 1898

SOUTH SPAFFORD

Samuel L. Churchill	Postmaster	May 19, 1879

SPAFFORD

Asahel Roundy	Postmaster	Dec. 21, 1820
Isaac Knapp	Postmaster	Apr. 24, 1824

POSTMASTER	TITLE	DATE APPOINTED
Isaac C. Knapp	Postmaster	Jan. 13, 1826
Joseph R. Berry	Postmaster	Mar. 11, 1828
Zara Berry	Postmaster	Dec. 6, 1834
Thomas B. Anderson	Postmaster	June 16 1836
John Collins	Postmaster	Sept. 7, 1838
William W. Legg	Postmaster	June 5, 1849
James H. Isdell	Postmaster	June 7, 1853
John R. Lewis	Postmaster	Jan. 31, 1855
Asahel M. Roundy	Postmaster	July 10, 1855
John R. Lewis	Postmaster	Nov. 1, 1856
VanDyke Tripp	Postmaster	Apr. 10, 1861
William W. Legg	Postmaster	Jan. 30, 1862
Benjamin McDaniels	Postmaster	May 10, 1869
Uriah Roundy	Postmaster	Mar. 4, 1878
George S. King	Postmaster	Dec. 22, 1885
George King	Postmaster	Dec. 30, 1885
Caleb E. King	Postmaster	Apr. 23, 1888
Uriah Roundy	Postmaster	Apr. 1, 1889
Caleb E. King	Postmaster	Oct. 9, 1893
Uriah Roundy	Postmaster	Feb. 3, 1898

SPAFFORD HOLLOW

William O'Farrell	Postmaster	Oct. 9, 1837
William O'Farrell	Postmaster	Feb. 13, 1844
Kelly Case	Postmaster	June 6, 1849
William O'Farrell	Postmaster	Sept. 29, 1851
Charles W. Skeel	Postmaster	Aug. 7, 1861

Postmasters in the Town of Tully

ASSEMBLY PARK

David H. Cook	Postmaster	May 14, 1897
Bromley		
John W. Howard	Postmaster	Nov. 30, 1892
Warren J. Howard	Postmaster	May 18, 1899

TULLY 13159

Jonathan Buell	Postmaster	Jan. 1, 1804
John Osgood	Postmaster	Apr. 1, 1805
Nicoll Howell	Postmaster	Jan. 28, 1815
William Trowbridge	Postmaster	Feb. 15, 1817

POSTMASTER	TITLE	DATE APPOINTED
Caleb Whitford	Postmaster	Oct. 1, 1821
William M. Allen	Postmaster	Oct. 1, 1825
William M. Ostrander	Postmaster	May 8, 1826
Harry F. King	Postmaster	Mar. 12, 1830
William M. Allen	Postmaster	Nov. 8, 1831
Harry F. King	Postmaster	Mar. 29, 1833
John B. Hall	Postmaster	June 8, 1849
Hiram Chapin	Postmaster	Apr. 27, 1853
Joseph Fletcher, Jr.	Postmaster	Dec. 18, 1856
Hiram Chapin	Postmaster	Apr. 10, 1861
Martin J. Bouttelle	Postmaster	Dec. 17, 1875
John B. Hall	Postmaster	Aug. 5, 1879
Judson S. Wright	Postmaster	Feb. 19, 1885
Joseph Fletcher	Postmaster	Sept. 4, 1885
William H. Brown	Postmaster	Aug. 2, 1887
William L. Stone	Postmaster	Mar. 29, 1890
William A. Dewey	Postmaster	Dec. 14, 1893
Richard R. Davis	Postmaster	Mar. 26, 1898

Information for postmasters after this time period not available

POSTMASTER	TITLE	DATE APPOINTED
John R. Houck	Postmaster	July 12, 1940
Charlotte M. Houck	Officer-In-Charge	June 30, 1970
Charlotte M. Houck	Postmaster	July 17, 1971
Timothy J. Milicich	Officer-In-Charge	Nov. 4, 1977
Martha M. Rogusz	Officer-In-Charge	Mar. 10, 1978
Philip N. Stitzel	Postmaster	Apr. 22, 1978
Judy Marshall	Officer-In-Charge	Apr. 15, 1983
Joeanne B. Simoneau	Postmaster	Aug. 6, 1983
Nancy A. Brown	Officer-In-Charge	May 31, 1991
Richard C. Knopp	Postmaster	Nov. 2, 1991
Theresa B. Furlong	Officer-In-Charge	Dec. 28, 2009
Marjorie L. Beebe	Postmaster	July 16, 2011
Laura W. Rankin	Officer-In-Charge	Mar. 9, 2015
Laura W. Rankin	Postmaster	Sept. 19, 2015

TULLY LAKE PARK

POSTMASTER	TITLE	DATE APPOINTED
George Tenker	Postmaster	July 23, 1890
Frank R. Slayton	Postmaster	Apr. 15, 1892
James W. Slayton	Postmaster	Apr. 5, 1894
James C. Rann	Postmaster	Apr. 3, 1896

POSTMASTER	TITLE	DATE APPOINTED
William H. Young	Postmaster	June 9, 1897
Henry F. Scranton	Postmaster	May 18, 1899

TULLY VALLEY

POSTMASTER	TITLE	DATE APPOINTED
Ornan King	Postmaster	July 25, 1833
John Henderson	Postmaster	Apr. 4, 1834
John Salisbury	Postmaster	Aug. 8, 1836
George Salisbury	Postmaster	Dec. 14, 1836
Job T. Irish	Postmaster	Nov. 11, 1839
John A. Bailey	Postmaster	Mar. 3, 1840
Job T. Irish	Postmaster	Sept. 7, 1841
William Salisbury	Postmaster	May 27, 1846
William Salisbury	Postmaster	Nov. 20, 1857
Avery P. Shue	Postmaster	July 19, 1862
Alvin Benjamin	Postmaster	June 12, 1882
Clark Estey	Postmaster	Mar. 17, 1888

VESPER

POSTMASTER	TITLE	DATE APPOINTED
William Clark	Postmaster	Apr. 3, 1820
Asa Knight	Postmaster	Feb. 9, 1830
Barak Morse	Postmaster	July 11, 1831
Jared G. Winslow	Postmaster	June 14, 1832
Samuel Ashby	Postmaster	Feb. 5, 1835
Charles Talllman	Postmaster	June 2, 1841
William Patten	Postmaster	Apr. 11, 1846
Chester M. Clark	Postmaster	June 16, 1849
Edward M. Hoyt	Postmaster	Apr. 27, 1853
Robert Earll	Postmaster	Jan. 30, 1856
Jesse Patten	Postmaster	Mar. 17, 1860
Robert Earll	Postmaster	Apr. 10, 1860
Nathan W. Fuller	Postmaster	Apr. 10, 1861
Eli H. Whitmore	Postmaster	Apr. 27, 1863
Cone Williams	Postmaster	July 25, 1864
Alfred B. Daniels	Postmaster	Dec. 28, 1864
Kirkland C. Arnold	Postmaster	Mar. 20, 1866
William Clowe	Postmaster	Mar. 22, 1869
George W. Babcock	Postmaster	Nov. 1, 1869
Alphonso French	Postmaster	Dec. 9, 1869
George W. Babcock	Postmaster	Jan. 11, 1870
Alphonso French	Postmaster	Mar. 17, 1870

Acting PM = Acting Postmaster

POSTMASTER	TITLE	DATE APPOINTED
George W. Ripley	Postmaster	Jan. 11, 1881
Benjamin F. Churchell	Postmaster	May 12, 1882
Joel A. Smith	Postmaster	Apr. 30, 1883
Jane Estey	Postmaster	June 2, 1884
James E. Henderson	Postmaster	Dec. 30, 1885
Charles Hoag	Postmaster	June 19, 1897
Harriet Hodge	Postmaster	Oct. 3, 1898
Charles W. C. Richardson	Postmaster	Jan. 29, 1900

Postmasters in the Town of Van Buren

CANAL

POSTMASTER	TITLE	DATE APPOINTED
Oliver Nicholls	Postmaster	Jan. 15, 1830
Job Nicholls	Postmaster	Jan. 3, 1835
David C. Lytle	Postmaster	Dec. 15, 1838
John D. Norton	Postmaster	Aug. 7, 1839
Leonard V. Mason	Postmaster	Dec. 23, 1843
Abel H. Toll	Postmaster	Feb. 24, 1849
Charles H. Toll	Postmaster	Oct. 16, 1851
John Lakin	Postmaster	Apr. 27, 1853
Andrew B. Conover	Postmaster	Dec. 31, 1857
Wilson Bates	Postmaster	Mar. 20, 1858

IONIA

POSTMASTER	TITLE	DATE APPOINTED
Charles H. Toll	Postmaster	Feb. 22, 1820

MEMPHIS 13112

POSTMASTER	TITLE	DATE APPOINTED
Wilson Bates	Postmaster	Dec. 10, 1860
Anson Dunham	Postmaster	Apr. 10, 1861
Chester D. Barnes	Postmaster	June 26, 1866
David Shapley	Postmaster	June 21, 1867
Seabury M. Higgins	Postmaster	Aug. 11, 1869
Henry Crouse	Postmaster	June 26, 1871
Irvin R. Burch	Postmaster	Sept. 4, 1885
Dwight M. Warner	Postmaster	June 17, 1889
Irvin R. Burch	Postmaster	July 10, 1893
William W. Suits	Postmaster	July 23, 1897
Frank Lee	Postmaster	Apr. 8, 1899
Information for postmasters during this time period not available		
Joseph W. Mannion	Postmaster	July 26, 1965
Judy C. Brinkerhoff	Postmaster	Apr. 18, 1981

POSTMASTER	TITLE	DATE APPOINTED
Suzanne L. Beck	Officer-In-Charge	June 5, 1992
Kathie M. L. Hall	Officer-In-Charge	
Kathleen A. Cwenar	Postmaster	Jan. 23, 1993
Richard J. Wood	Officer-In-Charge	Aug. 21, 1996
Carol A. (Robinson) Jerose	Postmaster	Dec. 7, 1996
Kathleen M. Wingood	Officer-In-Charge	Oct. 1, 2007
Kathleen M. Wingood	Postmaster	Oct. 13, 2007
Marcia L. Salo	Officer-In-Charge	June 20, 2013
Barbara Almonte	Officer-In-Charge	Sept. 19, 2013

VAN BUREN

POSTMASTER	TITLE	DATE APPOINTED
Charles Turner	Postmaster	Apr. 17, 1829
James T. Hough	Postmaster	Dec. 21, 1830
Adonijah White	Postmaster	Aug. 12, 1831
Hezekiah R. Dow	Postmaster	Sept. 4, 1837
Isaac Earll	Postmaster	Aug. 24, 1840
Christopher C. Clapp	Postmaster	May 10, 1842
Herman S. Stearns	Postmaster	Mar. 23, 1843
Asahel K. Clark	Postmaster	Oct. 11, 1843
Hezekiah R. Dow	Postmaster	Apr. 28, 1845
Lyman Peck	Postmaster	Oct. 1, 1849
John Bowman	Postmaster	June 30, 1851
Solomon Keller	Postmaster	Nov. 24, 1852
Horatio N. Howe	Postmaster	Mar. 22, 1856
Hezekiah R. Dow	Postmaster	July 22, 1856
Solomon Keller	Postmaster	Aug. 7, 1861
Emeline Keller	Postmaster	Feb. 15, 1862
Rufus Foster	Postmaster	Dec. 18, 1867
Augustus W. Bingham	Postmaster	Dec. 12, 1871
Bertha Smith	Postmaster	June 5, 1895
Susan P. Van Hoesen	Postmaster	Feb. 6, 1896

VAN BUREN CENTRE

POSTMASTER	TITLE	DATE APPOINTED
Jonathan Skinner	Postmaster	Dec. 27, 1837
George W. Marvin	Postmaster	Aug. 22, 1849
John Boley	Postmaster	Apr. 22, 1853
Sherburn Noble	Postmaster	Feb. 14, 1854
Stephen W. Betts	Postmaster	May 22, 1854

WARNER'S 13164

POSTMASTER	TITLE	DATE APPOINTED
Stephen W. Betts	Postmaster	Jan. 13, 1870
George W. Davis	Postmaster	Nov. 19, 1872
Alvah L. Spaulding	Postmaster	Sept. 8, 1884
Duane Van Alstyne	Postmaster	Dec. 22, 1885
Thomas H. Marvin	Postmaster	Mar. 26, 1889
Ann McAuliffe	Postmaster	Feb. 24, 1894
Duane La Du	Postmaster	Feb. 8, 1898
Frank B. Garnett	Postmaster	Dec. 24, 1914
Hannah B. Michels	Postmaster	Aug. 24, 1918
Caroline M. Belcher	Acting PM	Nov. 29, 1933
Anna M. Isbell	Acting PM	Dec. 11, 1933
Anna M. Isbell	Postmaster	June 8, 1934
Ella P. Olmstead	Acting PM	Dec. 31, 1953
Beatrice V. Conway	Acting PM	Mar. 31, 1956
Beatrice V. Conway	Postmaster	July 19, 1956
Michael D. Poulos	Officer-In-Charge	Oct. 29, 1982
Mary Susan Goleski	Postmaster	Jan. 22, 1983
Dawn M. Jackson	Officer-In-Charge	June 30, 2010
Donna L. Jenness	Officer-In-Charge	Oct. 9, 2010
Dawn M. Jackson	Officer-In-Charge	Dec. 22, 2010

Postmasters in the City of Syracuse

SYRACUSE 13220

POSTMASTER	TITLE	DATE APPOINTED
John Wilkinson	Postmaster	Feb. 24, 1820
Jonas Earll Jr.	Postmaster	June 26, 1840
Henry Raynor	Postmaster	Mar. 3, 1842
Wiliam W. Teall	Postmaster	July 23, 1845
William Jackson	Postmaster	Apr. 14, 1849
Henry J. Sedgwick	Postmaster	May 4, 1853
Patrick H. Agan	Postmaster	Aug. 27, 1861
George L. Maynard	Postmaster	Mar. 22, 1866
Dwight H. Bruce	Postmaster	Mar. 15, 1871
Austin C. Chase	Postmaster	Dec. 15, 1875
James M. Gilbert	Postmaster	Feb. 4, 1884
Milton H. Northrup	Postmaster	Mar. 14, 1888
Carroll E. Smith	Postmaster	Oct. 16, 1889
Milton H. Northrup	Postmaster	May 23, 1893

POSTMASTER	TITLE	DATE APPOINTED
Dwight H. Bruce	Postmaster	July 24, 1897
William Foure	Postmaster	Dec. 16, 1908
John J. Kesel	Postmaster	Aug. 27, 1913
James McLusky	Postmaster	Apr. 18, 1922
Edmund L. Weston	Acting PM	Apr. 22, 1933
Edmund L. Weston	Postmaster	Jan. 31, 1934
Cornelius J. Nugent	Acting PM	Mar. 1, 1941
Cornelius J. Nugent	Postmaster	Oct. 21, 1941
Myron J. Parkinson	Acting PM	Jan. 31, 1946
Myron J. Parkinson	Postmaster	July 7, 1947
George Sommers	Officer-In-Charge	Sept. 5, 1963
Anthony F. Caffrey	Acting PM	Sept. 20, 1963
Anthony F. Caffrey	Postmaster	Sept. 8, 1964
Lawrence T. Ryan	Acting PM	Oct. 21, 1968
Thomas DeYulia	Officer-In-Charge	Oct. 31, 1969
Thomas DeYulia	Postmaster	Feb. 20, 1971
William E. Peck	Officer-In-Charge	Feb. 4, 1972
William E. Peck	Postmaster	Feb. 17, 1973
John E. Doran	Officer-In-Charge	July 31, 1975
Alphonse J. Sarno	Postmaster	Jan. 31, 1976
Lewis R. Firley	Officer-In-Charge	Sept. 26, 1986
John W. Duchesne	Postmaster	Nov. 8, 1986
Jonathan A. Gale	Officer-In-Charge	Feb. 9, 1990
Ronald E. Odie	Officer-In-Charge	Mar. 9, 1990
Barbara A. Patterson	Postmaster	May 5, 1990
Jonathan A. Gale	Officer-In-Charge	Oct. 16, 1992
Edward F. Phelan Jr.	Postmaster	Jan. 23, 1993
Perry F. Kolodziejczyk	Officer-In-Charge	
David E. Boardman	Postmaster	Dec. 25, 2004
Lindsey B. Hicks	Officer-In-Charge	Mar. 5, 2007
John J. Phelan	Officer-In-Charge	Apr. 14, 2007
Gail A. Weeks	Officer-In-Charge	Oct. 13, 2007
Gail A. Weeks	Postmaster	Aug. 2, 2008
Cameron P. Whitmore	Postmaster	Aug. 27, 2011

SOUTH SYRACUSE

POSTMASTER	TITLE	DATE APPOINTED
John C. Larkin	Postmaster	Mar. 29, 1882

Acting PM = Acting Postmaster

Postal Locations in Onondaga County

Location Types:
B   Branch
S   Station
P   Post Office
C   Community Post Office (post office boxes and retail inside a non-postal facility)
E   Contract post office (nonpostal provider of limited retail services, no post office boxes)
I   Inspection Service/Office of Inspector General

Bold   Syracuse City operations, window services only – no carriers in this building

BOLD CAPS   Syracuse Main Post Office on Taft Road, distinguishing the carrier section of that big building (24 acres!!) from the front window services, but it is all one big building

Italics   Syracuse Vehicle Maintenance Facility is a separate outbuilding found in the far back of the property on which the Taft Road facility sits; it provides full bays of service to hundreds of postal vehicles on a regular basis

Location Type	Town/City	Address	City	State	Zip Code
B	Bayberry	7608 Oswego Rd	Liverpool	NY	13090
B	Solvay	1801 Milton Ave	Syracuse	NY	13209
B	**Mattydale**	1900 Brewerton Rd	Syracuse	NY	13211
B	De Witt	6581 Kinne Rd	Syracuse	NY	13214
B	Onondaga	4912 W Seneca Tpke	Syracuse	NY	13215
B	**Federal Station**	100 S Clinton St	Syracuse	NY	13261
C	Mottville	873 Crow Hill Rd	Mottville	NY	13119
E	Syracuse	5640 E Taft Rd	Syracuse	NY	13220
I	Syracuse USOIG	5640 E Taft Rd	Syracuse	NY	13220
I	Syracuse USPIS	5640 E Taft Rd, Rm 246	Syracuse	NY	13220
P	Apulia Station	979 Apulia Rd	Apulia Station	NY	13020
P	Baldwinsville	26 E Genesee St	Baldwinsville	NY	13027
P	Brewerton	5560 Bartel Rd	Brewerton	NY	13029

Location Type	Town/City	Address	City	State	Zip Code
P	Bridgeport	7901 Bridgeport Minoa Rd	Bridgeport	NY	13030
P	Camillus	120 Kasson Rd	Camillus	NY	13031
P	Clay	5601 State Route 31	Clay	NY	13041
P	Delphi Falls	2185 Oran Delphi Rd	Delphi Falls	NY	13051
P	East Syracuse	404 W Manlius St	East Syracuse	NY	13057
P	Elbridge	106 South St	Elbridge	NY	13060
P	Fabius	1306 Keeney Rd	Fabius	NY	13063
P	Fayetteville	599 E Genesee St	Fayetteville	NY	13066
P	Jamesville	6499 E Seneca Tpke	Jamesville	NY	13078
P	Jordan	9 Mechanic St	Jordan	NY	13080
P	Kirkville	6365 N Kirkville Rd	Kirkville	NY	13082
P	La Fayette	2507 US Route 11	La Fayette	NY	13084
P	Liverpool	300 Cypress St	Liverpool	NY	13088
P	Manlius	110 Wesley St	Manlius	NY	13104
P	Marcellus	9 E Main St	Marcellus	NY	13108
P	Marietta	2796 State Route 174	Marietta	NY	13110
P	Memphis	1749 State Route 173	Memphis	NY	13112
P	Minoa	115 N Main St	Minoa	NY	13116
P	Nedrow	6709 S Salina St	Nedrow	NY	13120
P	Plainville	8000 Plainville Rd	Plainville	NY	13137
P	Pompey	7360 Academy St	Pompey	NY	13138
P	Skaneateles	20 Fennell St	Skaneateles	NY	13152
P	Skaneateles Falls	4564 Jordan Rd	Skaneateles Falls	NY	13153
P	Tully	24 Elm St	Tully	NY	13159
P	Warners	6454 Newport Rd	Warners	NY	13164
P	**SYRACUSE**	5640 E Taft Rd	Syracuse	NY	13220
S	**Downtown Syracuse**	444 S Salina St	Syracuse	NY	13201
S	Colvin Elmwood	2200 S Salina St	Syracuse	NY	13205

Location Type	Town/City	Address	City	State	Zip Code
S	**Eastwood**	2509 James St	Syracuse	NY	13206
S	Teall	226 Teall Ave	Syracuse	NY	13217
S	Franklin Square	401 W Division St	Syracuse	NY	13218
S	**SYRACUSE CARRIER**	5640 E Taft Rd	Syracuse	NY	13220
S	**Syracuse University**	720 University Ave	Syracuse	NY	13235
V	*Syracuse VMF*	5640 E Taft Rd	Syracuse	NY	13220

BIBLIOGRAPHY

Abbott, Clifford A. *The Story of Case Settlement 1800-1952*

Baldwinsville Messenger

Beauchamp, William M., *Past and Present of Syracuse and Onondaga County, New York, from prehistoric times to the beginning of 1908* (NY:S.J. Clarke Publishing Co., 1908).

Bruce, Dwight H., *Onondaga's Centennial: Gleanings of a Century* (Boston, MA: The Boston History Company, 1896)

Christopher, Anthony J., "Sketches of Yesterday" *The Messenger*, 1960-1973

Clark, Joshua, *Onondaga; or, Reminiscences of earlier and later times; being a series of historical sketches relative to Onondaga; with notes on the several towns in the county, and Oswego* (Syracuse, NY: Stoddard & Babcock, 1849)

Clayton, Professor W.W., *The History of Onondaga County*

Crowell, Kathy & Moore, Ann & Schifffhauer, Nancy *A History of the Fayetteville Post Office*

French, J.H. *Gazetteer of the State of New York, 1860*

Gasciogne, Bamber, *History World*

Gazette and Farmers' Journal Newspaper

Kay, John L. and Smith, Chester M. Jr., *New York Postal History, the Post Offices and the First Postmasters from 1775 to 1980,* (Copyright 1982 American Philatelic Society)

Palmer, Miss L. Pearl, *Historical Review of the Town of Lysander* with additional name and subject indexes compiled by Robert F. Nostrant and Jane H. Kinsley, Margaret C. Bye (Baldwinsville NY: Town of Lysander, 1997, 1947)

Scholl, Fred L., (An unpublished compilation of Onondaga County Post Offices and first postmasters from photostats of official US Post Office records)

Scisco, Louis Dow, *Early History of the Town of Van Buren, Onondaga County, N.Y.* (Baldwinsville, N.Y., W.F. Morris Publishing Co., 1895)

Spafford, H.G. *Gazetteer of the State of New York, 1824*

Sweet's New Atlas of Onondaga Co. New York: from recent and actual surveys and records under the superintendence of Homer D.L. Sweet (N.Y.: Walker Bros. & Co.,1874)

Syracuse Post Standard

Tomasetti, Mario *Down Solvay's Memory Lane Moods and Images* Volume 13, No. 2

The United States Postal Service, *The United States Postal Service, An American History 1775-2006*, Bulletin 100

www.ingramcontent.com/pod-product-compliance
Lightning Source LLC
Chambersburg PA
CBHW080500110426

42742CB00017B/2951